The Impossible Conversation:

Choosing Reconnection and Resilience
at the
End of Business as Usual.

Dean Walker

ISBN-13: 978-0692900017
ISBN-10: 0692900012

DEDICATION

It is with great love and humility that I dedicate this book to all of the peoples before us who lived as one with the web of life. I honor your commitment to peacefully co-exist upon this miraculous planet, and I deeply regret our disconnection from that web.

Specifically, I honor two of my heroes,
who modeled living fully committed to the
beauty, truth and mystery that is Life:

Jacques Yves Cousteau
And
Rachel Carson

CONTENTS

Acknowledgments

Introduction

1   Exposure to Sober Data.   13

2   Life at 4°C.   41

3   Beyond greenhouse gas emissions: 47
    Other metrics of our impact.

4   What did corporations and governments know and when?   59

5   Our Shadow: On the scale of government and corporation.   77

6   Choices to Make at the End of Business as Usual.   123

7   Bridge Building Tools.   144

8   Reconnecting With Earth.   169

9   Reconnecting With Deeper Self.   191

10 Reconnecting With Others.   219

11 Chapter References and Resources.   2

What level of threat to life on Earth would need to occur

To motivate you to change your lifestyle, your presence,

Your relationship with the web of life?

"We can will the perfect future into being by becoming microcosms of the perfect future, and no longer casting blame outward on institutions or hierarchies of responsibility and control, but by realizing the opportunities here, the responsibilities here, and the two may never be congruent again, and the salvation of your immortal soul may depend on what you do with the opportunity."

Terence McKenna

What do you most love about being alive

on Earth at this time?

ACKNOWLEDGMENTS

It is a joy for me to acknowledge at least a few of the dear allies who have helped to make *The Impossible Conversation*, possible: Heather Ann Couch, Harvey Austin, Julian Spalding and Terry Brown, Carolyn Baker, Andrew Harvey, and my father, Don Seaman.

Thank you all for your encouragement and support.

The Impossible Conversation

Introduction

Not everything that is faced can be changed, but nothing can be changed until it is faced.

James Baldwin

Knowledge is the antidote to fear.

Ralph Waldo Emerson

I think everyone has that knowing. That the world is supposed to be much more beautiful and alive and authentic and gentle. But that knowing usually gets crushed.

Charles Eisenstein

*   *   *

What is important enough for you to stand for in life?

Who will you be in the face of our predicament?

Who will we be together?

I can remember as if it was yesterday the sense of anticipation and excitement as I was about to watch another episode of a most remarkable TV show. This show was like no other before or since, for me. It opened my eyes to a most miraculous world of beauty and wonder and it also offered an unflinching view of humanity's dreadful devastation of that beauty.

The show was *The Undersea World of Jacques Cousteau*. The series ran from 1968 to 1975 and always included gorgeous footage of the undersea world and some new sort of specialized diving gear that the team was testing. While all of that was enchanting to me, what hit me the hardest were Cousteau's vivid descriptions of the degradation of that undersea habitat, usually degradation caused by human beings.

I have no question that watching this series with its particular focus on how our human activity was impacting the planet's oceans set a foundation for me. This was the same foundation that more than forty years later I would use to put into perspective some of the most disturbing news and information I had ever heard— and help me to see a bigger picture or context for how that disturbing news came to be.

My teenage years found me constantly surfing or diving in the ocean or backpacking in remote sections of Baja California in Mexico. I also had a deep fondness for rock climbing that exposed me to a wonderful combination of enthusiastically pursuing excellence with the zen-like sense of just being present in the moment, with little attention to outcome.

As I look back, the requirement of presence in each of these outdoor activities is what blended with my undergraduate studies in psychology, to make me a good fit for my eventual career. That career started by working with a number of different providers of transformation-based training: *EST, LifeSpring, PSI, SuperCamps, InSpirit, On The Edge Productions, SportsMind* and others.

The work always involved the integration of very powerful curriculum with some form of engaging activity in the classroom or risk-perceived activities outside. Whether we were working with corporate executives or gang kids, couples desiring more intimacy or spiritual students seeking greater peace and grace, this blend of transformational methodologies with engaging experiential activities seemed to be a potent combination.

The core of this work seemed to be a predictable breaking open of people's hearts when they would experience these risk-perceived activities together. There was always a healthy dose of in-group sharing and bonding and often a sense of entirely new possibilities made available by engaging in the processes together.

What a dream career this has been. I am deeply grateful for the many years of working with people from all walks of life, sharing their vulnerable moments of growth and learning. I also am humbled by the remarkable trainers, facilitators, coaches and thought leaders I've had the privilege of working with around the world.

How this career history fits with this book starts back with a young teenage boy riveted to the next Jacques Cousteau special and learning to dive in the nearby Southern California ocean. The Cousteau exposés of the massive destruction of global ocean habitat hit me deep and hard. The conclusions to be drawn from these shows were not hard to discern.

If a twelve year old kid with no knowledge of life sciences or oceanography can figure this out surely anyone can. There were a few conclusions that came to me early in the TV series, and stayed with me to today. They each end up with their own place in the conclusions of this book.

A few of my Jacques Cousteau and personal observation conclusions:

- Human beings were and are having a massive negative impact on every ecosystem on Earth.
- The structures, methods and metrics of the human industrial and economic models have absolutely no useful inclusion of tracking impact or true sustainability regarding methods of extraction or of waste disposal.
- Anyone who advocates for human stewardship of the planet and its resources will be marginalized or worse.
- This human operating system is based on a single profound lie… That we will always have infinite growth of our system on this finite planet.

This last item is the one that rocketed to the top of the list a couple of years ago as I was attempting to make sense of some potentially devastating data I had learned about in a lecture presentation.

I'll get to the details of that presentation and the subsequent vetting and learning-how-to-learn about a remarkably complex field of study. I'll gladly share with you all of the many resources I've found to vet and validate the data and projections of that first presentation, and the many more I've found since then, that imply even greater acceleration and intensification of those projections.

This book is a recounting, a sharing of my own recent personal transformation. It is the story of my evolution from a regular guy living a regular life in the day to day routine we all call business as usual to a guy whose world view and orientation to life itself has been utterly disrupted and reinvented.

The tour I'm offering has to start where we all are. We are all children of our business as usual culture. We all (even those at the bottom of the economic ladder in the developed world) are enjoying the luxury and fortune that has been reaped by our global use of fossil fuels for the last couple of hundred years. We all have been born into a level of privilege and relative wealth that was unknown by royalty in past ages.

Arguably, this lifelong immersion in the privilege of a fossil-fuel-driven lifestyle has been so seductive and complete as to become a deep, collective addiction. It could also be said that the many well documented *Shadow** traits of an addict can readily be found in every expression of our global cultures. These *Shadow* traits appear most aggressively in the top most levels of our governments and corporations where the concentration of wealth and power from that fossil-fuel-based lifestyle has always been the greatest.

*   *   *

What I'm about to do is outline this entire book for you in a very condensed fashion. with the hope of orienting you, the reader, to the path that I took to go from the shock of the original presentation —through the many stages of grief, resistance and fascination that I encountered —to ultimately land in a position of empowerment, equanimity and grace, in the face of our shared global predicament.

I'm outlining the flow of the book hoping to circumvent the many human habits and neurological quirks that so many experts have warned me about. The relatively new field of neuroscience has studied us modern people and concluded that we all just don't want that much to do with scientific data or even civil public discourse.

In the many books I've read and classes I've attended I've basically been told that my experience of hearing some very disturbing data and projections, then vetting those same data through focused study, then integrating those data into my life and lifestyle and sharing these new insights with others makes me a very rare person indeed.

The thrust of what these neuroscientists and sociologists have concluded is that we are a people more divided than ever and less likely to be changed by any amount of data, no matter how scientifically sound. We tend to lock onto a politics-based point of view and burrow into our own little world and put ourselves onto a media diet formed exclusively by voices that echo our own point of view.

We will explore these notions later in the book. For now, I just want to share with you in the off chance that you might be a rare bird like me. Maybe, just maybe, you will find it useful to read the Sober Data portion of this book and learn how to vet this kind of information for yourself. (My apologies if you already know that you are this kind of person.)

Perhaps you will participate by doing the recommended exercises in this book and perhaps you will collate your responses to those exercises to form a strong foundation for a newly reinvented way of living in this world.

Perhaps you will use this book and these distinctions and exercises to bolster your efforts to crack out of your own version of our collective addiction.

So, in the first chapter, I'll detail how I ended up at this jaw-dropping presentation about Abrupt Climate Change.

In chapter 2, I'll share a bit about my vetting the material by studying articles and reports from numerous other climate scientists and agencies.

Chapter 3 tells of my search for other types of metrics to support the assertion that the destruction that humanity has wrought on Earth is far larger than our present fixation on CO_2 emissions. The assertion is that we are forcing so much extinction-level destruction that our times are now being called the Sixth Great Extinction.

Chapters 4 and 5 show us the corporate and governmental history of manipulation of our human presence on Earth —such that we have disconnected from our innate inter-relatedness with Deeper Self, Others and Earth—and come to rule all of humanity in terms of only one thing… the pursuit of profit.

Chapter 6 takes a look at how we as individuals have become fully immersed in all the addictive trappings of our lifestyle and the cost to our sense of agency and empowerment of our surrender to business as usual as the "only" way for us to live on Earth.

Chapter 7 is a primer for those who desire to get into action after engaging with the Shadowy and daunting earlier chapters. This chapter offers some empowering context, tools and suggestions for how we might learn and even thrive in the face of our predicament.

Chapters 8, 9 and 10 are intended to be sharing from pioneers and thought leaders who have courageously shifted from our societal disconnection from all sources of meaning to a reconnection to Deeper Self, Others and Earth.

*   *   *

So, now that you know where this book is headed, let me tell you, there is a really fast way to skip through the chapters and just do the written exercises... and still get some value out of the book without having to plough through all the data, projections and stories about how all of this stuff happened and so on.

Yes, you could do that, and that's probably better than not reading the book at all or picking this book up and putting it down somewhere in the middle of chapter 2.

What I ask of you, dear reader, is to give this book some real effort. This is not some personal favor to me, but a request for you to imagine yourself starting to assemble a tool kit for the next chapter of life on planet Earth.

This tool kit is different from any personal growth workshop or life-hack-filled inner tool kit we may have assembled in the past. This one is the real deal. All the self-help books, lectures and workshops of the past fifty years will have precious little value in the face of the predicament we have before us. Our current love affair with life hacks and listicles will be of little use in this journey. Maybe later on. But this part of the journey involves us really slowing down to look closely. To take a journey like this may require the most stamina and hard inner work of any we have attempted before.

I'm asking you to take your time with each chapter to let the scale and nature of our global predicament settle in to your heart and mind. I'm asking you to crack through any of those pesky neuroscience-based habits that might want to distract you...and really be present with the contents of each chapter.

I am asking you to reorient your attention from the usual default mode of judgment or entertainment or whether you agree or not, to just being present to the material and offering your sincere, truthful responses to the exercises.

As if I weren't already packing this book full of fatal writer's mistakes like, too much data, too much doom and gloom, no pictures, not many jokes, too long, and on and on, I'm now going to give you the punch line to this whole story.

The punch line is—we cannot continue to run our civilization on the lie of infinite growth on this finite planet. And, deny as we might, we must take responsibility at some point, for the waste and destruction of global habitat that we produce as we engage in business as usual.

Anyone courageous enough to read a book like this and seriously vet and consider the data and projections herein, like it or not, shall, be considered a leader in our times. And each of us has no real option but to experience ourselves as living two lives, or having a foot in two worlds. The relatively few people, at this time, who are aware of the collapse of business as usual, are uniquely challenged to co-create a way to bridge from our current, collapsing world to whatever world it is that shall replace this one.

Lastly, I strongly suggest that you not read this book alone. The "bridging" process pretty much impossible to take on alone and the more personal process work that is suggested here occurs, by its nature, in our blind spot. The best way to gain insight regarding our blind spots is to surround ourselves with caring allies who can powerfully "see" us.

If ever there was a book built for a book club or some kind of group read, this is it. While the exercises and practices contained in this book are plenty to get you engaged and started in this immense process, you might want to consider using *The Impossible Conversation Workbook* to give yourself some creative space in which to keep your responses and musings. At the very least, I encourage you to keep a journal of some kind next to this book to support your full engagement with the completion of the suggested exercises.

*   *   *

My wonderful allies and I would like to invite you to join us in crossing a bridge as we build it. We are looking for other courageous souls to join us in the massive project of gradually shifting our primary attention from our exclusive focus on the business as usual world, to reconnecting with our innate sensitivities and perceptions—reconnecting with our Deeper Selves, Others and Earth. We are committed to reconnecting with the primary sources of meaning, purpose and life that humans have had for millennia.

We're asserting that, while we indeed find ourselves in a predicament more cynical and daunting than anything in human history, we can still orient ourselves to lives reflecting deep inter-relatedness with other people, other beings on the planet and indeed with Earth herself. We can choose to locate ourselves in lives infused with authenticity, love and even core joy. It is well within our human ability to be resilient and thrive as we face the predicaments and challenges ahead.

But this is far more easily said than done. The destructive structures and processes of business as usual are deeply ingrained in us: the addiction to the supercharged energy source that is fossil fuel pumps through our veins every moment of every day.

To gradually turn our attention and intention from the business as usual world to any alternative will clearly be the hardest thing humanity has ever taken on—and the most contentious.

And, ironically, all of that business as usual expertise, all of those tried and true ways of operating, all of the concentration of wealth and power, all of the inequality and domination, all of the constant drum beat of war and the palpable threat of violence from those in control… all of it has to be reevaluated and transformed if we have any hope of creating a sincere, alternative way of operating in this world.

No Shit… this is an Impossible Conversation. And it's the only one we've got.

*   *   *

Lastly, this final rewrite and update of *The Impossible Conversation* has delayed the publishing from mid 2016 to mid 2017. What started out as my exposure to jaw dropping data and projections about our shared global habitat and human and Earth systems, eventually uncovered the depth and strength of the cultural, governmental and corporate influences that have accelerated us into this predicament.

This additional year has not only validated all of these Shadowy, conspiratorial influences but has both emboldened them and brought them fully into public view. What I first tentatively offered as the background influence of propaganda since early in the 20th Century is now in the 24/7 news spin cycle and includes: Alternative Facts and Fake News and the CEO of the world's largest fossil fuel company being confirmed as the Secretary of State of the US.

Basically all of the pieces of our global predicament that led me to call this book, The Impossible Conversation, have grown far larger, more bold and accelerated. I'm in search of a new title for the book so please contact me if you know of a term that represents the next order of magnitude of *impossible*. I figure, like the word, infinity, there are not relative sizes of infinity…or of impossible.

And, in the face of all that, we have also witnessed more overt activism and protest against aspects of our business as usual culture than I can recall in my almost sixty years of being alive. Prior to these protests and activist actions I was perpetually discouraged that we (regular folks around the US and around the world) didn't have it in us any more to get off the couch and stand up for something larger than our individual selves.

These actions are indeed inspiring and encouraging. They have even prodded the mainstream news media to do some no-kidding journalism for the first time in decades. But, reader, I have left the last few chapters in place in this book. All of my assertions about our collective blind spots and cultural weak suits still hold true. As you will see I cover the ground that is best described by the question, "How did we get ourselves into this predicament?"

We are only a few months into a new and deeply troubling administration that, as I said above, is promising to intensify and accelerate the Shadow-driven destruction of many rights, freedoms and privileges we have all taken for granted for as long as we've been alive.

The question is, can we muster the stamina, the strength, the resolve, the focus, the love of life necessary to stop the now imminent destruction of our shared habitat? Will we be able to keep up the protestation and resistance where needed? Will we be able to shift our stance from one primarily of resistance, outrage and protest to one of alignment FOR something?

There are so many causes and issues being surfaced at this time. So many different directions we could point our newfound political and ethical passion. My concern is that we have forfeited our agency and power for too long and we are still essentially disconnected from our most important individual and collective power sources. As you will see in later chapters, I am asserting what got us here is our disconnection from the innate sensitivities and power that come from our being fully inter-related with: our deeper selves, other beings and Earth.

To attempt to keep up the intensity of resistance and protest against a deeply sociopathic and eco-cidal business as usual system, without reconnecting ourselves to these primary sources of meaning, aliveness and purpose for human beings, will surely end in deep failure.

So, as you can see, I earlier gave you a couple of suggestions for how to get through this book quickly and relatively painlessly. But realistically, you and I both know this next era for human beings is going to take real work. This is the work that we all have done everything in our power to avoid.

Where we have become a pain-phobic, death-phobic and grief-phobic culture, we now must confront the fact that pain, death and grief are all natural parts of life and will cause even greater pain and pathology, if we continue to deny them.

Where we have suppressed or denied telling the truth about the dark side of our individual and collective nature, we are now grappling with the most grotesque expressions of Shadow the world has ever seen.

I am still very uncomfortable with the words in the last paragraph—the hyperbole, the seemingly toxic judgment implied in those sentences.

But reader, I invite you to carry these words with you as you read through these chapters. If you end up with any of the same conclusions that I have about our predicaments, you may just find yourself using the same hyperbole.

This is far beyond any notion of partisan politics. This is far beyond a calling for a set of bold new solutions for our pesky problems. The calling of our time appears to me to be a calling for nothing less than a reconnection of human beings to the web of life. It is a calling to co-create some kind of bridge from this collapsing paradigm to some new way of being on Earth in which we humbly return ourselves to being just one part of the web of life, rather than the crushers of the web itself.

I will be introducing you to exemplars, people who are already fully engaged with this process of reinvention. As we explore their lives and their work we can see that it is indeed possible to engage with this Impossible Conversation and quite possibly, be more alive than at any point in our business as usual lives.

We just may discover that this time of predicament and world-scale dismantling and reinvention, that our constant cultural fixation on being 'happy' and finding the next great life hack for 'success' were failed attempts to avoid this much needed reinvention. We just may discover that in inviting our own hearts to break open as we truly feel the pain of our lives and of Earth… we find the core joy and deep vitality we never found in business as usual.

After all of this research and in-depth exploration of our shared predicament, there is one thing I know above all else. Those who sincerely take on their part in building this "bridge" between worlds, will be the true heroes of our time. Perhaps the greatest heroes who have ever lived. Living this calling will take immense courage and immense love of life.

May we all find great blessing and grace in our experience of going on this immense journey together.

In love, in soul, and in spirit…

Dean

> The most important thing to do is find your gratitude for life. Take stock of your strengths and give thanks for what you have, and for the joys you've been given. Because that is the fuel. That love for life can act like grace for you to defend life.
>
> *Joanna Macy*

*   *   *

Self Assessment 1. What do you love about life?

This is an ongoing list or inventory of the aspects of life you appreciate, have gratitude for and love deeply.

This is as good a place as any to start a journal, if you don't already keep one. This listing of loves in life is foundational to accessing the profound fountain of inspiration, stamina and grace that lies, usually dormant, within each one of us.

The scale of the predicament and challenges that we will explore in this book together is such that we must bring out our most powerful tools to address it.

Starting now, today, list the aspects of life you appreciate, have gratitude for and love deeply.

Please keep this list as a living document. Allow it to grow and take the time to regularly add to it. You may also find it useful to circle or highlight an item or two that have bumped up to a higher position on your list. While it might be more your style to write this up using your computer, I recommend you do this list in your own handwriting.

Please don't let yourself be distracted by the order in which these items come to you. This list is most effective if you allow each item to come to mind in its own time. You also may want to leave a little room around particular items, to allow for some additional writing about each one.

---

* In <u>Jungian psychology</u>, **"Shadow"** or **"Shadow aspect"** may refer to an <u>unconscious aspect</u> of the <u>personality</u> which the conscious <u>ego</u> does not identify in itself. In short, the Shadow is the "dark side."

1. Exposure to the Sober Data.

The most radical thing any of us can do at this time is to be fully present to what is happening in the world.

Joanna Macy

*   *   *

In many ways, landing at the airport in Southern Oregon was a familiar routine. Flying in over lush green mountains, throw in a few lakes and rivers, really a storybook beautiful place to call home.

This time, fall 2014 was different. Very different. This time my partner and I were coming home after an attempt to become expats in Central America. We had flown down to live, explore and to start to put down roots.

What we did not, and evidently could not, anticipate was that one of us just could not get comfortable with our new living arrangements. It seemed that there was just too much of the unfamiliar and far too little of the precious familiar. Say what you will about that mysterious formula each of us carries inside—that formula determines our ability to relax in a place— and especially determines our ability to call a place "home."

There is probably a book to be written about that awkward and radical set of changes, but what seems to be more important for this book is a little bit of what preceded Central America and a lot about what has happened since we returned.

BEFORE…

I have been in the training business for most of my career life—decades of design and delivery of Corporate, Organizational Development, Personal Development, Communication skills, At-Risk Youth, Intimacy, lots of different types of training and coaching for different audiences around the world. Most of this training was highly experiential and transformational in nature. I am hard pressed to imagine a more fulfilling and enriching career path. It has been a great run.

In the 80s and 90s I would often alternate between facilitating training sessions for corporate executives and training adults to work with At-Risk Youth programs in major cities in the US, Asia and UK. Both of these engagements involved offering transformational workshops to people in communities and organizations—be they corporate managers, or concerned social workers or gang members in a crumbling urban environment.

One part of that work that my partner and I borrowed from the empowerment segments of a number of those trainings was to greatly reduce our footprint, to have only "just-enough" stuff in our space. We both committed to paring down our personal possessions to an absolute minimum in preparation for moving down South.

In looking back, we both repeated often that: "No matter how this whole Central America thing turns out, we are both committed and excited to be paring our footprint of possessions down to a minimum." Little did we know that just a few months after moving down, we would be returning to our little 10x10 storage locker half-filled with our remaining possessions.

Our preparations were not just about the material things of our life. We had both spent considerable time, care and attention on completing all of our personal relationships and of course tying up all the myriad loose ends: taxes, accounts, communications and the like.

The cleaning up of the paperwork stuff was good and important to do but the extra attention and intent on personal relationships being complete and in good shape was at least as empowering as the clean out of our material stuff. This type of cleanup and completion of personal relationships has been in my coaching toolbox for decades and one that I'd personally done many times before. This time, however, was by far the most comprehensive clean up and completion of both inner and outer "stuff" I'd ever done.

*　　*　　*

So we were landing back into an airport, a city, a valley, a region, a state and a country we thought we would see only rarely for years to come. For my partner it was a relief, a welcome return to family, friends, the familiar. For me it was massively disorienting.

When we had moved to Central America I had looked forward to starting up a whole new chapter in life. I was committed to expanding my video production and documentary film projects and was exploring new, possibly international, avenues for training design and delivery.

Moving back I had a massive decision point to confront in myself. This rapid fire 180 degree return to the States could either be "the death of a dream" and "a crippling disappointment," or I could shake off the victim drama and declare that this would be the greatest chapter of my life—ever.

I am very grateful to say that I have found a wonderfully inspiring (albeit occasionally very daunting and lonely) groove for the latter of the choices. But I am getting ahead of myself.

As our plane touched down in Southern Oregon, all I knew was that I had no idea what life held in store for me. Oh, and I had a single video gig to do in 48 hours. Maybe that could be a small first step forward in this new life chapter. Maybe.

*   *   *

What I experienced with the video recording and editing assignment was a lot like being shot out of a cannon. Even with all of my experience with transformation-based, experiential learning I can say that my experience of this two day workshop and the learning curve over the next few months were nothing short of mind blowing.

This video assignment I slipped into so soon after our return flight home was a very small, quiet gathering,. A loose-knit group of folks was presenting a day and a half long workshop about climate change and grief. It seemed like an unusual and intriguing combination of themes.

There were a couple of old friends of mine and a couple of new folks. One of the new ones was the presenter, a retired professor of Conservation Biology who had abandoned all of his past life in academia to go on the road to speak about climate change with anyone who would listen.

As the weekend progressed I was immersed with the rest of the participants in his disclosure of a raft of data and projections. All of this information had been assembled to wake us up to the high probability that everything we anticipated when we thought of climate change was actually coming toward us (the global us) much faster and with much greater ferocity than has been described in our traditional sources for news and information. This accelerated and intensified version of climate change is often called Abrupt Climate Change (ACC). It has also been called Anthropogenic Climate Disruption (ACD)—in other words, caused by Man.

For the last ten years or so, I had pieced together what I thought was a fairly well informed point of view about climate change and the state of our environment. I had assumed that global temperatures would rise to the point of some noticeable damage to our global habitat by 2100 or so. At least that was the year that was usually quoted in the news and special reports I occasionally watched.

I figured this would imply more extreme weather, more heat waves, some rising of sea level and perhaps some added difficulty in terms of survival of some fragile species.

This Abrupt Climate Change information took all of my vague estimates of far-off climate impacts, replaced them with painfully clear articulations of global hardship and, placed them on projected timelines that panned out long before 2100—long before.

The presenter, Professor Guy McPherson, laid out these predictions in a long rather subdued Power Point presentation. Other than the occasional quip of gallows humor the tone of this talk was like any other science-filled Power Point presentation I've ever attended. The absolutely unmistakable difference was the content. These data and projections which McPherson had collected from peer reviewed studies from a number of different climate science niches all pointed to the assertion that severe consequences of climate change are coming more quickly and more intensely than we ever hear from traditional news sources.

My vague, layman's predictions and timelines had some "fairly uncomfortable weather" occurring by the oft-quoted, distant year, 2100. McPherson's presentation listed, with uncomfortable precision, what kind of symptoms we could look forward to and followed that list with a projected timeline for those changes that literally dropped my jaw.

*   *   *

THE SOBER DATA: 2014.

The daunting punch line of Professor McPherson's 2014 presentation was that by combing through reams of data and projections from current studies in global climate science he estimated that Earth is likely to be experiencing average temperatures of between 3 degrees C and 5 degrees C (Celsius) by 2030 to 2050.

Of course, the presentation went into considerable detail about what effects we could expect to see with that temperature rise; but for that first moment all I could hear was that ridiculously close timeline of between 2030 and 2050.

For those unfamiliar with the technical jargon, these temperatures are in terms of the more commonly used Celsius measure (1 degree Celsius = 1.8 degrees Fahrenheit). And, the number of degrees 'C' indicates the number of degrees above the base, average, global temperature recorded at the beginning of the Industrial Revolution (approximately 1750).

THE CONTEXT: THE WORLD AT 4°C

At the center of this Abrupt Climate Change assessment of our world is the assertion that a global temperature rise of 3°C or more in less than a hundred years would be too fast and too radical a change in habitat for the plants upon which all species rely for food, oxygen and so much more. Too fast by a number of orders of magnitude.

In the next chapter, I will share with you some of the clearest and easiest ways to understand descriptions of life on Earth at 4°C. What captured my attention in McPherson's presentation was how, until this dramatic presentation, I had never heard another news source or government agency study mention what life would be like if we allow the global temperature to rise within our business as usual paradigm. I felt a tension and a sinking feeling in my stomach.

POSITIVE FEEDBACK LOOPS / TIPPING POINTS / EXPONENTIAL CHANGES

At the center of Professor McPherson's presentation about Abrupt Climate Change is his "essay" in which he gathers links to current research, articles and videos that describe what are often called: Positive Feedback Loops or Self-Reinforcing Feedback Loops.

In 2014, McPherson had gathered data on more than fifty positive feedback loops and included them in his online essay. One of the simplest examples of a positive feedback loop is the melting of the Arctic ice.[1]

As global temperatures rise (and Arctic temperatures tend to rise far faster than any other place on Earth) the ice cap has been steadily melting and decreasing in thickness and area of coverage. As the ice cap melts it reveals the much darker surface of the sea beneath the ice. As the darker water absorbs more of the sunlight that was previously reflected by the ice, the warmer water accelerates the melting of more ice. And so a "positive" feedback loop is created.

You might have guessed that the use of the word "positive" has nothing to do with our human judgment about the loop being good or bad. In this case positive means that there is an additive value implied to the looping process.

Just a quick word about the melting of Arctic ice. There has always been polar ice on both poles while humanity has been on Earth. The full summer melting of Arctic ice is predicted by the US Navy to be occurring in 2016, plus or minus 3 years. This has been given the nickname of a Blue Water Event.

*   *   *

It is probably important to mention here that many Abrupt Climate Change advocates, including Guy McPherson, assert that there has been no human life on Earth with a temperature above 3.5°C. A viewing of one of McPherson's many YouTube video presentations will also detail his assertion that the years between now and 2030 or 2050 promise to be a progressive, downhill slide regarding the habitability of Earth for us and millions of other species.

*   *   *

This might be a good spot to do a brief reality check with yourself. It certainly was for me.

What I had just been presented was an interpretation of current science data and projections that predicted such intense downgrade of global habitat that human life (and many other species) could be pushed to the edge of extinction. And, this downgrade of habitat could happen within the next fifteen to twenty years. The "long range" projections for this habitat and species destruction seemed to be around 2050.

When I did a reality check here, I could not get my head around these projections. I also noticed that I was barely breathing, taking in and exhaling only tiny wisps of air. I was not very present as I listened to the speaker finish up his talk.

The final segment of this workshop was a few hours of conversation and exercises inviting us to notice our feelings and reactions to the Abrupt Climate Change material. This made sense, giving us a chance to notice some of our emotions and thoughts about this dire information. And, possibly return to deeper breathing.

I was deeply moved by this information, and frankly, stunned by the implications of this Abrupt Climate Change orientation for our collective future. I was so confronted by the data and projections I literally couldn't believe some of them. Could temperatures rise that fast? Could we really be talking about the "Sixth Great Extinction" within our lifetimes? Could one of the species in question be Homo Sapiens?

*   *   *

I invite you to take a few moments and notice how you are experiencing these data and projections. Are you able to be fully present to these predictions? Are you aware of any inner changes in your mood, thoughts, reactions? Are you inspired to do your own validation of these data? What are you feeling?

I suggest starting a journal as you read this book. This material is extremely evocative and I have found it very valuable to set up a regular journal writing practice. Each chapter will include a set of questions to prompt your own progress through The Impossible Conversation.

*   *   *

I was invited to produce some video segments for this fledgling group of folks and offer some counsel regarding future course/workshop design and organizational development.

These were opportunities to bring both of my vocations to a field of study that has long held my interest and now was motivating me at my core—an amazing opportunity sparked by an awful set of predictions.

Like many other professions, Training Design and Video Production both require a producer to really do their homework to prepare for the design process and to assure the integrity of the offerings. To build a training offering or produce a documentary on ill-founded data is a sure way to sabotage even the most prestigious content or sincere motivation of the person or team.

Needless to say, I set about vetting the information, this "Abrupt" Climate Change information and (if this information is true) investigating how and why the world of mainstream culture, especially our conventional media sources, were not including these data and projections in their reports about climate change.

If these dire projections were even half true, I knew that this would be a life-changing threshold. I had no delusions of saving the world but I knew that I would want to bring the best of what I have to offer to a world that could be on track for such severe consequences.

I have always been attentive to the current trends in the world of corporate and personal development training and coaching. I know it is a fiercely competitive industry with everyone trying to find the next hot offering for the limited number of folks who are committed to growing themselves and or their business to the next level.

As of the publishing of this book, there is not one provider out there that is addressing these predicaments. Even at this very early stage of my involvement with this topic and what would become my research, I could see that this, in so many ways, is indeed an Impossible Conversation. As in, no one in their right mind would touch this topic, verifiable or not.

Before I could even begin my research into vetting this ACC data, I was already pondering a second question, "Why is it we are not talking about this anywhere in the world and why aren't all the trainers, thought leaders, life coaches, therapists, course leaders, clergy in the world actively designing and offering curriculum to address this?" Again, more on this later.

*　　*　　*

Full disclosure: I also had to determine if any of these data and projections were just plain wacko. I mean… this shit is crazy, right?!... This was like the REM song, "It's the end of the world as we know it…"

I just wanted to confirm that these abrupt climate change data and projections were solid and real. I had to cover my professional tail enough to know that this wasn't the unfounded babbling of a bunch of crazy, alarmist, conspiracy theorists.

My questions were pretty basic: "Are these data and projections verifiable and true?" And, if so, "Why isn't THIS what we see on the nightly news and on every news site on the Internet?"

Another version of my #1 question: "Are we seriously looking at a possible 3°C to 5°C global average temperature rise by 2050?" (Please notice here I was choosing to investigate figures that were on the very conservative end of McPherson's projected timeline. That reflected my inner capacity at that time, 5°C by 2050 was as far as I could go.)

At this point I need to mention my reading of the just-released, *This Changes Everything: Capitalism vs the Climate,* by Naomi Klein. To this day if I meet someone who only has the space to read one book about our global predicament, I recommend, *This Changes Everything.* There are precious few mainstream journalist-authors who are as thorough and thoughtful as Naomi Klein. At the particular moment I read *This Changes Everything,* I just didn't have the capacity to include all of Klein's message.

It was Klein's detailed inclusion of the ravages of the capitalist system and the dire strains of social justice issues that had me set down her book and not pursue the vetting of the social justice issues. Naively, I just wanted to vet the Abrupt Climate Change data, answer my first couple of questions and get on with my work projects.

I was intending to just isolate the factors involved with my questions, find the answers and move on, unencumbered by rafts of issues, data and metrics that were not directly involved with my inquiry. You can probably see how this choice may come back to haunt me later in the story.

*   *   *

At this stage in the story, let's look at the most superficial and practical justification for why one set of data and projections is on the nightly news and another set never sees the proverbial light of day. Let's take a look at how the climate scientists around the world (like any other self-respecting group of scientists in any other field or focus) use the long-standing scientific method to maintain the highest possible standards of quality control.

For someone not immersed in the world of peer review, scientific method and academia, it might not be immediately obvious just how serious these folks are about maintaining high standards for research and publishing. Suffice it to say that the closer one is to the mainstream center of a study (that would be the UN's Intergovernmental Panel on Climate Change [IPCC], for climate change science) the more rigid and rigorous the adherence to the letter of the scientific method. Many contend that the IPCC is one of the most conservative scientific bodies on the planet.

During the course of my research I would come to learn that the rigorous and meticulous methods used by the scientists in the field, combined with the sometimes frustratingly slow peer review process, make it very clear why these experts are accused of being very conservative in the reporting and analysis of their findings.

In the coming chapters, we will explore some of the other factors that prod the climate science community to distort, self-censor or suppress their findings. These influences could be said to change the descriptor from "conservative" to "suppressed" or "corrupted."

*   *   *

At this early stage of my research, and seeking the answers to my first couple of questions, I was directed, by the scientists I was questioning, to stay focused only on the scientists and data that were at the most rigorous center of the current research being done. Time after time I saw these experts literally frown on any source or data that wasn't fully vetted and peer reviewed within the IPCC standards. This peer review process could take five to seven years or more to reach the level of validation or confirmation.

*   *   *

In order to make my research process clear, I have made up my own Scale of Credibility to make it easier to establish where a given data set, scientist, advocate, denier or curious onlooker is in the grand scheme of vetting climate change data and projections.

My informal scale has 4 levels:

Level One: The science and scientists at this level are all fully vetted, fully approved for inclusion in the findings of the overseeing body of all things global climate change, the UN's IPCC. All of these data and contributors are active in the field of climate science and are fully committed to both the rigors of the scientific method at every stage of their research—and committed to the other scientific and political confines as mandated by the rather odd agency that is the IPCC.

Level Two: The science and scientists on level two are also fully committed to the rigors of the scientific method but may not be active in the field or involved in any form of current research themselves. The advocates of Abrupt Climate Change I mention in this chapter are good exemplars of level two analysts. There are a few journalists (precious few) that also seem appropriate to put here in level two. They are fully versed in how the scientific method works, how the IPCC works and how a given data set, model or projection might affect the findings related to specific

Earth and human systems. The common denominator for all of the people I gather in this home spun credibility scale is their commitment to associating all of the data and projections they mention— with current, vetted findings from the field.

It could be said that scientists and data that have not yet been subjected to the rigors of peer review for their particular project could also be a fit here in level two. We will have a few examples of this in the next couple of chapters.

Level Three: Level three involves the folks who know enough about an aspect of climate change to confirm or validate their particular point of view. As you might imagine this would definitely be the realm of climate change deniers. This is also the level where we would find most environmentalists or climate activists. What is similar between all of these folks is they have just enough knowledge to bolster their particular point of view—and probably not enough curiosity or interest to expand their knowledge beyond that point.

I humbly admit that, despite my staying fairly current with environmental concerns for most of my adult life, I have stayed somewhere between levels three and four. My motivation for writing this book was a result of getting a serious wake up smack and realizing that my desire to validate the Abrupt Climate Change projections would require me advancing my level of engagement from that of a layman at level three or four, to a layman who is conversant at least at level two.

Level Four: This is the level for everyone else. At level four a person occasionally hears something on the news in passing about climate change, knows it is somehow important, has little or no discernment regarding the accuracy or bias that might accompany that news, and sets up their life to conveniently avoid getting any more informed than that. There are many US citizens who sit smack dab in the middle of level four. All climate denial proponents are banking on the vast majority of people staying comfortably here in Level Four.

Level 2: Scientists and analysts with Abrupt Climate Change Projections:

I have included here four of the most prominent and vocal advocates of one version or another of Abrupt Climate Change projections. There are others, but I started my research project focusing on the work of these four in particular. Any reader who desires more sources, more pointed information to begin their own research, can find chapter references at the end of this book. I have also committed a substantial portion of *The Impossible Conversation* website to an extensive list of sources for climate science, other related science, activist organizations, supporting articles, books and films: www.ImpossibleConversation.net

1. Guy McPherson:[1] http://guymcpherson.com

Guy McPherson is Professor Emeritus of Natural Resources and the Environment at the University of Arizona. He has committed himself to gathering vetted, current climate change findings and relaying those findings to diverse audiences around the world.

Readers wishing to immerse themselves in the references **Professor** McPherson uses for his talks and books can refer to the extensive reference essay on his website:

http://guymcpherson.com/2014/01/climate-change-summary-and-update/

(Please check this site often for updates. It has been very difficult for me to keep up with Abrupt Climate Change updates and acceleration since beginning the writing of this book. I cannot overstate how disturbing it has been to see the dramatic increase in volume and acceleration of the ACC updates just in the last half of 2015, through 2016, and now faster still with the installation of the Trump administration and its anti-environmental stance.)

The link provided here is to an ever growing, often updated, "Summary" McPherson has produced in the past few years. While it covers many different elements and topics in the Abrupt Climate Change conversation, the center of this document appears to be McPherson's growing list of Positive Feedback Loops.

These well documented phenomena and measures are sometimes called "self-reinforcing feedback loops." When this type of loop is activated in the natural world, changes in element one in the system effect elements two and three. The subsequent changes in elements two and three then reinforce further changes in element one, which again effect elements two and three, and so on, ad infinitum.

I already mentioned the example of the melting of Arctic sea ice as one of these Self Reinforcing Feedback Loops.

To date, McPherson has catalogued more than sixty such Positive Feedback Loops regarding Abrupt Climate Change. We will explore a few more of these Feedback Loops in this book, particularly those involved with the release of methane in Arctic subsea and tundra environments. Each of these disturbing feedback loops has at least two things in common—one, they are not commonly included in the calculations of the IPCC, and two, they all tend to imply the possibility of a non-linear acceleration of a climate change symptom when fully activated. This effect can range from a rapid acceleration after a certain tipping point is reached, to an unpredictable, exponential jump in intensity.

In his 2014 talks, McPherson often estimated that, because of these feedbacks, global temperatures may rise to 5°C or more by as early as 2030. He went on to say that while humans may find some habitable pockets of habitat on Earth in those conditions, few or none of the plants we rely on for food will be able to adapt to those rapid changes. Yes, his is a dire prediction for humanity and for most other species on the planet as well. McPherson is quite well known for his particularly dark and dramatic predictions about the future of humanity given this acceleration and intensification implied in the Abrupt Climate Change scenario. In the original presentation I watched in 2014, McPherson estimated that human beings would no longer be living on the planet between the years 2030 to 2050.

*　　*　　*

An update: As I am finishing up writing this book, it is a full two years since my introduction to Abrupt Climate Change by Guy McPherson. In that two year span, McPherson and I, both, have updated our projections for Abrupt Climate Change. We both have landed on a range of probable temperature increases that are well detailed by Sam Carana below.

Both McPherson[1a] and Sam Carana[3] added together a number of climate impacting elements and Positive Feedback Loops to come to some stunning estimates of global warming that surpass the estimates McPherson used back in 2014. In the Carana graphic and text, the projected possible temperature rise was between 4°C and 10°C by as soon as 2026.

McPherson encountered some resistance to his estimates, using these analytical methods from Prof. Peter Wadhams—a world renowned climate scientist with extensive Arctic research credentials. He asserts that McPherson may well have erred on the side of being far too conservative by adding the elements together. Wadhams asserted, in a conversation with McPherson, that the elements may well have to be multiplicative, or be seen as multipliers for each other, rather than additive. A disturbing notion indeed. This could imply a 4°C to 10°C warming far sooner than 2026.

*　　*　　*

A must see, for a number of reasons, is Guy McPherson's guest appearance on National Geographic Explorer.[100] In that episode, Bill Nye is joined by Arnold Schwarzenegger exploring how grief is actually a very appropriate human response to the current projections about global, Anthropogenic (Human Caused) Climate Disruption.

I've got to say, this episode of National Geographic Explorer was astounding. It is the only mainstream media program that I've seen that explores in detail the projections of Abrupt Climate Change. Moreover, the episode wraps that data in an extraordinary context of just how healthy and appropriate it is to view these coming climate impacts through a lens of our individual and collective grief. (And it is primarily delivered through the lens of Elizabeth Kubler Ross' Stages of Dying/Grief.)

Someone had a stroke of genius when they cast Arnold Schwarzenegger as Bill Nye's therapist in this program. And McPherson holds his own in his role as the messenger of doom and gloom. While the plot line of this show implies some good-natured, tongue in cheek humor, the writers do a very solid job of addressing this deeply challenging topic without trivializing it or demeaning the grieving process virtually all of us will encounter some day soon—or may already be experiencing.

Additionally, we should not miss the irony that this show was aired within days of the announcement that Rupert Murdock, a world-class climate change denier, had purchased National Geographic, including the National Geographic Channel. My guess is that will be the last climate change/grief related content we will see on the National Geographic Channel or any other iteration of National Geographic content.

(As of August 2016, Murdoch's National Geographic purchased the rights to Leonardo DiCaprio's latest documentary about Climate Change, *Before the Flood*. The documentary was shown, free of charge, to thousands around the world, just before the US presidential elections in November 2016.)

If I may take a moment to review both DeCaprio's, *Before the Flood,* and Al Gore's, *An Inconvenient Truth*, both of these films are beautifully made, well researched and essentially useless from my point of view as tools to change humanity's direction. Both end up with what is quite common now—a sign-off that says, "if we all start serious action now to mitigate our global climate challenge then we still have a strong chance of staying below the COP21 limit of 2°C."

As you will see in the coming chapters, this is a deceitful declaration that the most powerful countries, companies and consumers on the planet have repeatedly chosen to broadcast while doing exactly nothing of any import in the twenty-five years of climate mitigation negotiations.

2. Sam Carana, *Arctic News.*

http://arctic-news.blogspot.com/p/posts.html

Sam Carana is the nom de plume of an anonymous curator, editor and contributor at Arctic News, among many other publications and blogs. Carana's forte appears to be the combining of astute analysis of current research findings regarding aspects of Abrupt Climate Change with a remarkable ability to generate clear and informative infographics to make the analysis even more accessible to the lay reader and expert alike.

While you will find hundreds of such postings on Carana's site, *Arctic News*, the posting of Sunday, March 13, 2016 titled, *February Temperature*, is one of the most disturbing articles I have read from any source. In his usual style of presenting referenced data and projections with simple, clear graphics, Carana adds up the projected cumulative effects of a number of the Positive Feedback Loops articulated by many current Arctic researchers and Guy McPherson on his website and in his talks.[1a]

In the February Temperature article, Carana lands on a range of land-based, global temperature increase between 3.9°C and 10.4°C. As if these estimates weren't staggering enough, the timeline for this projected temperature rise is by 2026.

This is a full four years sooner and more than double the temperature increase than the projections that launched me into this research project in the first place.

3. **February Temperature**.

http://arctic-news.blogspot.com/2016/03/february-temperature.html

Again, this is a projection of 3.9°C to over 10°C in global, land-based temperature rise by 2026, less than 10 years from the time this book is being written.

A Global Temperature Rise of More Than Ten Degrees Celsius by 2026? "Arctic News Blog," Sam Carana. July 15, 2016. All of the graphs, data and projections from February article with more detail and context.

http://arctic-news.blogspot.com/2016/07/a-global-temperature-rise-of-more-than-ten-degrees-celsius-by-2026.html

In this article all of the estimates and projections that were first offered in Carana's February piece are articulated in clear layman's terms. Each of the climate affecting elements is described as are some of the methods of estimating and calculating that were used for his 10°C by 2026 projection.

These elements are added together, in Carana's scenario, to yield a 10°C global temperature increase by 2026.

These descriptions of the climate warming elements is a fine primer on not only Abrupt Climate Change but also what constitutes a Positive Feedback Loop or a Tipping Point and how those events can yield non-linear or exponential changes in an Earth system.

As I have mentioned in the sections describing the work of Guy McPherson and Peter Wadhams, Wadhams suggested to McPherson that the positive feedbacks that were added up to form Carana's 10°C by 2016 graphic may be better described as "multiplicative." If this is the case, then the already devastating estimate of a global temperature rise of up to 10°C by 2026 could occur even sooner and imply an even greater temperature rise.

*   *   *

The *February Temperature* article mentioned above does include Arctic methane release as one of the positive feedback loops that combine to project a possible global temperature rise of 3.9°C to 10°C. Carana is not alone including methane in his projections and modeling.

Current and historical data show that atmospheric methane measured at 700ppb in pre-industrial times, now ranges between 1800-1945 ppb. (parts per billion). The other Abrupt Climate Change advocates I mention, Peter Wadhams, David Wasdell and of course Guy McPherson—with his hefty list of positive feedback loops—also have their attention on the release of Arctic methane into the atmosphere.

Methane is more than eighty to one hundred times as powerful a green house gas as CO2 during its first twenty years of its lifespan in the atmosphere. Its effects diminish over time after that.

Methane is a considerable part of the exhaust and waste produced in many human technologies and a huge part of our global fossil fuel and animal agriculture industries.

During the writing of this book, a massive methane leak in Southern California brought the world's attention to this otherwise little-known greenhouse gas. This leak also brought our attention to the almost nonexistent regulation of methane and its handling.

McPherson, Wadhams, Carana and Wasdell, among many others, have drawn attention to the greatest storehouse of methane on the planet. This storehouse consists of methane trapped in the frozen layer of permafrost in the Arctic and trapped in the undersea equivalent of permafrost – primarily in the East Siberian Sea off of Arctic Russia.

Like the positive feedback loop mentioned before, Arctic sea ice melting and giving way to darker seas, it is estimated by some Arctic and climate scientists that as much as fifty gigatons (a gigaton is equal to one billion metric tons) of methane could be released in the rapidly warming Arctic between 2015 and 2025.

A fifty gigaton release of methane would be ten times as much methane as currently exists in the atmosphere. Atmospheric methane levels have more than doubled since the start of the Industrial Revolution, but this predicted Arctic thaw would amount to a much sharper increase in a dramatically shorter time frame.

I have included a few links to the work of a climate scientist, Natalia Shakhova, later in this chapter to add important detail to this subject of arctic methane release. Shakhova and her fellow researchers have first hand experience of large scale Arctic methane release and equally disturbing accounts of corporate and government representatives' attempts to suppress their findings.

It should be mentioned that, in all of my research, there was no more disputed climate change projection or metric than this notion of a large scale, near term release of methane from Arctic sea floor and permafrost. The more conservative scientists estimate that there is no concern about a large scale Arctic release of methane in the near future. Obviously Abrupt Climate Change advocates think and speak quite differently.

Interesting that there is so much controversy about how to measure the potential impact of methane in our climate change calculations and to date there has been no inclusion of methane in any IPCC projections or public reports.

4. **David Wasdell:** (included in greater detail in chapter 3), Director, Apollo-Gaia Project. Accredited reviewer for the IPCC's 2007 Fourth Assessment Report.

http://www.apollo-gaia.org

Lead on Feedback Dynamics in Coupled Complex Global Systems for the European Commission's Global System Dynamics and Policy (GSDP) network.

Wasdell has articulated an elaborate alternative method for modeling global atmospheric sensitivity that yields a far faster and more intense impact on global temperatures than IPCC modeling. He asserts that we are already far over budget re carbon emissions to even consider a 2°C temperature target and on track to decimate our habitat/Earth well before 2100.

*   *   *

Many of the above findings probably would not be accepted in the IPCC reports because either they have not yet been subjected to peer review or they could be judged to include personal opinion, analysis or interpretations that could be seen as contrary to the ultra conservative IPCC/mainstream message or deemed to be "alarmist."

Level 1: Scientists with Abrupt Climate Change Projections:

The scientists at this level are solidly in level one.

These are all long-standing experts in their field with impeccable credentials and track records for very strong findings, projections and peer review validation. I have included each of these scientists because they have shown an unapologetic, full-throated warning of and advocacy for what can easily be called, Abrupt Climate Change projections.

James Hansen[5 a-c] : As of 2014, Hansen directs the Program on Climate Science, Awareness and Solutions at Columbia University's Earth Institute. Formerly (1981 to 2013) head of NASA Goddard Institute for Space Studies.

James Hansen is credited with being one of the first climate scientists to publicly declare that climate change is real and human caused and advancing more and more rapidly.

Professor Hansen has become one of the most vocal and activist members of the climate science community. His opinion regarding the COP21 proposed cap of

2°C on CO2 emissions: "It is crazy to say that 2°C would be safe."

Hansen has recently been researching large scale, land-based ice melt. He and his team have not yet had their recent findings peer reviewed, but they project a global sea level rise far faster (up to a meter every twenty years for the foreseeable future) than the ultra conservative IPCC projects (up to one meter of sea level rise by 2100).

While we will be filling in much more detail about the catastrophic effects of projected sea level rise in later chapters, suffice it to say that the economic costs of adapting to meters of rise will be calculated in the trillions of dollars. And the world is already starting to see the human costs of rising seas with the disappearance of numerous islands and low-lying inhabited deltas around the world.

6. Michael Mann. It could be said that climate scientists have been under attack from corporate, governmental and media representatives for years now. The motivation for these attacks is purely because the data and projections of these scientists are seen as alarmist threats to the continuation of our global business-as-usual system. Michael Mann has arguably been the climate scientist who has suffered the most direct threats, vilification and inquisition for the data and projections he has produced regarding the damage of climate change to Earth systems.

The interested reader is recommended to read any of Mann's books or view any of the many *YouTube* videos of his presentations. In my eyes Michael Mann is a strong exemplar of strength of character, integrity and an obvious love of humanity and Earth. My main question is, How does he keep doing his work in the face of yet another interrogation by Congress and how does he keep his even temperament and sense of humor? Truly he is an example to us all.

8. Professor Peter Wadhams. Professor of Ocean Physics. Emeritus Head of the Polar Ocean Physics Group at the University of Cambridge.

Professor Wadhams suggests that Guy McPherson may be underestimating the combined impact of a number of Self-Reinforcing Feedback Loops. (Carana Article above.) They may indeed be multiplicative, rather than additive,as McPherson has asserted.

Wadhams helps us understand what is meant by Tipping Points. He points to the analog of when a spring is loaded beyond a certain limit, it will be stretched beyond its capacity and will no longer recoil to its prior, unloaded shape. Similarly when our Earth systems are stressed beyond a certain "tipping point," the system will not return to the cycle of average or normal that had been observed prior.

Professor Wadhams is one of the finest Climate Change Communicators on the planet today. I have included a link to a recent interview with Prof. Wadhams at the end of this chapter. I strongly recommend watching the entire twenty minute clip to get a vivid notion of what he and other experts are seeing in the field now. The viewer will also be offered a remarkable layout of how methane affects our climate and how the current situation should be perceived now. Wadhams makes a case that any layman can understand, for how important it is for humanity to take massive, immediate action to have any chance of slowing the accelerating progression of positive feedback loops.

This is particularly appropriate as a way of understanding the dynamic when one or more positive feedback loops are activated and intensified beyond the carrying capacity of that system. As you will hear in the video clip, there are a number of significant tipping points which we appear to have crossed, or soon will.

Please take note how Prof. Wadhams finishes the interview with a rousing cheer for the possibility of being saved by geoengineering and carbon capture technologies. He calls for a Manhattan-Project-scale campaign to invent and bring into global production some kind of technology to remove CO_2 from our atmosphere.

I respect and admire Professor Wadhams and his research findings. I think you will see that I have concluded that the geoengineering and carbon capture technologies he hopes for in this interview are just that—hopes. Like the IPCC we will talk about in later chapters, Wadhams is relying on non-existent technologies as a solution for our predicament. There are no geoengineering methods extant that show any chance of reducing CO_2 emissions from our atmosphere. The two major bottlenecks in current research are: 1) How to extract the CO_2 and or deflect the solar radiation absorbed by our planet without causing even more drastic problems in our wake and 2) The cost. In our world of polluters who are unwilling to pay the cost of our daily extraction, production and use of fossil fuels we are unlikely to rally to the cause of paying for the clean up of our atmosphere.

Professor Kevin Anderson[7, 7a]. Deputy Director of the Tyndall Centre for Climate Change Research; holds a joint chair in Energy and Climate Change at the School of Mechanical, Aerospace and Civil Engineering at the University of Manchester and School of Environmental Sciences at the University of East Anglia; and is an honorary lecturer in Environmental Management at the Manchester

Business School. He is an adviser to the British Government (as of 2009) on climate change. He asserts, re COP21,

> The fundamentals of the whole process are wildly optimistic. It starts with climate models that assume too much, spills into unreal scientific advice and ends with rosy media reports that say that we can keep on growing without wrecking the climate. Our Western lifestyles won't be too greatly inconvenienced, say the IPCC and media projections.

Anderson's findings contradict the popular narrative that change will be "challenging but incremental," and compatible with continued conventional economic growth in markets around the world. According to Wikipedia, early in 2011, Anderson co-authored a paper with Alice Bows in a special issue of a Royal Society journal with other papers from the above conference. The Anderson and Bows "**analysis suggests that despite high-level statements to the contrary, there is now little to no chance of maintaining the global mean surface temperature at or below 2°C. Moreover, the impacts associated with 2°C have been revised upwards, sufficiently so that 2°C now more appropriately represents the threshold between 'dangerous' and 'extremely dangerous' climate change.**" (Emphasis mine.) Anderson says,

> Put bluntly, while the rhetoric of policy is to reduce emissions in line with avoiding dangerous climate change, most policy advice is to accept a high probability of extremely dangerous climate change rather than propose radical and immediate emission reductions.

I have included a substantial number of quotes and bullet points from Kevin Anderson because he is both a Level One climate scientist and boldly expresses what I agree to be the most sober and accurate way of describing our existential human predicament.

Anderson pulls no punches. Here I am excerpting from a recent talk professor Anderson did in Iceland. Of all of the Level One and Two scientists, journalists and advocates I mention here, Kevin Anderson is the one that really tells it like it is. Guy McPherson may tend to speak just a bit too much about near-term human extinction for my taste and ALL of the others are based far too much in a business-as-usual context; but these quotes and bullet points will take you to the center of Anderson's (and my own) assessment of the truth of our situation.

*   *   *

7b. Here are a number of bullet points from the *Ostrich and Phoenix* video I link to at the end of this chapter.

• Anderson calculates that our proposed global "Carbon Budget" will be completely used up by 2034.

• Global temperature is about: Cumulative Emissions and Carbon Budgets. Period.

• The word "economics," from the Greek, oikonimia, originally implied stewardship of the home. But it has been co-opted by the world of finance and now implies the singular focus on the extraction of profit, the hoarding of wealth, banking and finance: the commodification of everything.

• The main message of climate science has not changed in the twenty-five years of meetings that have been held about climate change.

Since 1990...

• World has dumped another 200 Gtns of CO_2 into the atmosphere.

• Annual emissions have risen 65% since 1990.

• Emissions have risen steadily @3% per year since 80s.

• We will not feel the effects of CO_2 emitted today for at least ten to forty years.

• CO_2 levels are higher than last 800k yrs. (about 3x longer than humans on Earth).

• We need deep and immediate reductions in energy demand, especially in the developed countries.

• Optimists are fond of saying, "We can do it with low carbon energy supply." (Renewable Sources)

NO. There is not nearly enough renewable energy supply to deliver

34

a comparable energy supply within the brief time we have.

• 2050 is an irrelevant date re mitigating CC. To project for this date for policy making decisions, is seriously misguided. In other words, it's too distant a target.

• We have missed, chosen to avoid, all easier mitigation choice points for twenty-five years.

• UK considers itself a "leader" on climate mitigation while offering tax breaks on shale gas development, proposing thirty new gas powered power plants, making highest investment ever in N Sea oil, reopening Scottish coal mines, expanding aviation and ports, reducing emission standards for cars, supporting Arctic exploration for hydrocarbons, and opening a consulate next to tar sands operations in Alberta.

Imagine how the US stacks up now—and will stack up in comparison with these UK statistics—as we see how the new Trump administration focuses its energy policies.

• Globally, if we continue with business-as-usual emissions, we are predicted to produce 5,000 gigatons of CO_2 between 2000 and 2100. **This alone will yield a 4°C to 7°C temp rise by 2100 (conservative estimate).**

• IPCC global budget was for 1,000 Gtns CO_2 (2011 budget projection). Approximately 20% less now at end of 2016 = 800Gtns.

• "The CO_2 trend is perfectly in line with a temperature increase of 6C, which would have devastating consequences for the planet." Faith Birol, IEA chief economist (International Energy Agency)

• We are now on a business-as-usual track toward 4°C to 6°C by 2050. We need to get to zero CO_2 emissions by 2050to stay under 2°C (Abrupt Climate Change estimate).

• From an engineering perspective, we can't engineer or build our way out of this situation.

• How about nuclear as an alternative energy source? Very low CO_2 emissions (per kwh produced). This doesn't account for the CO_2 footprint of the cement used in initial construction. Estimates that include accounting for the large CO_2 footprint of the construction of any nuclear plant show approximately thirty years for this CO_2 to be fully "paid for" by the project. Most current nuclear plants have a functional lifespan of thirty years.

• World uses 105,000 terawatt hours of energy per year. Electricity consumption is about 20,000 TWH or about 20% of total.

• Nuclear provides apprx 11.5% of global electricity: 435 stations. To bring that up to 25% of global electricity production between three and four thousand new plants would have to be built around the world in the next thirty years. (There are currently seventy new nuclear stations being built around the world.)

• No matter if one is talking about nuclear, wind, solar or Carbon Capture and Storage— the facilities cannot be built fast enough to keep us from surpassing our budget of fossil fuel based CO_2 emissions.

• WE HAVE TO REDUCE OUR ENERGY CONSUMPTION... YES, US... ALL OF US. NOW— especially the heaviest consumers and emitters in the most developed countries.

So what would we (in the US and other developed countries) have to do to come anywhere near meeting the COP21 2°C target? This means that the US and other high emissions developing countries would have to reduce emissions by approximately 15% per year, starting now:

• a 40% reduction from 2014 levels by 2018. And a 70% reduction by 2024. And 90% by 2030 to 2035.

• This is the truth of the Budget.

• What if we gave ourselves a new target of 4°C?

We would have far more strange weather: We would lose thousands more to heat waves around the world. Electrical grids would suffer massive deterioration and failures in such heat. Tarmacks would melt. Food and other essentials deliveries would fail. Train tracks would buckle. Approximately 40% drop in crop yields due to heat. **4°C is not compatible with a global organized community. Anderson: "4°C is beyond adaptation."** Massive refugee migrations in far greater numbers than 2016, devastating to ecosystems. Tipping Points (as mentioned by Guy McPherson) triggered frequently. Like World Bank mentioned in chapter 2—4°C is to be "avoided at all costs."

We, the elite in the developed world, will choose to do nothing.

Some Anderson Solutions:

• Retrofit cars and trucks to be far more efficient. He suggests a 50 to 70 % drop in emissions in ten yrs. with no change in infrastructure or more cost. And we aren't even doing that.

• There are now refrigerators that use 1/3 of the energy of the average one—and yet we still sell the average ones because we are more committed to the choices for the consumer than to any real change in our carbon footprint. This one change would yield a 60% saving of CO2 in ten yrs.

These are but two examples that cost virtually nothing—that we are not doing.

• Technology could help with efficiency, scaled tech and reductions.

We must throw out the delusion of infinite growth on a finite planet. There are alternative measures of a good life.

Pareto's 80:20 rule: e.g. 80% of something relates to 20% of those involved. 80% of emissions from 20% of population. "Run this 3 times" and you get…50% of emissions from 1% of population.

"The emissions we are putting out now mean other people will die. We as climate scientists cannot pretend not to know this."

"And this is about poor people in other countries now, but it will soon enough be about the deaths of our own children."

Most people in the world do not fly in airplanes. 2°C and mitigation are not about population. It is about US, the biggest consumers, reducing our consumption and emissions immediately.

There are 300 million people in China who currently enjoy what we in the developed world call a middle class lifestyle.

For a 2°C budget to be realized, we will need to choose between…

a) OUR flying to another conference, family visit or sun-kissed holiday.

or

b) THEIR access to energy for basic needs.

This means every time we choose a), we imply that poor people should be kept poor longer and have them suffer more the effects of climate change. This is what we all just don't want to think about.

GROWTH…

Economists assert… "any mitigation over four percent per year is incompatible with economic growth."

Why on Earth are we listening to the economists whose failed economy we live in, e.g. Alan Greenspan, 'I am shocked by the failure of the markets to self regulate.' We have the foxes guarding the chicken coop. (Add Trump's administration to that. CEO of Exxon, Rex Tillerson, is Secretary of State; Rick Perry is Secretary of Energy; Scott Pruitt heads the EPA.) More on this later.

We have an unprecedented opportunity to create an entirely new economic model for the world. Growth makes the heterogeneous homogeneous. In itself it has no meaningful value. Notice how growth, as a core metric of our world, forces us to monetize and commoditize everything. Everything.

And yet, all the things that matter the most for us are priceless. De-commodifying our world must be at the center of any new economic model and lifestyle model. We also must radically reduce our energy consumption and emissions. Now through 2030. Even the most conservative interpretations of the IPCC COP21 calculations, indicate we must create a Marshall-style-plan of low-carbon energy supply with 100% penetration by 2030-2040.

Ultimately, we must escape the shackles of a twentieth century mindset of business as usual, if we are ever to resolve twenty-first century challenges. This will demand leadership, courage, innovative thinking, engaged teams and difficult choices.

*   *   *

At every level the greatest obstacle to transforming the world is that we lack the clarity and imagination to conceive that it could be different.

Robert Unger

Thank you reader for reading through this particularly long section. I promise that this level of detail, combined with Professor Anderson's passion, will be extraordinarily useful as a reference when we get to the governmental and corporate forces at work on the other side of this Impossible Conversation.

We need thousands of climate scientists to step up and communicate with Kevin Anderson's passion, clarity and imagination. We then need millions of regular citizens to understand the gravitas in this Sober Data as described by Kevin Anderson, Guy McPherson, Michael Mann, James Hansen and many others. This is clearly a time for standing up for the continuity of life on Earth.

*   *   *

At this stage in my learning-how-to-learn about Abrupt Climate Change I started the sometimes uncomfortable process of expanding my elementary and fragmented understanding of some small aspect of this field, to include more of its context.

What is delivered as a single issue or single metric for a situation (e.g. COP21 in Paris and our sole fixation on global CO_2 emissions) is ridiculous when considered alone and removed from its native systems: the atmosphere and all the other elements and dynamics within it, the biological systems that interact with and rely on CO_2 as an essential part of those systems and on and on.

As you will see in the coming chapters it is literally impossible to separate our biosphere into its many individual elements. Or more importantly, to attempt to interact with only one element of our biosphere to measure how "sustainable" our human industrial processes might be.

In fact, we will see that the same systems dynamics and interrelatedness that is at the core of our home, our habitat, the biosphere, Earth are also to be found at the core of our human systems. And, yes, this has become more than a little problematic given our huge cultural and individual blind spots caused by our disconnection from our deeper awareness of Self, our essential relationships with Others and our most essential interrelatedness with Earth.

We will be exploring some of the costs of that core disconnection and some of the most powerful ways to reconnect ourselves to life itself.

Thank you again for your courage in taking this journey. It is a journey that I promise will deeply change and empower all who take it on.

2. Life at 4°C

In fact, we are almost guaranteed to reach 4 degrees of warming, as early as 2050, and may soar far beyond that—beyond the point which agriculture, the ecosystem, and industrial civilization can survive.

Kevin Anderson

Even in the unlikely event of us succeeding at staying below 2°C, millions of poor people will die as a result of our collective, insufficient action at mitigation.

Kevin Anderson

Beyond 1° C may elicit rapid, unpredictable and non-linear responses that could lead to extensive ecosystem damage."

United Nations Advisory Group on Greenhouse Gases. October 1990

We are at about 490ppm, (CO_2 equivalent, including methane and other greenhouse gases) today. The likelihood of going over 500ppm is almost a certainty. There is a reasonably high probability of going over 600. And so, this is very scary. Because if you look at what we are doing now—the rate of CO_2 we're putting up (in the atmosphere— and we look at how seriously countries are taking these reduction targets, they are not taking them seriously) it is very hard to see us stopping at 550ppm. I can tell you that 1°C temperature rise is really bad, so to contemplate 2°C, 3°C, 4°C and higher is obviously far worse. And, this is all happening in a non-linear fashion.

Steven Chu[1a]Former US Secretary of Energy

So we now have data and projections from Abrupt Climate Change advocates that point to possible effects of continuing our business as usual ways that include global average temperature rise as high as 3°C to 10°C by as soon as 2026 to 2050 and sea level rise projections of up to one meter every twenty years for the foreseeable future.

We can contrast these projections against the ultra conservative, business as usual projections of the IPCC of 3°C to 5°C of temperature rise and one meter of sea level rise by 2100.

What we need here is a bit more basic information about what these projections mean. Perhaps the central question here is, What does life on Earth look and feel like at say, 4°C? (4 degrees Celsius above the pre Industrial Revolution average temperatures.)

For this, and many other pieces of what I am calling the Sober Data, I am pursuing sources that are as conservative and middle of the road as I can find. What I'm after is the clearest, least biased projections available from respected mainstream sources.

For the answer to the question, "What does life on Earth look and feel like at 4°C?" I went to that wacky, left-wing bunch of tree huggers at the World Bank.

In their 2012 report[1] *Turn Down the Heat: Why a 4°C Warmer World Must be Avoided*, the authors detail the extraordinary global damage that will occur should we allow our emissions to take us to a 4°C temperature rise. They predict that global crop production would fail by as much as 25% to 50% and much more.

The 4°C scenarios are devastating: "the inundation of coastal cities; increasing risks for food production potentially leading to higher malnutrition rates; many dry regions becoming dryer, wet regions wetter; unprecedented heat waves in many regions, especially in the tropics; substantially exacerbated water scarcity in many regions; increased frequency of high-intensity tropical cyclones; and irreversible loss of biodiversity, including coral reef systems."

And most importantly, "a 4°C world is so different from the current one that it comes with high uncertainty and new risks that threaten our ability to anticipate and plan for future adaptation needs."

"The lack of action on climate change not only risks putting prosperity out of reach of millions of people in the developing world, it threatens to roll back decades of sustainable development."

Turn Down the Heat continues…

"Despite the global community's best intentions to keep global warming below a 2°C increase above pre-industrial climate, higher levels of warming are increasingly likely. Scientists agree that countries' current United Nations Framework Convention on Climate Change emission pledges and commitments would most likely result in 3.5° to 4°C warming. And the longer those pledges remain unmet, the more likely a 4°C world becomes.[1] "

*   *   *

New research is showing that when Earth's vegetation, traditionally a primary carbon sink for the planet, is exposed to 4°C temperatures it would soon shut down its ability to absorb CO_2…

The modeling shows that global warming of four degrees will result in Earth's vegetation becoming "dominated" by negative impacts— such as "moisture stress," when plant cells have too little water on a global scale.

Carbon-filled vegetation 'sinks' will likely become saturated at this point, they say, flat-lining further absorption of atmospheric CO_2. Without such major natural CO_2 drains, atmospheric carbon will start to increase more rapidly, driving further climate change.[2]

As far back as 2008, some of the world's top climate scientists were warning us that we would be wise to plan for at least a 4°C rise. Bob Watson should know— he is the former chair of the Intergovernmental Panel on Climate Change (IPCC), but was kicked out at the behest of the Bush administration for being too vocal about the threat presented by global warming.

Professors Bob Watson and Neil Adger spoke in a *Guardian* article[2a]:

"There is no doubt that we should aim to limit changes in the global mean surface temperature to 2°C above pre-industrial," Watson, the chief scientific adviser to the Department for the Environment, Food and Rural Affairs, told the *Guardian*. "But given this is an ambitious target, and we don't know in detail how to limit greenhouse gas emissions to realize a 2 degree target, we should be prepared to adapt to 4°C."

Globally a 4°C temperature rise would have a catastrophic impact.

According to the government's 2006 Stern review on the economics of climate change, "between 7 million and 300 million more people would be affected by coastal flooding each year, there would be a 30-50% reduction in water availability in Southern Africa and the Mediterranean, agricultural yields would decline 15 to 35% in Africa and 20 to 50% of animal and plant species would face extinction."

One big unknown is the stage at which dangerous tipping points would be reached that lead to further warming. For example the release of methane hydrate deposits in the Arctic. My own feeling is that if we get to a 4 degree rise it is quite possible that we would begin to see a runaway increase.

You will recall the mention of positive feedback loops or self-reinforcing feedback loops in chapter one. The tipping points mentioned here are thresholds reached within those loops after which mitigation or stopping the effects is no longer possible.

"At 4 degrees we are basically into a different climate regime," said Prof. Neil Adger, an expert on adaptation to climate change at the Tyndall Centre for Climate Change Research in Norwich. "I think that is a dangerous mindset to be in. Thinking through the implications of 4 degrees of warming shows that the impacts are so significant that the only real adaptation strategy is to avoid that at all cost because of the pain and suffering that is going to cost. **There is no science on how we are going to adapt to 4 degrees warming. It is actually pretty alarming**,"

In yet another *Guardian* article[2b] from 2008 Watson:

"Mitigate for two degrees; adapt for four" has long been the catchphrase among climate negotiators and campaigners. Translated, that means: try to reduce emissions to stay below two degrees of warming, but also prepare for the worst."

The problem with the "mitigate for two degrees; adapt for four" strategy is that it is doomed to fail. Yes, we should certainly prepare for the worst as far as possible— with flood defenses, drought-resistant crops and strategies to ameliorate the loss of wildlife, at the very least— but a look at the likely impact of a four-degrees temperature rise suggests that such a dramatic change would probably stretch society's capacity for adaptation to the limit, not to mention having a disastrous effect on the natural ecosystems that support humanity as a whole.

By the time global temperatures reach four degrees, much of humanity will be short of water for drinking and irrigation: glaciers in the Andes and Himalayas, which feed river systems on which tens of millions depend, will have melted, and their rivers will be seasonally running dry. Whole weather systems like the Asian monsoon (which supports 2 billion people) may alter irrevocably. Deserts will have spread into Mediterranean Europe, across most of southern Africa and the western half of the United States. Higher northern latitudes will be plagued with regular flooding. Heat waves of unimaginable ferocity will sear continental landscapes: the UK would face the kind of summer temperatures found in northern Morocco today. The planet would be in the throes of a mass extinction of natural life approaching in magnitude that at the end of the Cretaceous period, 65m years ago, when more than half of global biodiversity was wiped out.

Four degrees of warming would also cross many of the "tipping points" which so concern climate scientists: the Amazon rainforest would likely collapse and burn, as part of a massive further release of carbon from terrestrial ecosystems— the reverse of the current situation, where trees and soils absorb and store a good portion of our annual emissions. Most of the Arctic permafrost will lie in the melt zone, and will be steadily releasing methane, accelerating warming still further. The northern polar ice cap will be a distant memory, and Greenland will be melting so rapidly that sea level rise by the end of the century will be measured in meters rather than centimeters.

You will read in another chapter that Greenland's ice sheet is already melting 600% faster than the most recent projections predicted.

The harsh truth is that the latest science shows that even two degrees is not good enough, never mind four. And since four degrees would be a catastrophe that many of us, or our children, would not survive, it is surely our absolute duty to do everything in our power to avoid it.

This isn't just about reducing emissions, it is about getting emissions quickly down to zero (by 2050 or earlier). And, to repeat, many of the researchers and analysts quoted in this book are asserting that we have passed so many critical tipping points that we will actually see no relief even if we were to reduce our emissions to zero today.

Lastly I can recommend a book to any reader who wishes to get a fuller picture of the impact on our habitat at each degree of projected temperature rise. *Six Degrees: Our Future on a Hotter Planet*, by Mark Lynas.[2c] Lynas paints a vivid picture for us calling on research findings from the paleo-records of the ancient past and the advanced climate and systems modeling of the present day.

I hope that it is clear why I've included this short chapter in *The Impossible Conversation*. The primary reason was to provide some of the context for the Sober Data we are using in this exploration of our near-term future.

I am asserting from here on that our mainstream media as well as governmental agencies are welded to a very restricted language in describing climate change issues and other negative impacts of human activities on Earth. This language is deliberately kept vague and rarely includes the kind of detail that we just read from the World Bank and Professor Watson and the others.

I am very uncomfortable asserting that there is a large scale control of messaging about climate change, but in the course of my research it has become crystal clear to me that this issue, among a number of others, is perhaps the most controlled and corrupted global propaganda campaign the world has ever seen.

We will be exploring aspects of my assertion in the coming chapters.

*　　*　　*

The engaged reader may want to assess for yourself here just how alert you may be to the scale of propaganda and message control in which we are immersed. You might want to start with a few simple questions:

"What climate change impacts do you foresee from your perspective?"

"When do you predict them occurring?"

"Do you access unbiased, vetted updates regarding Abrupt Climate Change or the stress on other global systems?" If so, "What sources do you use?"

3. Beyond green house gas emissions: Other metrics of our impact.

Learn to see and understand that
everything connects to everything.

Leonardo DaVinci

*   *   *

Having compiled a substantial stack of data and projections to validate the Abrupt Climate Change assertions about the effects of more business-as-usual CO_2 emissions, I noticed that I had landed smack dab in the middle of the land of the climate deniers.

I had zero respect for climate deniers before my learning-how-to-learn project and had even less now that I was at least conversant in some aspects of climate science and our collective, almost disregard for sincere climate mitigation.

We will address the global conversation about climate change, including denial, in later chapters.

For the moment suffice it to say that the powerful global entities that control most of the conversation about climate change and mitigation, have a tremendous investment in controlling the conversation so that it is only CO_2 emissions that are talked about and any conversation about climate change must include a large dose of doubt and uncertainty about whether humans are causal in climate change and even whether climate change itself is real.

A reminder of the sobering clarity of Kevin Anderson's words from chapter one: Anderson again is one of the very few climate scientists that hasn't been bullied into complete silence about the obvious implications of our not reaching our COP21 emissions reductions targets. He is also one of a ridiculously few experts who freely states the premise that sits at the center of *The Impossible Conversation*—that we have hit the end of business as usual. We have finally reached the point where we can no longer prop up our collective lie: that we can have infinite growth on a finite planet. THIS is The Impossible Conversation.

With that being said, it became more and more obvious that a singular focus on CO_2 emissions is a very constricted and misleading metric of our collective damage to our habitat. Surely there are other measures of our impact on Earth, and particularly there must be measures that are not tainted by the cynical, delusional, denial of basic science that is, deniers.

Somehow we have allowed a twisted subculture of science deniers to gain a powerful foothold in all of our media, our government, our corporations and even our daily discourse.

So my research advisors suggested that I might expand my study to include other global measures that would offer very different depictions of the impacts we humans are having on our home planet. If I found other evidence of our destruction of habitat or other species or other measures of climate-related impact from our human systems, I could circumvent the noxious, internet-troll-laden world of climate deniers and their singular focus on global warming and CO_2 emissions.

These different measures rather than projecting into some imagined or modeled future climate scenario, are primarily based on what is directly observable now. And these findings are not scrutinized, edited and suppressed by corporate and governmental representatives like so many of the IPCC findings and reports tend to be.

Of course you will see for yourself but I can tell you the data you are about to read shocked me just as deeply as the original Abrupt Climate Change projections. Perhaps even more so. With these findings I suddenly had a face or an image I could associate with each data point.

In a conversation about vaguely defined climate impacts in some far off future it was very difficult for me to really understand the dangers and costs. With these findings I could easily remind myself of a particular species or habitat. Not eighty years from now. Not so abstract. Not so easy to ignore.

This learning moment in my process also involved expanding both the context and content of my initial questions. It is here I had to see beyond the isolated metrics of the IPCC and the common parlance used in mainstream media about climate change. In recommending my inclusion of other fields of study, my research coaches were inviting me to see how interrelated virtually all systems of the planet are. It was extremely eye opening to see that the few metrics used by the ultra conservative, IPCC were in no way a complete picture. They were just the metrics that had been carefully chosen to carry out their mandate to "address" climate issues on a global scale.

Hopefully you will see what I saw with this more Systems-Theory orientation. I saw that there are hundreds, perhaps thousands of data sets, metrics and projections that all show an important part of the total picture of our impact on the planet we call home.

To establish a baseline for this exploration of other metrics we will start with literally the baseline of our human operating system. Earth, or more specifically, the soil in which we grow our food. In a December 14, 2012 edition of TIME magazine online, an article, *What if the World's Soil Runs Out?* Researchers estimate that globally we have about sixty years of topsoil left. They go on to say that seventy percent of topsoil around the world, has been lost since the advent of large scale, modern farming techniques. The rate of soil loss currently is between 10 and 40 times the rate at which it can naturally be replenished.

There is not space in *The Impossible Conversation* for any detailed layout of the massive amount of fossil fuel that is involved with every single calorie of food we consume. Suffice it to say that not only are we destroying the production capacity of our global soils, but we are propping up that diminishing food production with fossil fuel based fertilizers and supply chain methods that show no sign of slowing down as we prepare for a world with nine billion mouths to feed arriving just about the time these researchers are estimating the collapse of our soils.

From this baseline subject of world soil health we move to other indicators that will be refreshingly clear of the arguments of cynical deniers. While we may have few arguments as we cover these subjects, unfortunately we will also find few, if any advocates for these endangered species and swathes of our biosphere.

Let's start with a field of study that is in no way included in the IPCC calculations or reports, but offers starkly obvious and critically important data as we examine the impact of our global Human Operating System. Here we will explore the Extinction of Species, the immense reduction in global biodiversity and the severe reduction in population of species.

Species Extinction.

Earth has lost half of its wildlife in the past 40 years. The vast majority of this extinction is human caused either by habitat destruction or other activities that fit under the heading of Anthropogenic Climate Disruption triggering activity.[3]

Elizabeth Kolbert details the depressing facts in her book entitled *The Sixth Extinction: An Unnatural History*. She estimates that about half of the species of plants and animals currently in existence will die out by 2050. This is not due to any natural catastrophe, but rather due to destructive effects of human activities. [2a]

Pope Francis issued a dire warning to the world when addressing the UN General Assembly: "The ecological crisis, and the large-scale destruction of biodiversity, can threaten the very existence of the human species."

Twenty-two million trees have died from a beetle infestation, exacerbated by California's now four year drought. Governor Jerry Brown declared a state of emergency and stated: "California is facing the worst epidemic of tree mortality in its modern history. A crisis of this magnitude demands action on all fronts."[5b]

In a recent study from the University of California one author stated: **"If the trend (human caused climate change and habitat destruction) continues, within two human lifetimes we are in danger of losing three of four species on Earth. And, a continued trajectory is "like going into the world's most famous museum— say the Louvre in Paris— and slashing with a razor blade three out of every four paintings.** In one century, we're destroying works of art that evolved over millions of years." There is a broad consensus among scientists that extinction rates are the highest since dinosaurs died out 66 million years ago. "We emphasize that our calculations very likely underestimate the severity of the crisis." [4]

"The Earth is in the midst of a mass extinction of life. Scientists estimate that 150-200 species of plant, insect, bird and mammal become extinct every 24 hours. This is nearly 1,000 times the 'natural' or 'background' rate and, say many biologists, is greater than anything the world has experienced since the vanishing of the dinosaurs nearly 65m years ago." [5]

He urged governments to invest in nature. "If you do not, you will pay very heavily later. You will be out of business if you miss the green train. Mounting losses of ecosystems, species and genetic biodiversity is now threatening all life," said Djoghlaf. "In immediate danger, he said, were the 300 million people who depended on forests and the more than 1 billion who lived off sea fishing.[5]"

"Cut your forests down, or over-fish, and these people will not survive. Destroying biodiversity only increases economic insecurity. The more you lose it, the more you lose the chance to grow. The loss of biodiversity compounds poverty. Destroy your nature and you increase poverty and insecurity. Biodiversity is fundamental to social life, education and aesthetics. It's a human right to live in a healthy environment." Djoghlaf lambasted countries for separating action on climate change from protecting biodiversity. "These are the two great challenges. But the loss of biodiversity exacerbates climate change.[5]"

Another vital aspect of our miraculous biosphere that is far too vast to be covered well in these pages, insects. I offer here two examples of insects that are now considered endangered, and are iconic representatives of the essential place in the web of life held by all insects. First is the Monarch butterfly. The global population of Monarchs has dropped by 90 percent in the past two decades. The second species is the Rusty Patched Bumble Bee. Of course all bumble bees are pollenators. And, it should go without saying that when we lose our pollenators, we lose our food. Pretty simple.

A single mine in Canada's tar sands region moves 30 billion tons of sediment annually, double the quantity moved by all the world's rivers combined.

World Wildlife Fund and Zoological Society of London's biannual report, *Living Planet*,[5c] assesses how the natural world is reacting to the stresses implied by an ever growing human population. Their study of over 3700 vertabrate species shows that global wildlife populations have decreased by nearly 60% since the 70s. The loss of fresh water animals is far greater, closer to 80%. Since we have lost 58% of wildlife in forty years... what will happen in the next forty?

WWF report, list of causes for these losses:

1. Habitat loss from forest to farms or human development.

2. Taking/extracting too much—poaching, hunting, fishing.

3. Pollution

4. Invasive species

5. Climate Change effects on habitat and range.

*   *   *

Ocean indicators:

> We forget that the water cycle and the life cycle are one.
> Thus, if we destroy the oceans, we destroy ourselves.

Jacques-Yves Cousteau
Oceanographer and Conservationist

I've always had a very special relationship with the ocean. As I grew up in a house and family filled with the tensions and dysfunction of alcoholism, I found myself escaping to the beach at every opportunity. It always seemed like no matter how much upset and pain I brought with me, the great ocean could receive that pain and send me home more whole and open-hearted.

In this part of my research I allowed myself to really get personal instead of trying to focus only on the data and projections. While I could easily quote numerous articles, I am inclined to share with you some of the vetted information that was delivered in a biographical documentary about one of the preeminent oceanographers on the planet, Sylvia Earle, *The World is Blue*[7].

In this film we get to share a bit of her story and a lot of her love for the Earth's oceans. This was very impactful for me, to include interviews and commentaries from a scientist so active, for so long, in the field.

I feel that we do ourselves a great disservice if we attempt to view our global challenge with climate change as somehow separate from our human reactions and emotions about this situation. In fact I would assert that our long-standing tradition of over-riding our normal reactions and emotions about our impact on the Earth is at the center of how we ended up on this nasty brink.

*   *   *

In the Sylvia Earle documentary, *The World is Blue*[7], a few choice pieces of information are shared including a few comparisons between when Dr. Earle started her career in the 50s and current times:

Number of ocean Dead Zones: 1975 = 1   2014 = 500+
(caused primarily by toxic runoff of fertilizers, pesticides and other chemicals)

Number of nuclear bomb tests in oceans between 1950 and 1998 = 100+

Number of oil rigs in Gulf of Mexico in 2014 = 33,000+

Amount of global coral reefs dead due to acidification and other human caused
impact = 50%. If current rate of warming and destruction continues, 90% of coral
reefs will be threatened by 2030, and all of Earth's coral reefs could be dead by
2050. Within those same projections, The Great Barrier Reef would die by 2030.
(Truthout, May 2017)

Coral reefs absorb nearly one-third of the carbon dioxide generated from burning
fossil fuels. They produce 17% of all globally consumed protein.

Oceans have become 30% more acidic since pre-Industrial times.

Amount of these fish species that remain (compared to 1950s estimates of
populations)

Blue fin Tuna	10%
All breeds of Tuna	5%
Sharks	10%
Cod	5%

Amount of oxygen we breathe –produced by marine plants: 70%

Amount of Earth's water supply contained in oceans: 97%.

Amount of human-produced CO_2 emissions absorbed by oceans: 30%

Amount of the Gulf of Mexico devoid of life because of pollution as of 2014:
5,000 sq. miles

The world's oceans will be empty of fish by 2048 due to overfishing, pollution,
habitat loss and climate change. This projection from an international research
team that studied data from thirty-two related experiments on marine
environments, analysis of 1,000 year history of twelve coastal regions, fishery data
from sixty-four large marine ecosystems and the recovery of forty-eight protected

ocean areas. "This isn't predicted to happen. This is happening now."
Nicola Beaumont, PhD, Plymouth Marine Laboratory, UK.[3b]

The Great Barrier Reef (GBR) is the world's largest, living thing. A 2012 study showed that half of the GBR had died in the past 27 years. Two years later, the world's most qualified coral reef experts reported that, without dramatic intervention, the GBR would die completely by 2030. A related study estimates a 60% probability of all global coral reefs bleaching in 2017.[3d]

*   *   *

When all that coral goes, all that diversity of fish that depends on it goes. The entire food chain is in big trouble. If we lose the coral, we lose habitat for all the marine life that depends on it. We might see ecosystem collapse, as we know it.

John Rumney, managing director, Great Barrier Reef Legacy.

*   *   *

In a recent article from the journal, *Nature Communications*[3e], researchers estimate that climate change impacts, continuing at a business as usual pace, will disrupt more than half of the world's ocean habitat in the next fifteen years, and 86% by 2050.

The symptoms of this disruption include large swaths of ocean growing unusually hot, acidic and barren of life. This report further validates the others mentioned here regarding the bleaching and death of coral reefs around the world.

Phytoplankton population drops forty percent Since 1950. "Their identification of a connection between long-term global declines in phytoplankton biomass and increasing ocean temperatures does not portend well for [ocean] ecosystems in a world that is likely to be warmer," they wrote. "Phytoplankton productivity is the base of the food web, and all life in the sea depends on it."[5a]

*   *   *

The AP's Seth Borenstein (here excerpted from the Seattle Times[8]) summarized recent findings regarding the rapid acceleration of ocean warming in the past few decades. For those who follow the toxic banter of climate change deniers, this absorption of heat by the world's oceans has proven to be the real reason why there has been any let up in global temperature rise in the past few years. Clearly we are hitting the saturation point of the oceans' ability to take on both heat and CO_2.

It is both fascinating and devastating that the scientists quoted in this article use the metric of "atomic-bombs-worth of warming" on Earth and particularly within the Earth's oceans. Scientists have long known that more than 90% of the heat energy from man-made global warming goes into the world's oceans instead of the ground.

> The world's oceans absorbed approximately 150 zettajoules of energy from 1865 to 1997, and then absorbed about another 150 in the next eighteen years, according to a recent study published in the journal *Nature Climate Change.*

> To put that in perspective, if you exploded one atomic bomb the size of the one that was dropped on Hiroshima every second for a year, the total energy released would be two zettajoules. So, **since 1997, Earth's oceans have absorbed man-made heat energy equivalent to a Hiroshima-style bomb being exploded every second for 75 straight years.**

> But the study's authors and outside experts say it's not just the raw numbers that bother them. It's how fast those numbers are increasing. Jeff Severinghaus at the Scripps Institute of Oceanography praised the study, saying it 'provides real, hard evidence that humans are dramatically heating the planet.'

It is the double whammy of the warming of our oceans and its long-standing tendency to absorb massive amounts of human caused CO_2 that, among other things, is causing the bleaching and killing of coral reefs around the world.

> The worst thing that can happen during the 1980s is not energy depletion, economic collapse, limited nuclear war, or conquest by a totalitarian government. As terrible as these catastrophes would be for us, they can be repaired within a few generations. The one process ongoing in the 1980s that will take millions of years to

correct is the loss of genetic and species diversity by the destruction of natural habitats. This is the folly that our descendants are least likely to forgive us.

E.O. Wilson, 1985
Professor Emeritus,
Biology, Harvard University

This last quote is there for a reason. It is based in the 1980s. There are plenty of reminders like this quote— reminders that our situation is not new, it has not snuck up on us. This remarkable, species-survival level situation is an obvious outcome of decades of choices that have been made regarding human impact on Earth systems.

Once again I ask us to take a moment to slow down and consider deeply— what have you just read? The data and projections that I assembled about extinction were, for me, flat out devastating. With the intensity of this information it seemed like my fixation on a particular measure of temperature rise or CO_2 parts per million by a particular date was starting to matter less and less.

This, you could say, was the real beginning of my crafting my own, Informed Inquiry. Instead of quickly searching and finding a couple of cut and dried answers to my first, very simplistic questions, I was exploring the world of extraordinary, high integrity, scientists and their immense efforts to report honestly and clearly about our world of inter-related systems.

This more in-depth and nuanced research, this Informed Inquiry, was really a natural outcome of seeing just how detailed and multi-faceted the study of climate change is. Even my very basic level of study and research showed early on how there really is no way to study only one element of a system expecting to get a clear picture of what I'm studying.

It is downright silly to try to do what I originally set out to do. I wanted to get a couple of short, sweet answers to questions that defied being simplified. I had to learn how to learn about how human and Earth systems are monitored and measured, at least enough to be conversant about what is changing, what is causing the changes and what can be done about it.

I had to surrender to the fact that no object on Earth exists outside the context of one or more systems— and no system can be understood outside the context of inter-related systems.

It is just impossible to do this kind of research and see a given challenge or climate change symptom as separate from all other aspects of our natural world. It is equally impossible to see any one element as separate from our human endeavors, especially our economic structures and systems.

It was at this point in my pursuit of answers to my original questions when this process became not only an exploration of what we as human beings have done to our planet, but also a very personal level exploration of what my part is in all of this. How had we gotten this far down this destructive path without seeing our impact and changing course? How had I, who prided myself on being environmentally aware and concerned, let myself ignore so many red flags for so long?

I've become fond of saying: "We human beings have a collective blind spot big enough to drive extinction through."

I had two purposes in writing this chapter. The first was to bolster the case for the slow down and even stopping of large parts of our human operating system. By focusing on these non-climate-related elements of our world we could see the immense destructive impact humanity is having on Earth, without the incoherent, cynical babel of climate deniers to distract us.

The second purpose here is to offer you, the reader a method of deepening your understanding of an element of our miraculous planet. With this greater understanding also comes the added benefit of reconnecting us, in some small way, with a part of our world for which we have some affinity.

This method is what I've come to call, an Informed Inquiry. Probably the biggest example of an informed inquiry that I've ever known is the extensive vetting process I've taken on that includes writing this book. I'd have to guess that this scale of informed inquiry is far too extensive for most folks. I do understand that this level of study is only for the people that are driven toward a subject. And yes, I've been driven for these past few years.

What I am suggesting is for you to review your list of loves in life from the Introduction of *The Impossible Conversation*. I invite you to scan through your list and see if any of the animals or Earth features on your list are mentioned in this chapter. If so, it is realistic to imagine a sincere informed inquiry being done in a few hours of browsing related articles and reports in internet searches.

As I mentioned before, the information above, about the ocean, was an example of a much smaller scale informed inquiry. At the end of my search I felt so much more knowledgeable and, more importantly, I felt better equipped to scan the activist groups around the world and see where I might put my focus and energy, to slow or stop some of the impact.

Most important of all for me, I was able to feel the very normal and healthy grief, knowing the truth about our oceans. By feeling this grief and learning more, I have reconnected a bit of myself with the oceans I have loved for so long.

My invitation to you is to create a series of informed inquiries about aspects of our living Earth that warm your heart. Take the time to get to know how they are doing now. Take the time and space to grieve the many losses that have gone unnoticed in our frenzied business-as-usual world.

*   *   *

4 What did corporations and governments know ...and when?

UN PREDICTS DISASTER IF GLOBAL
WARMING NOT CHECKED

Noel Brown, director of the New York office of the UN
Environment Program said: "Governments have a 10 year
window of opportunity solve the greenhouse effect before it goes
beyond human control."

Associated Press, 29 June 1989

If at any point in that journey Exxon—largest oil company on
Earth, most profitable enterprise in human history—had said:
"Our own research shows that these scientists are right and that
we are in a dangerous place," the faux debate would effectively
have ended. That's all it would have taken; stripped of the cover
provided by doubt, humanity would have gotten to work.

**Instead, knowingly, Exxon helped organize the most
consequential lie in human history.**

Bill McKibbon

This is the biggest emergency we've had to face since we came
out of the caves. There is nothing bigger.

Van Jones.

We now have a substantial foundation of understanding —that even the most conservative projections show us barreling ahead toward an unlivable planet by 2100. The Abrupt Climate Change projections have us there by mid-century or sooner.

We also have a huge number of life-critical metrics (the extinction projections in the previous chapter) to add to the measurement of CO_2 in our atmosphere. These combined metrics indicate that the lifestyles we lead (particularly in the developed world) are having a devastating impact on other species, on our shared habitat, on the biosphere we call home.

I finished up the last chapter asking, how did we get ourselves to this brink and pondering how have I been complicit in this.

While these are strong questions for us all to ponder I'm going to hold off on the exploration of our personal culpability in this predicament until later chapters. I'd like to share with you some of the most stunning pieces of our collective story I have found in the course of my research. These historical elements add substance and gravitas to the notion that senior corporate executives across multiple industries and government leaders at the highest levels have known for decades, with great precision, that our business-as-usual burning of fossil fuels would create an unlivable planet by the middle of the 21st century.

At this point in my process I did my best to stay focused on the research at hand and not let myself be overwhelmed by the scale of this cynical, deeply destructive system. I can't count how many times I've found myself shaking my head at the simple but piercing truth of the Bill McKibben quote above.

*   *   *

It is here I will share with you some of the significant data I found regarding US government complicity in avoidance and cover up of accurate climate change data (from the George HW Bush administration). But as you will see, my stumbling into this article was almost trivial when compared with the 2016 disclosure of oil companies' alleged fraud, duplicity and distortion of data.

With this exploration of some of the most prominent large scale structures and influences and how they affect our world, let's start with the global agency that has been tasked with articulating and measuring the entire issue we have come to call, climate change.

The UN's association of climate scientists who establish for us all: the jargon, metrics and standards with which we talk about climate change, is the IPCC, the Intergovernmental Panel on Climate Change.

This grouping of scientists are volunteers who focus on vetting any and all current research that is being done in the climate sciences. It has been called one of the most conservative scientific bodies on the planet.

On a regular basis, the IPCC issues public reports, more or less a State of the Climate report to keep the public, the business world and government agencies up to speed with our collective climate situation.

When we have global conferences about climate policy like, COP21 in Paris in December of 2015 or COP22 in Morocco in 2016, It is the IPCC that provides all the statistics, projections, data and jargon that are needed to have the public understand what is going on with our global climate and to have the policy makers and decision makers draft their policies using the best possible data and context.

So in the name of a much-shortened book, with fewer of those pesky details and numbers, I will list a few compelling facts about the IPCC and the other agencies that influence them.

$$*\quad*\quad*$$

Climate scientists are "self- censoring" their own findings. We dare not report findings that in any way indicate the need to change our global model of perpetual growth. To do so threatens both our perceived credibility and future funding of research. We all know the situation is much more severe. It is a collective façade.

Prof. Kevin Anderson

$$*\quad*\quad*$$

- At COP21 the first truly global agreement to limit CO^2 emissions was formed. The agreement was to reduce global emissions enough to avoid a 2°C temperature rise. An additional "stretch target" was detailed, one that would keep emissions to a level that allowed only a 1.5°C temperature rise.

- All of the COP21 Paris Agreements are voluntary in nature. There is no enforcement structure in place for noncompliance by any party.

- In order to accomplish these goals, a global Carbon Budget was estimated. This articulated how much CO_2 could be emitted over the coming years— and still keep our temperatures below 2°C.
- Every word of the IPCC's public reports or "Summaries for Policy Makers" is edited and filtered by delegates from all participating governments and numerous corporate representatives.
- Any climate scientist who is accused of going too far with her own interpretation of data or being an "Alarmist" can and will be vilified and threatened by any number of different propaganda sources. The US is by far the guiltiest of this vilification of climate scientists. (Michael Mann, James Hansen, Jason Box to name but a few)
- The IPCC has not included any of the Positive Feedback Loops that are shown to accelerate and intensify Abrupt Climate Change advancement. (As mentioned in chapter one.)
- The IPCC has been prohibited from including any tracking of the global airline industry, global shipping industry or the US military (the world's largest institutional consumer of fossil fuels) in any of its calculations regarding CO_2 emissions and the COP21 Paris Accord.
- When calculated at the end of COP21, all of the reduction targets by all of the countries were clearly not sufficient to avoid 2°C. Further projections of business-as-usual emissions yielded IPCC projections of between 3°C and 5°C by 2100.

OUR GLOBAL CO_2 EMISSIONS BUDGET:

This set of bullet points should be combined with the more current data that was quoted in chapter one by Kevin Anderson. I trust the reader will be able to understand that each of these projections regarding our global fossil fuel/CO_2 emissions was generated at different times by different experts using different modeling methods. That being said, all of these models show that we have a very small budget of CO_2 left to emit before we collectively trigger a tipping point of large scale acceleration of temperature rise.

About two-thirds of the available budget for keeping warming to below 2°C have already been emitted, global emissions urgently need to start to decline.[1b]

Fossil fuel use will have to fall twice as fast as predicted if global warming is to be kept within the 2°C limit agreed internationally as being the point of no return." Article in *Nature Climate Change* proposes that all previous budgets for CO^2 emissions have been "too generous" and: "We have been overestimating the budget by 50% to more than 200%. At the high end, this is a difference of more than 1,000 billion tons of carbon dioxide.

Climate News Network (1),Tim Radford February 2016.

* * *

Probably the most well known of the estimates of our global CO_2 emissions budget is the one presented by environmental activist, Bill McKibben in his *2013 US, Do The Math Tour*

https://www.youtube.com/watch?v=KuCGVwJIRd0&t=1030s

Here McKibben asserts that our budget includes:

- We must reduce our CO_2 emissions by 80 to 90% by 2050.
- To have a 50/50 chance of staying below a 2°C global temperature rise we must stay below an emissions cap of 565 Gigatons of CO_2.
- We (globally) currently emit about 30 Gt/yr. Calculating a modest 3% growth rate of those emissions McKibben estimates we would over shoot our budget by 2028, a mere 15 years from that 2013, Do the Math Tour.
- Perhaps the most important data point from McKibben's presentation is the estimate of the known reserves (fossil fuel resources located but still in the ground). Fossil fuel companies are estimated to own enough reserve supply to yield 2,795 Gt / CO_2 of emissions, if burned: **Five times the amount of our global "budget."**

Additionally I can tend to be over-encouraged by the news that renewables are being installed at a rapidly increasing rate. Another recent article[1a]states that even with more than a million solar power installations in the USA, those installations only represent 1% of the USA power consumption. If the 2°C global warming cap is to be honored, then global climate-changing emissions will have to drop by as much as 70 % by 2050.

(Other estimates range from 70% to 90% reduction in emissions by 2050.)

> Just to level off emissions over the next 50 years, the world's solar capacity would have to increase 100 fold. Renewables are adding capacity, but now only helping to cover new, additional demand. Not yet enough to cover existing demand.
>
> *Center for Environmental Climate Research. Oslo.*

I will not take the time here to detail the immense expense of a 100-fold increase of solar installations. Let's just say it is astronomical.

*   *   *

As with most of the data provided in this book, additional references and sources can be found in chapter 11, References and Resources for Each Chapter, and on the Impossible Conversation website.

In an Open Letter to world leaders ahead of the Paris Climate Conference 2015, academics from around the world articulate what they see as the more sobering version of our climate situation and their requests regarding binding policies that might come from COP21:[2]

> ...it looks unlikely that the international community will mandate even the greenhouse gas reductions necessary to give us a two-thirds chance of limiting global warming to two degrees Celsius above pre-industrial levels. At the moment, even if countries meet their current non-binding pledges to reduce carbon emissions, we will still be on course to reach three degrees Celsius by the end of this century. This is profoundly

shocking, given that any sacrifice involved in making those reductions is far overshadowed by the catastrophes we are likely to face if we do not: more extinctions of species and loss of ecosystems; increasing vulnerability to storm surges; more heat waves; more intense precipitation; more climate related deaths and disease; more climate refugees; slower poverty reduction; less food security; and more conflicts worsened by these factors. Given such high stakes, our leaders ought to be mustering planet-wide mobilization, at all societal levels, to limit global warming to no more than 1.5 degrees Celsius.

Perhaps it would be good to summarize here all this talk of the IPCC and who controls climate change policy making.

Let's start with a reminder that all of the Abrupt Climate Change data and projections were shocking primarily because they differed so greatly from the mainstream media delivery of the IPCC version of the story. Where the IPCC predicts business as usual warming of 3°C to 5°C by 2100… The Abrupt Climate Change advocates speak of 3°C to up to 10°C by between 2026 and 2050.

Where the IPCC offers a projection of one meter of sea level rise by 2100, The Anthropogenic Climate Disruption advocates (this time it's James Hansen in recent findings) predicting as much as one meter of sea level rise every twenty years for the foreseeable future.

> We conclude that continued high emissions will make multi-meter sea level rise practically unavoidable and likely to occur this century. Social disruption and economic consequences of such large sea level rise could be devastating. It is not difficult to imagine that conflicts arising from forced migrations and economic collapse might make the planet ungovernable, threatening the fabric of civilization.
>
> *James Hansen*

*   *   *

In November of 2016, the total amount of sea ice (both Arctic and Antarctic) was measured to be the greatest deviation from the historical average since the beginning of record-keeping of this type. At 1.5 million square miles below average, this equals ice covering an area 40% the size of the continental US to be gone at end of warm season, 2016.

On a parallel note, scientists are now estimating that between 70% and 99% of the world's glaciers will be completely gone by 2100.

*   *   *

A recent article from *Slate* online magazine (July 20, 2015) offers a bit more detail about recent research on ice melt on the planet...

> The science of ice melt rates is advancing so fast, scientists have generally been reluctant to put a number to what is essentially an unpredictable, nonlinear response of ice sheets to a steadily warming ocean. With Hansen's new study, that changes in a dramatic way. One of the study's co-authors is Eric Rignot, whose own study last year found that glacial melt from West Antarctica now appears to be 'unstoppable.' Chris Mooney, writing for *Mother Jones*, called that study a 'holy shit' moment for the climate.

When I reached this point in my researching Abrupt Climate Change, it seemed very unlikely that this was a significant moment of any kind for any policy makers, certainly not policy makers from the major developed countries.

I was plagued by the unshakeable knowledge that the IPCC is a collection of world-class climate scientists doing their best to provide the strongest data possible to inform the public and global policy makers— and they are under the constant scrutiny and pressure of corporate and corporate-owned government representatives who want nothing more than the complete suppression or manipulation of accurate climate data.

With the combination of the ongoing threatening and vilification of climate scientists and intricately woven fog of media ineptitude, climate denial and doubt, there appears to be a seamless membrane that keeps us from having the kind of "holy shit" moment described by Eric Rignot above.

*   *   *

It was almost exactly at the moment when I started drafting this chapter that *Inside Climate News* released its stunning expose, "Exxon: The Road Not Taken." In this series of revelatory articles, *Inside Climate News* described Exxon's decades-long practice of sponsoring world-class climate research specifically to determine just how damaging CO_2 emissions would be for life on Earth and simultaneously funding climate denial campaigns around the world to promote the prolonged lifespan of fossil fuel use (and, obviously, their profits).

Subsequent articles showed that Exxon and other major oil industry corporations and agencies had full knowledge of CO_2's derogatory effects as early as the 60s.

At this time a number of states attorneys general are pursuing criminal prosecution for Exxon and other corporations for charges including fraud. The implication is that the disclosure of the data uncovered in the early research of Exxon and others would have motivated timely and powerful action at a far more opportune time for humanity and Earth. By keeping the data secret and cloaking it with a full-fledged campaign of denial, Exxon and others clearly set us on a track toward large scale destruction—possibly existential destruction.

This may be a good moment to return to the top of this chapter and read Bill McKibben's quote about this very topic.

*   *   *

Climate Denial Crock of the Week
with Peter Sinclair

Exxon Sues to Make Lying "protected speech"
June 18, 2016

CLIMATE MODELING - CONCLUSIONS

· GLOBAL AVERAGED 2.5°C RISE EXPECTED BY 2038 AT A 3% p.a. GROWTH RATE OF ATMOSPHERIC CO_2 CONCENTRATION

· LARGE ERROR IN THIS ESTIMATE - 1 IN 10 CHANCE OF THIS CHANGE BY 2005

· NO REGIONAL CLIMATE CHANGE ESTIMATES YET POSSIBLE

· LIKELY IMPACTS:

  1°C RISE (2005): BARELY NOTICEABLE
  2.5°C RISE (2038): MAJOR ECONOMIC CONSEQUENCES, STRONG REGIONAL DEPENDENCE
  5°C RISE (2067): GLOBALLY CATASTROPHIC EFFECTS

Conclusions from an early 80s vintage Exxon Briefing on Climate Change

Screenshot from *Climate Denial Crock Website.*

As you can see in the screenshot above the "Conclusions from an early 80s vintage

Exxon Briefing on Climate" shows an estimate of a 5°C global temperature rise by 2067. Sound familiar?

Exxon is hardly apologetic about any of this. The corporation is fighting any and all efforts to hold them to account for this deadly secretiveness. [4,4a,4b]

> When asked at a recent conference of fossil fuel giants, What about the current research that shows that 30% of known oil reserves and 50% of gas reserves cannot be burned if the world wants to avoid warming of beyond 2°C, the panel said it was "down to economics, not science. In the end it will be economics that is driving it. The value of public companies is based on proved reserves…and it is rather unlikely these reserves will not be produced."

> *Shell CEO, Bill Van Beurden*

A response from environmental groups protesting the conference stated, "Oil demand projections by BP and Shell are consistent with warming well over 2°C— and in some cases over 4°C.[5]

In two articles from *Climate Home*, Exxon's CEO, Rex Tillerson perfectly exemplifies the voice of the status quo with regard to mitigating climate damage in our global emissions-driven predicament: [6,6a]

Tillerson, speaking at an Oil and Money conference, asserted:

> Global demand for energy will grow 25% in the next 25 years and countries will guzzle oil five times the size of Saudi Arabia's reserves.

…dismissing any concerns that the UN's new climate treaty will limit near-term consumption of oil and gas.

> "His scenario would blow efforts to contain global warming to below the 2°C danger zone sky high, unless nascent carbon capture technologies come online fast." (Article.)

Note here that Tillerson/Exxon is relying on Carbon Capture technology that presently shows no sign of being deployed at scale. This is also the thinking of the IPCC as they project out to 2100. The buzz phrase for this is "Negative

Emissions." Meaning, one way or another, a currently non-existent technology will be implemented and suck CO_2 out of the atmosphere.

The conclusion of that logic string is that when this carbon capture technology is in place and fully functional we will all be able to go back to business-as-usual and stop all this pesky chatter about reducing CO_2 emissions and the dangers of climate change.

We will revisit this point in later chapters but hopefully it is clear to you by now that our predicament is not one of CO_2 emissions alone. We are confronted with a multi- layered predicament here and I have seen exactly zero mitigation solutions that might give us the green light to return to the business-as-usual scenario of limitless growth on a finite planet.

"While greenhouse gas emissions in developed countries will likely peak in 2030, developing economies will struggle as they burn more fossil fuels," Tillerson told the "Oil and Money" conference.

The article notes that:

> Leaked internal documents clash with the company's public position over the past decades and funding of lobbying to cast doubt on the veracity of climate science. It is facing an inquiry from a coalition of Democrat attorneys general led by New York State's, Eric Schneiderman into what the company knew. Tillerson avoided mentioning the issue, but insisted the company he has run since 2006 was committed to doing the 'right thing the right way. Integrity is in everything we do. It's the foundation of trust and cooperation. A focus on integrity makes a corporation more effective,' he said.

*   *   *

A late breaking update[6b,6c] *Inside Climate News* has continued their breakthrough investigation into "Who knew what, when?" and has landed damning evidence that every major oil producer knew about the dangers of CO_2 emissions back in the 70s:

> The American Petroleum Institute together with the nation's largest oil companies ran a task force to monitor and share climate research between 1979 and 1983, indicating that the oil industry, not just Exxon alone, was aware of its possible impact

on the world's climate far earlier than previously known.

In addition, API task force members appeared open to the idea that the oil industry might have to shoulder some responsibility for reducing CO_2 emissions by changing refining processes and developing fuels that emitted less carbon dioxide.

Later the same ICN article describes a 1980 American Petroleum Institute meeting in which they were briefed by Stanford climate scientist, John A. Laurmann:

Laurmann told his audience several times that the evidence showed that the increase in atmospheric CO_2 is likely 'caused by anthropogenic release of CO_2, mainly from fossil fuel burning.'

In his conclusions section, Laurmann estimated that the amount of CO_2 in the atmosphere would double by 2038, which he said would likely lead to a 2.5 degrees Celsius rise in global average temperatures with "major economic consequences." **He then told the task force that models showed a 5 degrees Celsius rise by 2067, with 'globally catastrophic effects.'** (emphasis mine)

*　　*　　*

Now let's take a quick look back in time to get a sense of what our US government knew and when it knew it. After all, it wouldn't be of much use if all of this important climate impact data was kept only with the oil industry.

*　　*　　*

In an article from the *Washington Post*, December 3, 2015.[7] reporter, Joby Warrick describes a series of recently declassified State Department documents from 1989 that address a number of environmental concerns facing the administration of George H.W. Bush.

In these documents, drafted by Assistant Secretary of State OES, Frederick M. Bernthal (OES = Oceans, Environment and Science.) Bernthal is summarizing administration policy positions and assessments for a then new Secretary of State, James Baker.

I am including only a few of the most salient quotes from these documents. I recommend that the reader follow the link to the full text. It is truly amazing how political stances and language have changed in less than thirty years. A reminder, these are documents from a Republican administration.

(February 27, 1989 memo)…

> **If climate change within the range of current predictions (1.5 to 4.5 degrees Centigrade by the middle of next century) actually occurs, the consequences for every nation and every aspect of human activity will be profound.** (emphasis mine)

This one paragraph is a smoking gun of sorts. I believe that the temperature range quoted here is a very standard estimate of temperature increase projections based on a doubling of atmospheric CO_2 using climate modeling available in 1989. What is interesting is the inclusion of "by the middle of next century."

In my research on this topic, it is very difficult to find mainstream or IPCC timelines for climate impact with anything other than 2100 as the benchmark.

Given how many sources offered by the Abrupt Climate Change advocates warn of daunting climate change impact occurring by as soon as 2030—and the revelation of this 1989 memo including, "up to 4.5°C by the middle of next century"—it becomes hard to deny that these closer timeline projections have been intentionally dropped from the public discourse.

Here are more excerpts from the briefing document for Secretary of State, James Baker:

> The president-elect is committed to U.S. leadership in addressing global warming, and I believe you will see that reflected in his (GHW Bush) early words and actions.

> While it is clear that we need to know more about climate change, prudence dictates that we also begin to weigh impacts and possible responses. **We simply cannot wait— the costs of inaction will be too high.** (emphasis mine)

> To be effective, we (US) must provide leadership in two key areas: <u>Analyzing</u> the problem and strategies to manage or resolve it; and, <u>Acting</u> to limit greenhouse gas accumulation if scientific evidence demands we do so. (emphasis theirs).

The US played a lead role in bringing the IPCC into being. A working group of the IPCC will review the state of international scientific understanding. U.S. scientists are actively involved in development of that review. This full international scientific analysis will not be available until mid-1990.

This addresses a phrase we still (26 years later) hear quite often, "We just don't have enough evidence... we need to do more research." Evidently they anticipated having "enough evidence" by mid-1990. The briefing document continues,

> **Global climate change is the most far-reaching environmental issue of our time**. If the climate change within the range of current predictions actually occurs, the consequences for every nation and every aspect of human activity will be profound. (Emphasis mine.)

> There is no way that the US can develop a credible international strategy on climate change unless it addresses US emissions of CO_2 from fossil fuel combustion. Once we have developed a domestic strategy for stabilizing and then reducing our use of fossil fuels over time, we can then develop an international strategy which is consistent with our domestic strategy.

> Similarly, we will not be able to forestall consideration of a framework climate convention. It would be better to incorporate our own ideas into a draft convention than to react to someone else's.

I am asserting here that the core data and projections that make up what I like to call the Sober Data of Abrupt Climate Change has been available to and known by every high level corporate executive and every high level government official around the world since at least the 1980s.

And, at the risk of putting too fine a point on it, I am asserting that the evolution of the climate change denier propaganda campaign has been intricately and richly choreographed by big money interests and the government officials who are, and long have been, in the pockets of those interests.

Shall we take a quick look at the current status of the corporate/government partnerships today? Obviously things have changed quite a bit since the Exxon and US government anecdotes described above.

*   *   *

So we now can see that Exxon and other corporations knew full well that the use of their products would cause catastrophic damage to our biosphere by mid 21st century. We can see that they intend to take zero responsibility for the incalculable damage done by hiding their research findings from the public with a massive, decades-long denial campaign (which continues to this day).

A truly last minute addition to this writing: Rex Tillerson, the Exxon CEO mentioned above, is now the Secretary of State in the Trump administration. It also coincides with a number of States Attorneys General investigating Exxon for what may be the largest, most cynical and destructive fraud ever perpetrated on humankind—the allegations that Exxon simultaneously funded research about the damaging effects of CO_2 emissions from fossil fuels *and* funded multi-million dollar campaigns to deny the existence of those effects.

This news coincides with the revelation that both Donald Trump and Rex Tillerson/Exxon have extensive business ties with Vladimir Putin and Russia. At the center of Tillerson's recent deal-making with Russia is an as yet unrealized $500 billion project to drill for oil and gas in the Russian Arctic. At the risk of being repetitious, I will remind us that there is NO global CO_2 budget for more fossil fuel infrastructure or increase of extraction. There is no shortage of irony that this massive example of the survival of millions of species, including human beings versus the profit margins of global fossil fuel interests is being played out in the Arctic.

Temperatures have been and will continue to be rising far faster in the Arctic than any other area on Earth. And for those who took the time to watch any of the suggested videos in chapter one, you will recall that the area proposed for the half trillion dollar Exxon/Russia Arctic drilling is right in the methane-rich permafrost and Arctic ocean shelves at the center of that critical positive feedback loop. Ironic and lethal.

There is some talk of creating independent investigatory panels to uncover just how much relationship exists between Russia and Trump and Tillerson. The investigatory panel mentioned above is actually related to the CIA and FBI allegations that the 2016 US elections had been hacked and influenced by covert Russian spying and manipulation. All of this Exxon/Tillerson/Russia oil-deal drama is occurring on top of that espionage investigation.

It appears that Tillerson, has received Russia's highest civilian award for his work in forging business relations between Exxon and Russia. Putin was recently heard stating that the Trump cabinet is a "dream team" from Russia's point of view.

We will explore this topic in more depth in coming chapters. Suffice it to say that we never could have predicted this level of cynical, government-corporate inter breeding. We have obviously crossed a line indicating a dramatic movement of the entire subject matter of this book— further in the direction of "Impossible."

Did I mention that as Secretary of State, Tillerson will be the US representative diplomat at future COP meetings, like the COP21 Paris meetings mentioned earlier? Tillerson and Trump both have stated that they don't believe that climate change is a serious concern. Trump has called it a "hoax perpetrated by the Chinese."

The Trump administration has formed an aligned front to not only officially deny climate change, but to repeal any US promises or agreements from COP21 and eliminate the US Environmental Protection Agency.

What could possibly go wrong?

*　　*　　*

So Exxon and other industry majors predict very prosperous years ahead for the fossil fuel industry. They have unrestricted access and editorial control over the IPCC reporting process and unhindered access to and control over the entire US government.

They appear to have complete control of the public discourse about all matters of climate, environment, social justice, environmental justice, national and international policy making regarding further extraction of fossil fuels in the Arctic and elsewhere around the world.

Pretty sweet deal, eh?

With this new administration at the helm and a Republican Senate, House and Supreme Court right behind them, it is hard to imagine a worse nightmare for the health and well being of all Earth systems and, of course, humanity.

*　　*　　*

It was at this point in my research efforts that I was again reminded of the

74

poignancy of Naomi Klein's choice of words for the title of her book, *This Changes Everything: Capitalism vs the Climate*.

It is extremely uncomfortable for me to land in this part of *The Impossible Conversation*. It is here that all I can see is how close to the brink we are. There are times when all I can see from this vantage point is how we collectively appear to be choosing a few more years of the most comfortable lifestyle humanity has ever known rather than doing what it would take to create a more sustainable way of living on Earth.

With a track record of twenty-five years of absolutely no significant mitigating action, it appears we have made our ultimate choices.

The initial purpose of this chapter was to share with you one of the last fragments of my naïveté and my life-long assumption that government and big business were looking out for the best interest of life on the planet. I had assumed that I could keep my focus on my own day to day living, projects and future—and the powers of global governments and the market would keep on evolving and finding solutions for our many problems.

I was hoping that you, dear reader, would join me in this process of asking more penetrating questions about our assumptions about this world and how we might, together, shed some light on how important those "ultimate choices" have been.

That purpose has morphed some, especially with the inclusion of the most recent information about the new US administration and its apparent antipathy for any and all consideration of climate science. It also morphed as I've heard and read so much analysis about what fueled the election of Trump and his cronies.

At this point I generated a new direction for this research project. I had started with what turned out to be the simplest question to answer, "Is this Sober Data verifiable, is it real?" The next question was "Are there other data and measures to support the CO_2 emissions projections and to support the notion that we have arrived at the end of business-as-usual?" (This was the chapter on Extinction of Species, Ice Melt/Sea Level Rise) The next questions in this chapter poked into the arena of "How long have governments and corporations known about this predicament?"

The new direction for my research questions was the most disturbing of all. I found myself wondering how we, collectively, had gotten to the brink that is described in this book.

With a combination of sincere ignorance and willful ignorance we appear to have arrived at a point in human history and evolution in which we have surrendered the last vestiges of authentic democracy, surrendered our personal sense of agency in life, surrendered our experience of connection with core elements of being alive.

We have disconnected from our experience of our own, innate wisdom, our connection with other human beings and finally, and perhaps most disturbingly, we have disconnected from our inter-relatedness with our original mother, habitat and home, Earth.

In the next couple of chapters we will explore what elements and dynamics of our shared Human Operating System have resulted in our surrendering such rich human treasures as listed above. How could we be in a world in which willful ignorance, loss of agency and deep divisiveness are now our primary motivators?

How could we be responding to twenty plus years of virtually unanimous warning calls from our climate scientists with either a sneer of doubt and annoyance or a disinterested yawn?

How could we seriously be considering the next chapter of human history to be one described by words like: collapse, chaos, divisiveness, habitat destruction, sea level rise, Abrupt Climate Change and even, extinction?

*   *   *

5. Our Shadow: On the scale of government and corporation.

The contrarian efforts have been so effective for the fact that they have made it difficult for ordinary Americans to even know who to trust.[4]

> *Justin Farrell,* Yale University sociologist and author of a recent study on corporate funding of climate denial, in the peer-reviewed journal,
> *Proceedings of the National Academy of Science.*

The latest election a couple of days ago, you could almost interpret it as the death knell for the species. There was an article in *Bloomberg Business Week*, not a radical rag exactly, they're worried about the Republicans in Congress. One of the reasons is that they are global warming deniers, almost all of them. That means that the powerful House committees, like Science and Technology and so on, are going to be in the hands of people who think there is nothing-to global warming, or that is what they say anyway. What they really think may be a very different story. One of them was quoted as saying 'This won't be a problem because God will take care of it.'

If this was happening in some small country it wouldn't matter much, but when it's happening in the richest, most powerful country in the world, it's a danger to the survival of the species. So we're essentially saying, you can just kiss it all goodbye.

> *Noam Chomsky: How Climate Change Became a 'Liberal Hoax'.* YouTube. January 2011.
> https://youtu.be/FJUA4cm0Rck

It is difficult to get a man to understand something when his salary depends on his not understanding it.

Upton Sinclair

Anyone who has tried to talk to someone with different opinions about the election of Donald Trump, or the British exit from the European Union, or climate change for that matter, will know   that there is a madness in the air right now which goes far beyond the facts of any particular case, and which engulfs them until they are lost in the fog.

When people argue about Brexit, they are not really arguing about Brexit. When they fight about Donald Trump, they are not really fighting about Donald Trump. These things have become symbols, archetypes of the kind of future we want and don't want, the kind of people we think we are and the kind of people we think others are.

It's as if we are fighting over myths, stories, representations of the world as it is and as we want it to be.

Paul Kingsnorth, Dark Mountain Project. 2016

We are all very worried here. We should assume our worst fears will be realized.

Stefan Rahmstorf
Pottsdam Institute for Climate Impact Research, regarding the Trump administration's stance on environmental policy.

What good is it to save the planet if humanity suffers?

Rex Tillerson, Trump's US Secretary of State, Former CEO of ExxonMobil, in a statement to ExxonMobil shareholders.

> This is precisely why there will be no voluntary
> transformation…I wish I would have had this quote when I
> wrote the human supremacy book.
>
> *Derrick Jensen*

*   *   *

Steve Bannon has some past experience as a broker at Goldman Sachs but it is
assumed he honed his skills as a racist, Islamophobe, anti-semite and misogynist
during his time running the toxic website, *Breitbart*.

Political and public service novice, Steve Bannon, is Trump's chief strategist and
senior advisor, and some would say, chief puppeteer. What are the goals that
Bannon sets for himself?

> I want to bring everything crashing down, and destroy all of
> today's establishment.
>
> *Steve Bannon*, As quoted in *The Daily Beast*, 2013.

> Darkness is good. Dick Cheney. Darth Vader. Satan. That's
> power.
>
> *Steve Bannon*, after Trump presidential win. As
> quoted in the *Hollywood Reporter*.

*   *   *

When I arrived at this point in my research project, I had to expand the frame
through which I had been viewing this predicament. By far the majority of my
focus had been on gathering the most current data, modeling and projections I
could find to validate Abrupt Climate Change and species extinction reports.

To address the new question, "How could we be responding to twenty-plus years
of virtually unanimous warning calls from our climate scientists, with either a sneer
of doubt and annoyance or a disinterested yawn?" I had to look for longer-term
trends and historical influences in our collective past. This deeply disturbing blend
of apathy, denial and distraction had to have come from somewhere. It is well
within my memory that we (the USA in particular) considered ourselves to be

79

caring and hard working and well-intentioned.

If you go back to chapter four, you can read how an earlier Republican administration positioned itself with the then-nascent challenge called climate change or global warming.

We weren't always this divisive and we didn't always have this seamless wall of denial of basic science and facts. As far back as the sixties we seemed to be able to set aside differences and have some very difficult conversations in the name of addressing deep national problems or accomplishing great things— as a nation. (I am thinking here of the NASA program to put a man on the moon, addressing water and air pollution: we actually had rivers that caught fire here in the USA and discontinued the use of hydrofluorocarbons to stop our damaging of Earth's atmospheric ozone layer.)

We basically saw ourselves as the good guys in the world and even saw ourselves as the "world's police force for good." We touted our Christian values and our generosity and charity for those in need. We generously funded R&D in many different scientific fields. And, perhaps above all, we saw ourselves as the premier exemplars of how a Democracy is meant to be run.

So, the question, repeated above, is really quite a serious one. If we see ourselves as such a morally, economically, militarily and politically superior nation, how have we landed ourselves into the middle of this global predicament with such a disinterested response to our very survival?

We always considered ourselves to be savvy. Not smart, because it is just not cool to be too smart these days. But savvy—we prided ourselves on having good, common sense and an always-on bullshit meter. Not so much any more.

We have all collectively thrown ourselves in a strange pond where there is no more common sense, there is no more "savvy." We now swim together in this putrid pond where truth is no longer welcome. We sneer at common sense. We spit at any facts that don't match our narrow political opinions. We have, quite obviously, severed the last remaining threads of relatedness we once had, relatedness that came as a birthright, relatedness with our own innate wisdom, relatedness with other people and other beings, and relatedness with Earth.

If any of these assertions are true, then what the heck got us to this point of denial, apathy and deep division? What took us from being the moral ones, the good-guys, the Christians with the family values, the ones who could set aside differences and accomplish overcome any obstacle—to being the ones (flying in the face of almost every other nation on Earth) who are willing to hold on desperately to our business-as-usual ways and watch as our habitat withers before our children reach adulthood?

It was obvious that the scale and scope of this book would not accommodate a full detailing of the historical path that culminated in what we now call business as usual.

With the exception of one jump back to the early 20th Century and a few brief quotes from early political and economic philosophers, I believe we will find plenty of context for a sober reply to the question above, by tracking our human activity just since the 1970s.

*   *   *

It turns out that my own lifespan has overlapped with the vast majority of the acceleration and intensification of our global human endeavors—particularly those that have yielded the greatest impact on Earth's biosphere and on sustainable living standards.

So, starting with the 1970s and the vivid reporting of Jacques Cousteau about massive human-caused damage to our oceans— and the creation of the EPA and the support of Earth Day by Republican politicians—we see the last fifty years bringing with them the largest increase in damaging CO_2 emissions, and other industrial destruction of habitat, the world has ever seen. That increase also occurred far faster than the planet has ever seen, no matter what the source of CO_2 or destruction might have been in past epochs. (Yes, even faster than the climate changes that caused the great die-off of the due to an asteroid hitting Earth.)

As I mentioned at the beginning, my career track overlapped with a number of important business-as-usual trends that were clearly at odds with healthy human systems and even downright adversarial with Earth systems.

The singular focus on corporate profit, backed by unbridled political power, was honed to a razor sharp point in the last fifty years. It was not difficult to see how that fixation of focus created the greatest profit accumulation ever seen in humanity's history. It was also very easy to see that that accumulation and extraction left great devastation in its wake. First came the devastation of the empowering jobs and wages that formed the middle class since the 50s. Next came the devastation of the environment that would gradually grow into the Sober Data we have detailed here.

*   *   *

In my corporate training engagements I was able to sit in on dozens of executive meetings in which the one and only topic was how to maximize profit. There was rarely a mention of any other sincere focus for the company's attention. So, there was talk-a-plenty of which third-world country to move manufacturing or other divisions to, which developing country would yield the lowest costs in terms of wages (none of the contenders required any benefits for the workers), and which would have the least concern for environmental damage done in the manufacturing process.

Across the board, there were precious few mentions of the fate of the US workers whose jobs would be eliminated, nor the communities in which they lived.

The conversations were always focused on maximizing profits and minimizing costs. The jargon eventually shifted to privatizing all of the profit and wealth— and socializing all of the costs, or "externalities" as they have come to be known. In other words, manufacture in a far off country where we can pay people a fraction of the US wages, and leave all of the environmental damage over in that poorer country and, before you know it, two externalities are no longer on our balance sheets.

The massive ramp-up of the global industrial extraction machine has been truly a parade to behold. Retail analyst Victor Lebow, who in 1955 wrote in the Journal of Retailing:

> *'Our enormously productive economy demands that we make consumption our way of life, that we convert the buying and use of goods into rituals, that we seek our spiritual satisfactions, our ego satisfactions, in consumption ... We need things consumed, burned up, worn out, replaced, and discarded at an ever increasing pace.*
>
> This message sums up the advertising world of the last half century. It's insidious, pervasive, and deliberate -and it's consuming us.
>
> *Madeleine Somerville, The Guardian.* November 2015.

In those last few decades of the 20th century and first few years of the 21st, we saw the greatest increase ever recorded: of global CO_2 emissions—the greatest decimation of biodiversity ever seen by humans—and of the elimination of industry and jobs from communities in the US.

As we now understand in hindsight (having completely disregarded the early warnings of James Hansen and many others), we also saw the decimation of more than half of the world's fauna, 40% of the oxygen producing phytoplankton in Earth's seas through human caused ocean absorption of heat, CO_2 and pollution. As you may recall from chapter three, we are currently losing 150 to 200 species each day to extinction.

But we still aren't any closer to seeing the elements and dynamics that influenced us in the last forty years. What were the influences that had us collectively vilify our scientific community and turn away in willful ignorance from their many warnings in recent decades?

What influences drove us to the current remarkable brink where we are feeling a collective sense of helplessness and anger about our political and economic situation—yet we sit in a position of willful ignorance of the causes of our economic malaise?

Nor are we any closer to seeing what influences resulted in a US populace that didn't seem to notice when the hard-won, good paying jobs were "off-shored" to countries where wages were a fraction of the US and environmental regulations were non-existent. In fact, during those same decades, US unions have contracted to a tiny fraction of their former numbers.

How could we have spent so much emotion and bluster blaming illegal immigrants for our decline in decent employment –when those jobs were being moved out of the US by corporations that had zero interest in, or loyalty to, the success of the US economy?

How could we repeatedly vote against our own interests and against the interest of relating with Earth as stewards and protectors of our finite and fragile home?

We have a populace in which less than half participate in voting. We seem content that in 2016—the second year of the most recent presidential campaigning—the amount of mainstream news time spent reporting about the candidates' actual policy platforms (all channels) was less than sixty minutes.

Indeed in the last forty-five years we have seen the transformation of global corporate presence, from entities that maintained some modicum of identity with and appreciation of their home nations and communities, to a now seamless presence in all nations on Earth. These massive corporations are enjoying more "personhood" and power in the US and other nations, than any human citizen ever will. They exercise their almost limitless power over national and local governments with a profound commitment to continue the rocket propelled, over-reaching, over-riding, extraction system that our Human Operating System has become— even in the face of the indisputable evidence that that operating system is on rails to destroy life on Earth as we know it.

This last detail has come to a particularly fine point with the appointment of the Exxon CEO as Secretary of State and the many business-as-usual "foxes" that have been installed in cabinet posts (the proverbial chicken coop). We will address that in the next chapter.

So let's get to it. Let's look at some of the powerful influences on the peoples and cultures of the world. Particularly I will articulate some of the larger influences on the people of the US, influences that have culminated in the election of a most unlikely character for president, a populace that vacillates between not believing in or just not caring about a deeply damaged climate and global habitat and a country that is screaming at the top of its lungs to return as quickly as possible to our good old days of business as usual, or as the campaign placards said: "Make America Great Again!"

*   *   *

Edward Bernays and Carl Jung. Disempowering the Masses and Inviting the Shadow.

To pursue this track, we could go back hundreds or even thousands of years to look for early examples of how large numbers of people (nations) have been influenced in the past.

In the name of making this book more readable and compact, I will limit this sifting in the past to the early years of the 20th century. I first want to introduce you to Edward Bernays— the nephew of one of the pioneers of psychoanalytic theory, Sigmund Freud.

Bernays has long been considered to be the founder of the field that has come to be called, Public Relations. His early career years were spent working within the US government advancing the foundation of his body of work. This iteration of his work— influencing mass populations with carefully crafted communications— was known initially as, propaganda.

Bernays' efforts were of particular value to the US and our allies in World War I. The messaging of the Committee on Public Information was designed to promote the idea that America's war efforts were primarily aimed at "bringing democracy to all Europe." This was a far more flattering motive than the actual motives that included profiting both politically and economically by participating in the war effort.

An interested reader can track Bernays' very long and illustrious career that focused on generating propaganda campaigns to disguise the often cynical corporate and US Governmental intentions in countries around the world including: Iran, Guatemala, Nicaragua and many more.

As is mentioned elsewhere in this book, the writing of John Perkins in his book, *The New Confessions of An Economic Hitman*, would be a powerful addition to this description of the US's sinister influence and use of propaganda around the world.

Should there be any question of Bernays' propaganda work being taken seriously or having substantial impact in those early decades of last century, it is well known that Bernays' books were an important part of Joseph Goebbel's library. (Goebbels headed the Third Reich's Propaganda Ministry.)

In addition to the government leaders and agencies with whom Bernays consulted, he found a hungry audience in academia and in the business community in the US. He was invited to teach at New York University and published a number of books, which immediately became essential texts for students of government or business communications.

It was obvious to Bernays that the power and potential of influencing mass populations with crafted communication was only partially being utilized in the context of war. He had grudgingly limited his use of the now tainted name for mass influence, propaganda. He sought out a far more benign and even likeable title, "public relations." His work would also play an important role in the creation of the curriculum of the Tavistock Institute, an early think tank which focused on the development of in-depth studies of group dynamics and group psychology. This Tavistock work formed much of the foundation of the corporate group facilitation and organizational development work I mention in my own career history.

Bernays continued to have a significant following in the government's use of public relations or propaganda to put an intentional and often deeply misleading twist on America's press releases to its citizens regarding its intentions and operations both at home and abroad.

As I mentioned before, his work was also of profound interest to the US corporate business community. His mastery of mass communication and influence would become a center piece to corporate sales and marketing departments as well as in the cloaking of the cynical corporate manipulation of government policies in the next hundred years.

In all of Bernays' work, his primary focus was to influence people in the subtlest ways possible. Yes, much of his body of work was active on a very surface and simplistic level, such as the use of self image, emotions, contrived needs and much more to motivate people to consume more and perpetually. But his preference by far was to craft corporate and government communications so as to have the desired results actually appear to have been born out of the public's own mind.

Bernays considered himself most successful in a campaign of propaganda when public opinion had been shifted to the desired notion and none of the machinations of the propaganda agency had been visible at all.

Let's explore some of the history of how Bernays' propaganda methods and some of his own political philosophy helped American business and government leaders direct 20th century Americans to fully buy into a market model of infinite growth and consumption and, even more cynically, to buy into the entire message that the powerful leaders of business and government have everything under control—the consumer public need not concern itself with governmental or political issues—and what's good for US business is always and unquestionably, good for us all.

*   *   *

One of Bernays' first ventures to show off the power of this new way of communicating to and influencing the masses was a campaign he produced for one of his clients, Lucky Strike Cigarettes. In a 1929 Easter parade in New York City, Bernays had staged dozens of women, participating in the parade and smoking while doing so. Today that might be no big thing— then smoking in public was likely to get a woman arrested. After that very public event, women began lighting up in public in ever-greater numbers, making Lucky Strike a very happy client.

Bernays had a long and very lucrative relationship with the tobacco industry, up to and including assisting in the creation of the methods of generating denial, misinformation and doubt regarding Big Tobacco's culpability in deceptively selling lethal products. These methods, as mentioned elsewhere in this book, have also been used to boost the power of the climate denial campaigns from the eighties to present day.

There is no way I can track the evolution of sales and marketing in this book. Suffice it to say that it has become the water we swim in in our everyday lives. I am not the first to assert that sales and marketing to promote ever growing consumption is not just a ubiquitous form of messaging in our world— it has become our defining story—it is who we are—consumers before anything else.

The core of Bernays' propaganda-based sales and marketing methodology was to shift advertising from the detailing of a product's value and features, to the promise of how the product will bring the consumer new levels of health, wealth, status, sex appeal and even self-worth. Another way of describing this dynamic was the planting of the background communication to the consuming public — that a person would be of lesser status, less beautiful, less manly, less whole and well, if they didn't purchase and use product X.

I use the metaphor of advertising being "the water we swim in" quite intentionally. Indeed the power of propaganda comes from the message being virtually invisible to the mass audience. There will be little or no resistance to the message if it is delivered repeatedly from the voices of trusted authority, and always wrapped in a rhetoric that addresses the base emotions (fear, anger, desire for comfort), concerns and self-image of the masses.

I am asserting that, starting after the growth of US industrial and corporate strength in WW I and WW II, the government and corporate interests of the USA began a systematic campaign to intentionally redirect the population at large to shift their consumption habits, from being essentially frugal and measured, to being compelled to purchase and consume ever more products driven by the manufacturing of contrived needs.

Again, this has become such an integral part of the "water we swim in" that most of us in the developed world have no real idea what is a real need vs what is a need that has been invented from whole cloth to motivate us to consume.

Comedian Lee Camp does a magnificent routine[2] asking us, "What if advertising was some guy you just met?" This "guy" spews a rapid-fire monologue of piercing judgments at us the viewers, repeatedly cutting us down to size for our lack of the right deodorant, or phone or anti-depressant, or our girlfriend's use of the wrong shampoo, shoes or lack of the right cosmetic surgery.Camp is asking us if we would hang out with "that guy'" if advertising were an individual, real person?

It is daunting to take notice of just how much judgment, criticism, shame, status and self worth have been woven into this—far and away, the most prevalent communication content in our daily lives.

There can be little argument that the desired results have been produced in the plan to influence Americans to be the greatest consumers of all time. Of course, adjustments have also been made on the production side of this plan. In order for consumption to stay on an eternal growth trajectory, consumer goods would have to be designed to break down after a relatively short time. Alas, built-in, or planned obsolescence was born.

Dean Walker

Ending the Depression Through Planned Obsolescence, Bernard London.
- 1932 Pamphlet title.

Keep the consumer dissatisfied.
- *Charles Kettering,* 1929, Director of GM.

We must shift America from a needs to a desires culture. People must be trained to desire—to want new things even before the old have been entirely consumed. We must shape a new mentality in America.

Paul Mazer, Wall Street Banker, 1929

*   *   *

The last of the elements that have evolved to deepen our immersion in constant consumerism that I will mention here, has been the expansion of the use of credit. When added to consumers who have been groomed to consume continuously and ravenously to feed contrived needs and planned obsolescence, credit acts as an explosive amplifier of a consumer culture.

This massive growth of the use of debt, in excess, is now an integral part of business as usual at every level of society. From birth, we are told to live beyond our means. We are encouraged to rack up massive debt load on cars, education, home mortgages, travel— even while barely covering the daily expenses of life.

On the macro scale, it is obvious that any economic growth that has been realized in the past twenty years or more has been through the many and varied instruments of debt used around the world. In order to continue the delusion of infinite growth on a finite planet, especially in a time of diminishing resources, the only vehicle that could offer any hope of growth, has been the expansion of debt. And that expansion is itself, completely unsustainable.

An S&P prediction quoted in the same episode three of *Culture In Decline*, mentioned above, estimated that 60% of all countries on Earth would be bankrupt by 2050.

There are many experts who have pointed to the fact that we simply cannot continue to accumulate personal and national debt at a volume far greater than our income.[3]

These changes in consumer behavior imply a profound use of propaganda, but they are not the only results that the captains of government and industry had in mind when they crafted their platform for mass communication and influence. There were philosophical underpinnings that had been well articulated and implemented in governments prior to the birth of the USA. These guidelines and admonitions were intended to guide those in positions of great power and wealth on the best ways to retain and strengthen those positions.

In addition to the comedic piece about the toxic blather that is advertising in the reference mentioned above[2], *Culture in Decline* Episode 3 includes a very enlightening segment about Edward Bernays and a few of the early philosophers who provided the aforementioned guidelines and admonitions.

*   *   *

First, since we're talking about the profound influence of Edward Bernays through his contributions to the fields of propaganda, public relations, sales, marketing and manipulation of mass communications, let's take note of some of the philosophy Mr. Bernays carried behind his messaging.

In a BBC interview with Bernays' daughter Anne, she recounted her father's belief that the public's democratic judgment was "not to be relied upon" and feared that the American public "could very easily vote for the wrong man or want the 'wrong thing', so that they had to be guided from above." Anne interpreted "guidance" to mean that her father believed in a sort of "enlightened despotism."[1]

Here begins the most important thread of all. The thread that extends from the early political and economic theorists mentioned here (and plenty before them) to the most current events of our present day.

I am asserting that in the quotes from Bernays, Adam Smith, David Ricardo, Thomas Malthus and others, we will see the roots of what has come to fruition in these first two decades of the 21st century— a politics and economic model of, by, and for those already wealthy and in power.

Additionally, a politics and economic model that depends entirely on the disempowerment and suppression of any public expression other than complete compliance with the dictates of our now bankrupt business-as-usual paradigm.

Another way of saying this is: "those already holding power and wealth are somehow more deserving than the masses of population who have little or no wealth or power, and there is NO alternative."

*   *   *

A few quotes from early political and economic theorists that helped to form the philosophical underpinnings of the early US Government:

Adam Smith, famous for distinguishing the, "Invisible Hand of the Market."

> Civil government, so far as it is instituted for the security of property, is in reality instituted for the defense of the rich against the poor, or of those who have some property against those who have none at all.

> *Adam Smith*, 1776

Inevitable poverty and deprivation of the poor was a "societal law of nature."

> By gradually contracting the sphere of the "poor" laws; by impressing on the poor the value of independence, by teaching them that they must look not to systematic or casual charity, but to their own exertions for support, that prudence and forethought are neither unnecessary nor unprofitable virtues, we shall by degrees approach a sounder and more healthful state.

> *David Ricardo*, British political economist, 1817

In Ricardo's and Smith's words, we can read the beginnings of a philosophy of the wealthy class being enlightened overseers or observers of the inferior, poorer class. It should be mentioned here that many of these same philosophical underpinnings surfaced again in the writings of Ayn Rand, mid 20th century— and then again in the 90s when Rand's works came back into fashion with neo-liberals and libertarians.

Our current system has evolved from these roots and become a mythology that asserts: we only get that which we deserve. As if our world is a level playing field, as if there is no corruption in our system, as if there is no innate advantage bestowed upon those who already have greater wealth or access to power. The myth continues: that the poor are poor because they are stupid and even implying they are less than human.

> You only do harm to the poor by trying to help them. Instead of recommending cleanliness to the poor, we should encourage contrary habits. In our towns we should make the streets narrower, crowd more people into the houses, and court the return of the plague.

The Impossible Conversation

Thomas Malthus, 1798

In one final quote, directly from Bernays' book, *Propaganda*, we can vividly see his context for the work of propaganda and his assumptions regarding who is really in control when propaganda is being deployed.

> The conscious and intelligent manipulation of the organized habits and opinions of the masses is an important element in democratic society. Those who manipulate this unseen mechanism of society constitute an invisible government, which is the true ruling power of our country. We are governed, our minds are molded, our tastes formed, our ideas suggested, largely by men we have never heard of…in almost every act of our daily lives, whether in the sphere of politics or business, in our social conduct or our ethical thinking we are dominated by the relatively small number of persons…who understand the mental processes and social patterns of the masses. It is they who pull the wires that control the public mind.

*   *   *

So where we are now is with a US population that grows and prospers through the 40s, 50s and 60s. The New Deal and growth of unions were begrudgingly accepted by the elite, corporate community, but at no point was there any lessening of the intent of the overseers to be the overseer despots mentioned by Bernays and Rand.

It could be said that the fossil-fuel-driven economic escalation from the 30s through the 70s was (particularly in the US) the greatest expansion of a middle class ever seen on Earth. With a number of hard won benefits and safety nets in place and unions giving workers more collective bargaining power than ever before, there was something of a challenge to the philosophies and control strategies mentioned above.

Sure, corporations and the world's power players were doing very well, but there was a lot of pesky empowerment going on among those working classes that seemed to reduce the real profit potential of the global markets and reduce the direct power of government and corporate leaders.

Going back to Edward Bernays' body of work, the advent of TV had been like a super charger for the grand plan to make the global marketplace a consumer driven parade of infinite growth. It didn't take long for the American ethos to be entirely motivated by the need to consume and consume big.

*   *   *

I am vividly aware that we are deep into the weeds here in a conversation that could easily be seen as paranoid delusion about a secretive power elite that seeks ultimate control in the US and ideally, the world. I am also very clear that this thread of research into "What has us react to our global predicament with indifference or willful ignorance?" has led me along this path and lands us in the precise location we find ourselves in today.

We appear to have landed where there is utter disdain or contempt for such quaint relics of America's 20th Century history as: Civil Rights, Social Justice, Collective Bargaining/Unions, Rule of Law, Gender Equality, truth, respect for science, and so much more.

To give just a bit more credence to this historical track we are on and to make plain how this background shadow agenda in American and global politics has massively influenced our daily lives, let's go back to 1980 and look at that usually well hidden, background agenda.

In 1980, one of the wealthiest people on the planet decided he would get on the ticket for the 1980 presidential race in the USA. David Koch positioned himself to be the Libertarian candidate for vice president. Here are some of the platform planks put forth by Koch and the Libertarian party in 1980 (excerpted from the website of Bernie Sanders):

- We urge **the repeal of federal campaign finance laws**, and the immediate abolition of the despotic Federal Election Commission.
- We favor the abolition of **Medicare and Medicaid** programs.
- We oppose any compulsory insurance or tax-supported plan to provide health services, including those which finance abortion services.
- We also favor the deregulation of the medical insurance industry.
- We favor the repeal of the fraudulent, virtually bankrupt, and increasingly oppressive **Social Security** system. Pending that repeal, participation in Social Security should be made voluntary.
- We propose the abolition of the governmental **Postal Service**. The present system, in addition to being inefficient, encourages governmental surveillance of private correspondence. Pending abolition, we call for an end to the monopoly system and for allowing free competition in all aspects of postal service.
- We oppose all personal and corporate income taxation, including capital gains taxes.
- We support the eventual repeal of all taxation.
- As an interim measure, all criminal and civil sanctions against tax evasion should be terminated immediately.
- We support repeal of all law which impede the ability of any person to find

employment, such as **minimum wage** laws.
- We advocate the complete separation of education and State. Government schools lead to the indoctrination of children and interfere with the free choice of individuals. Government ownership, operation, regulation, and subsidy of schools and colleges should be ended.
- We condemn compulsory education laws … and we call for the immediate repeal of such laws.
- We support the repeal of all taxes on the income or property of private schools, whether profit or non-profit.
- We support the abolition of the **Environmental Protection Agency**.
- We support abolition of the **Department of Energy**.
- We call for the dissolution of all government agencies concerned with transportation, including the **Department of Transportation**.
- We demand the return of America's railroad system to private ownership. We call for the privatization of the public roads and national highway system.
- We specifically oppose laws requiring an individual to buy or use so-called "self-protection" equipment, such as safety belts, air bags, or crash helmets.
- We advocate the abolition of the Federal Aviation Administration.
- We advocate the abolition of the Food and Drug Administration.
- We support an end to all subsidies for child-bearing built into our present laws, including all welfare plans and the provision of tax-supported services for children.
- We oppose all government welfare, relief projects, and "aid to the poor" programs. All these government programs are privacy-invading, paternalistic, demeaning, and inefficient. The proper source of help for such persons is the voluntary efforts of private groups and individuals.
- We call for the privatization of the inland waterways, and of the distribution system that brings water to industry, agriculture and households.
- We call for the repeal of the Occupational Safety and Health Act.
- We call for the abolition of the Consumer Product Safety Commission.
- We support the repeal of all state usury laws.

In other words, the agenda of the Koch brothers is not only to destroy Obamacare. The agenda of the Koch brothers is to repeal every major piece of legislation that has been signed into law over the past eighty years that has protected the environment, the middle class, the elderly, the children, the sick, and the most vulnerable in this country.

It is clear that the Koch brothers and other right wing billionaires are calling the shots and are pulling the strings of the Republican Party. And because of the disastrous Citizens United Supreme Court decision (and a number of similar court rulings) they now have the power to spend an unlimited amount of money to buy the House of Representatives, the Senate and the next President of the United States.

This list now includes the installation of party-line judges at every level in the USA including, of course, numerous Supreme Court judges in the near future.

* * *

But we're getting ahead of ourselves here. Let's explore a bit of the next chapter of American political and cultural history—the chapter from the 1980s to now. It is within this chapter of our history that we went from the resounding defeat of Koch and the Libertarians to the "shocking" win of Donald Trump in 2016.

It is in this time frame that we went from a news media that prided itself on being the "Fourth Estate" and a vehicle for sincerely informing our populace about the deeds and misdeeds of the leaders of corporations and governments— to an embarrassing shell of its former self, gorging on corporate funding to promote the next great iteration of the business-as-usual party line.

We went from a society with a profound respect for journalistic and scientific integrity, to one that gives birth to its newest vile offspring: Fake News, Alternative Facts, suppression of science and vilification and threatening of the world's best climate scientists.

So let's make note of some of the steps that were taken and changes that were made in the last thirty-five years or so, to propel the shadow elite out of the shadows and onto center stage.

* * *

While the unprecedented use of TV as the primary vehicle for the delivery of the all-important advertising message was growing by leaps and bounds, the other dimensions of Bernays' public relations/propaganda couldn't quite get as much traction because of the FCC regulation of both media outlet ownership and the actual content that went out over the airwaves.

Starting in the 80s, those in power began seriously chipping away at both of those aspects of American media regulation. In 1987, we saw the elimination of the Fairness Doctrine[5] which held stations accountable to present contrasting points of view about current issues in the news. This could be said to be the birthplace of a 'fair and balanced" presentation of the news. Ironic that this has become one of the strongest memes of the most pungent propaganda voice extant today—Fox News. Another Fox meme, dripping with irony, is "The No Spin Zone."

Additionally, since the eighties, not only have all previous regulations limiting media ownership by volume and region been eliminated, it is now estimated[6c] that

90% of all media in the USA is controlled by six major corporations.

The elimination of the Fairness Doctrine and other regulations controlling media content and ownership clearly set a new tone for news and media outlets to grow into profit-driven mouthpieces for whatever their corporate owners wanted to be reported—and whatever content gained the most viewership, regardless of its nature.

*　　*　　*

Lest we forget that these powerful sources of propaganda and doubt regarding such issues as global climate change and social justice are more powerful now than ever, let's take a look at the money and covert structures used by infamous right-wing think tanks and institutions to continue their campaigns in the present day.

> Money amplifies certain voices above others and, in effect, gives them a megaphone in the public square.
>
> *Robert Brulle, PhD*, Environmental Sociologist.

A recent study by climate sociologist, Robert Brulle, in the journal, *Climactic Change*, reports that the industry of right-wing propaganda and public relations that includes climate change denial campaigns, is funded in the neighborhood of $900 million per year.

> Brulle's report states:
>
> Numerous right wing think tanks[140] and institutions are funded by the fossil fuel industry. 78% of these foundations and agencies are listed as charitable foundations. Yet clearly they are denier-based think tanks and political and profit driven by their nature. Their activities include: lobbying, political contributions, media campaigns along the lines of those described in *the Merchants of Doubt*—Searle Freedom Trust, John William Pope Foundation, American Enterprise Institute and Heritage Foundation, to name a few.

These last two named institutions receive 30% of all right wing donations to denier causes.

> Between 2003 and 2010 these organizations received $900 million per yr. in donations, totaling more than seven billion dollars total

for those eight years.

Those funds were spread over a number of different right wing propaganda campaigns, including climate change denial.

Funding has only increased since 2010—13% more in 2016.

In 2010 alone, $1.2 billion was contributed to these think tanks.

These organizations can now completely hide all donations via Donors Trust and Donors Capital Funds, often called, Dark Money. There is no way to track the sources of any donations that are granted through these organizations to our political representatives.

Our representatives in the federal government spend an average of 40% of their time in office fundraising for their next reelection campaign.

This is a good place to weave in additional information about David and Charles Koch.

While David's political career was short and unsuccessful, the family business, Koch Industries, is one of the largest and most powerful in the world. The so-called Koch brothers have also made it their business to create, fund and direct lobbying groups, think tanks and super PACs, all designed to forward their libertarian, extremist agenda. Much of that agenda is a logical extension of the 1980 platform listed above.

As fits the focus of this book, it should be noted that the Koch brothers were huge contributors to the Trump campaign, among others. And, Koch brothers' money can be traced into the funding of virtually all major climate change denial groups and campaigns for the past few decades.

For a full picture of the influence and methodology of these immensely wealthy brothers and their fossil-fuel=driven empire, I recommend reading *Dark Money: The Hidden History of the Billionaires Behind the Rise of the Radical Right*, by Jane Meyer.

*   *   *

Again, here it would be good for the curious reader to dive into a couple of Bernays books on propaganda to get a sense of the inner workings of powerful propaganda methods.

Suffice it to say that it is no accident that we've become a country of deep divisions and hatred and fear. These elements are powerful destabilizers of a mass audience, if the background desire of those controlling the message is to rally that audience to unthinkingly adopt those destabilizing emotions as the emotions that are good and right and even patriotic. It is no accident that our media is world renowned for immersing their viewers in content laden with divisiveness, fear, vilification of entire cultural groups and doubt of any facts that run counter to the business-as-usual narrative.

This evolution of news from being a somewhat subtle vehicle of propaganda messages to being a 24/7 mouthpiece for pre-produced press releases, profit making faux debates and celebrity gossip has taken a few decades to come to its zenith.

As we turn our attention to the present day, we find ourselves in an accelerating whirlwind of now-fully-visible propaganda and highly advanced methods of mass influence. What may have started early in the 20th Century as powerful but far less sophisticated tools of message control, now has become a seamless machine propelling those in power to ever greater levels of wealth and power.

*   *   *

Another interesting overlap of the historical roots of propaganda and methods used today to shape political messaging is the use of Big Data to create the verbiage used by Trump and other savvy politicians to get the desired response from their target electorate.

Turns out that our deep love affair with social media and an Internet that records our every breath and wink not only feeds the grandest intelligence gathering apparatus known to man. It also feeds the campaigns of wealthy candidates with all the data they could want, data with which they can craft their stump speeches and talk straight into the ear of their target voters.

This was one method Trump's campaign used to determine what to say and how to say it, in all those über successful Trump rallies. What? You thought he was just talking extemporaneously? You thought he just stumbled onto just the right topics with just the right dog-whistle emphases? Nope. This was all the Bernays-basics of manipulative mass communications, turbo-charged by the massive, Big-Data-driven talking points, assembled into speech form by political campaign wizards.

In a recent article in Vice's Motherboard column, *The Data That Turned the World Upside Down*[9], Vice describes the consternation of the inventor of a particular Big Data app, Michal Kosinski, as he watched his powerful technology being used by someone else, to essentially shoehorn Trump into winning the election.

Kosinski's methodology uses brilliant search and aggregating algorithms combing through Facebook data, and data from other public sources, to form readily usable and deadly accurate profiles of people from all walks of life. He calls this profiling system, the Big Five Personality Profile.

"What would happen," wondered Kosinski, "if someone abused his people search engine to manipulate people?" He began to add warnings to most of his scientific work. His approach, he warned, "could pose a threat to an individual's well-being, freedom, or even life." But no one seemed to grasp what he meant.

The company that was hired to propel Trump's campaign in this way is Cambridge Analytica. It was Cambridge Analytica that Kosinski worried would abuse this powerful tool and produce results that caused more harm than good. In this next quote you get a sense of what sources are used in creating the Big Five Personality Profile and just how detailed these profiles can be.

> "First, Cambridge Analytica buys personal data from a range of different sources, like land registries, automotive data, shopping data, bonus cards, club memberships, what magazines you read, what churches you attend. Nix displays the logos of globally active data brokers like Acxiom and Experian—in the US, almost all personal data is for sale. For example, if you want to know where Jewish women live, you can simply buy this information, phone numbers included. Now Cambridge Analytica aggregates this data with the electoral rolls of the Republican party and online data and calculates a Big Five personality profile. Digital footprints suddenly become real people with fears, needs, interests and residential addresses."

As this book goes to press, a number of investigations are being done into the use of cyber espionage on an international scale. Russia has recently boasted that it has, and is deploying, the use of "weaponized" social media. This means that they are carrying out a mass-scale program of disinformation, propaganda and manipulation of other nations' media environments. This program allegedly includes influencing the 2016 US presidential elections.

It seems hard to overstate the potential power of this weaponization of media and social media. It is clear that the use of this methodology will have devastating impact on the subject country's trust and stability with its media/news sources and trust and discernment regarding what is real news and what is "fake news."

*   *   *

With the last two segments, I hope I have conveyed some of my biggest concerns about the disempowerment of the American electorate. First, I am utterly convinced that we have a political system that only vaguely resembles the democracy we once had. It has been replaced by an entirely money-driven oligarchy. We've known for years that all the political influence in the US is wielded by the top 10% of wealthy citizens. All the rest of us—no influence at all.

Second, we are ridiculously easy to manipulate via tools like the one described above, primarily because we have long-since stopped being an informed populace (the core component of a true democracy) and we have become accustomed to a 24/7 immersion in "truthiness," False News and Alternative Facts. We have become so disillusioned with our political process that we don't hear a single complaint that, in the entire 2016 stretch of the presidential election season, all candidates in all forums and in all major media outlets spoke of actual policy issues for a total of less than sixty minutes.

The focus of the next chapter is how the elements of this cultural, political, economic and environmental predicament occur on the individual level.

*   *   *

So, what on Earth have we been doing with all this talk about 18th century political philosophy and the early 20th century roots of propaganda and PR and deregulation and monopolization of American media? What does this have to do with anything, much less our country's tepid response to some climate change data?

In a word—Everything.

> The control of information is something the elite always does, particularly in a despotic form of government. Information, knowledge, is power. If you can control information, you can control power.

> *Tom Clancy*

> You, The media, are the enemy. You are the opposition party."

> *Stephen Bannon*, Trump Senior Advisor.

In earlier chapters we explored a range of climate projections ranging from the most conservative: approximately 4°C of global temperature rise by 2100 to the most rapid and aggressive: between 4°C and 10°C by 2026.

We then spent some time articulating how unlivable and devastating 4°C would be on humans and millions of other species on Earth.

We then inventoried a few of the most dire calculations of species extinction and habitat depletion occurring now and in the very near future. This was done to bolster the case for humanity to focus not only on CO_2 emissions, but to also inventory the many other damaging practices we have mastered during our brief frenzy of resource extraction on Earth.

Then on to a bit of history of what we (corporations and government) have known and for how long. Implying, how much misinformation and deception has been used to keep us from knowing the desperate costs of our business as usual ways.

And now we find ourselves searching for answers to the questions: "How can we (Americans primarily) have a response to our situation that is either skeptical or nonchalant?"

And...

"How can we sit back silently as our representatives vilify and attack the world's climate scientists?"

And...

"How can we sit back silently as every one of our mainstream media sources have allowed and encouraged a faux climate debate industry to materialize— an industry entirely the creation of perhaps the world's most high profile, cynical and powerful propaganda campaign?"

This chapter is pointing toward the answers I have found as I've asked these questions. It is also the forum for us to articulate some of the powerful propaganda tools that have been used and are being used more than ever in our new presidential administration.

*   *   *

What we have is a rather cynical and twisted faceoff between two choices. One choice is to take on-board the warnings of climate scientists for the past twenty-five-plus years and the CO_2 budget that has been plainly detailed by the COP21/IPCC agreements, and get into global action—on a scale never seen before—to mitigate the immense damage we have done and continue to do to our own habitat… immediately.

The other choice is to do nothing —to continue on with life and business as usual. Simple as that, really.

And why all the stuff about propaganda and media deregulation and an elite overseeing the "inferior," lower classes? Because it appears to me that each of these pieces has played an important role in getting us to where we are today. Additionally, this administration is overtly utilizing propaganda and mass message control like no other US Government in history.

And where are we today? Well, the CEO of Exxon Mobil has been confirmed as Secretary of State under the new Trump administration. He and Exxon Mobil are also being investigated by a number of attorneys general for Exxon's withholding of life-critical climate research data while simultaneously funding climate denial on a global scale.[7]

Anyone watching the parade of contenders for cabinet positions in the Trump administration, and specifically the Tillerson hearings, will be able to see, in full color, what a State Department would look and feel like, if run by an oil executive. It is abundantly clear that the intention of this administration is to give full, unbridled power over US policy, in every dimension, to corporate interests.

With a very high profile history of business relations between Vladimir Putin, Donald Trump and, separately, Rex Tillerson and Exxon Mobil, it was inevitable that Exxon's close ties with the Russian government regarding oil exploration would surface. They have indeed surfaced.

During Tillerson's confirmation hearings, he denied Exxon's efforts, and his own efforts, to lobby to prevent US sanctions against Russia. In response, Republican Senator Bob Corker said, "I think you called *me* at the time."

He also flatly declined to answer any questions about Exxon's duplicity of sponsoring world-class science regarding the effects of CO_2 emissions from fossil fuel use and suppressing those findings— while simultaneously funding a multi-million dollar, decades-long campaign of climate denial.

As if that weren't abhorrent enough, Tillerson punctuated his testimony with some of the tropes of that climate denial campaign again, as if they hadn't been disproven countless times in the past five and more years. He stated that scientific literature on climate change is still, "inconclusive."

Tillerson repeatedly showed how little he knows about foreign policy and diplomacy. He showed no interest at all in speaking plainly about the human rights records of such countries as Russia, Iran, Indonesia and more. There should be no doubt that Tillerson's only focus as Secretary of State, will be to negotiate corporate access to fossil fuel resources around the world.

It is predicted that the first such effort will be to remove the penalizing sanctions against Russia imposed by the Obama administration. These sanctions include the prohibition of American corporations from doing business directly with Russia, its state controlled oil industry or other Russian oil corporations.

When this prohibition is lifted Tillerson will be freed up to realize the estimated $500 billion dollars in profits to be had in a joint, Exxon Mobil and Russia Arctic drilling project.

This is but one example of the Trump administration's orientation. I doubt there is any hyperbole in saying that this administration will take the USA far in the opposite direction from the few positive steps taken by the Obama administration as it has endlessly tangled with a fully resistant Republican congress. Oh, and did I mention that it is the job of the US Secretary of State to represent the USA in any international talks regarding climate change?

Lastly, it should also be mentioned that dozens of high level State Department staff were either fired or resigned as the Trump administration took office. This unprecedented crippling of the US's diplomatic corps does not bode well for the future of US diplomatic efforts around the world.

*   *   *

Substantial investigative journalism has been done by *The Los Angeles Times*, et al. in which they have uncovered yet another cynical motive for concealing their climate research and prolonging their climate denial propaganda campaign.

In the LA Times article[8], it is disclosed that Exxon, their Canadian subsidiary, Imperial, and BP had purchased the mineral rights to more than a million acres of the Arctic's Beaufort Sea in anticipation of easier access after human-caused global warming made Arctic drilling more accessible by melting the ice cap,

"Today, as Exxon's scientists predicted 25 years ago, Canada's Northwest Territories has experienced some of the most dramatic effects of global warming. While the rest of the planet has seen an average increase of roughly 1.5 degrees in the last 100 years, the northern reaches of the province have warmed by 5.4 degrees and temperatures in central regions have increased by 3.6 degrees.

"Since 2012, Exxon Mobil and Imperial have held the rights to more than one million acres in the Beaufort Sea, for which they bid $1.7 billion in a joint venture with BP. Although the companies have not begun drilling, they requested a lease extension until 2028 from the Canadian government a few months ago. Exxon Mobil declined to comment on its plans there.

"Croasdale said the company could be 'taking a gamble' the ice will break up soon, finally bringing about the day he predicted so long ago—when the costs would become low enough to make Arctic exploration economical."

> Greenhouse gases are rising due to the burning of fossil fuels, Nobody disputes this fact, nor is there doubt those levels will double by the middle of the 21st century.
>
> *Ken Croasdale,* Senior ice researcher for Exxon's Canadian subsidiary, at an Engineering Conference, 1991.

> We are at about 490 parts per million CO_2 equivalent today. Not 400. That's counting methane, that's counting nitrous oxide and other greenhouse gases. The likelihood of us going over 500ppm is almost a certainty. And, there is a high probability of going over 600. And, so, very, very scary. If you look at what we are doing now, the long time it takes to make any significant changes in our emissions, it is extremely unlikely that we will avoid hitting 550. Since we are at 490 today. I can tell you that one degree is really bad. So the 'S' hits the fan."
>
> *Steven Chu,* Former US Secretary of Energy, December 2016 panel discussion at The Commonwealth Club/Climate One. YouTube video: *Steven Chu Shares Some Sobering Climate Change Math.*

So here we have abundant evidence of the singular focus of the US for the next at least four years. And, we have a few chapters full of evidence that corporate and government executives have known full well the consequences that await us when we continue in a business as usual fashion. Let's take one more stroll through some of the methods those business and political leaders have used to manipulate the voting populace to react to climate-focused, Sober Data with doubt, skepticism even with contempt and derision for the world's climate scientists.

So successful has this climate denial campaign been that our populace can be divided into a few rather depressing camps: those who doubt or fully deny human caused climate change (approximately 50% by some polls), those who don't deny climate change and see that it is important but still rather distant and requiring no particular action by the average person (approximately 47% by my unofficial polling) and the remaining roughly 3% who are actively engaged in mitigation and policy making, as if climate issues mattered now.

If you haven't picked up on the main point here, what I'm trying to say is we are facing an existential predicament here—one that is looming far closer than 2100—and we have almost unanimously bought into the not-at-all-subtle propaganda strategy to have us doubt what the scientists are saying and trust the media presentation that loudly declares the invincibility of the business-as-usual paradigm and its ability to innovate us out of this predicament.

As we will cover in more detail in the next chapter, we human beings are extremely fond of our luxurious, fossil-fuel-driven lifestyle. It appears that we are collectively more than happy to be reassured that government and corporations have everything under control, the experts will soon be discovering the solution to our pesky CO_2 emissions problem and finally we can get back to life and business as usual.

*   *   *

That climate denial campaign has been immensely successful. To even the casual observer it would appear that, at this most important global juncture, the greatest consumer of fossil fuels in human history (the US) is preparing to double-down and recommit to perhaps its greatest chapter of extraction, consumption and emissions yet.

To make it ok for us to double down on consumption and emissions at a time when we are being barraged with vetted science telling us we must reduce— and reduce immediately— those in control of the messaging did not have to counter each and every data point and projection offered by the scientific community.

All the folks in power had to do was create an atmosphere of doubt. They didn't have to prove anything. They just had to manipulate the public discourse in such a way as to cast doubt on the obviously well established and fully vetted science.

For the reader who wants more of the story of this insanely powerful propaganda program, I recommend the book and documentary, *The Merchants of Doubt*. In this remarkable book and film, Naomi Oreskes and Erik M. Conway, uncover the cynical motives and methods used by the fossil fuel industries to intentionally distract and confuse the public about the damaging effects we can expect from our continued use of fossil fuels.

Oreskes and Conway draw clear connections between the methods used by cigarette manufacturers in their attempts to avoid prosecution for knowingly selling a dangerous product—and the fossil fuel interests' actively withholding damning data and promoting a propaganda of deadly denial.

Myron Ebell, President Trump's senior advisor during their transition into office, is a well known climate denier of the highest order. He is mentioned in *The Merchants of Doubt* as one of the tobacco–cancer-connection deniers that migrated to creating the climate denier campaign.

Any guesses what the future enforcement and research measures of the EPA and other related agencies will look like regarding CO_2 emissions? Trump and Ebell both have declared great interest in eviscerating and perhaps dismantling the EPA and removing the USA from all aspects of the COP21 agreements. Similar stances have been declared by almost every one of Trump's cabinet appointees, including Scott Pruitt, the head of the EPA.

*   *   *

Edward Bernays on the press being in a state of "harmony" with their sources (those in power) vs. being a source of balance, skeptical inquiry and independent investigation:

> But being dependent, every day of the year and for year after year, upon certain politicians for news, the newspaper reporters are obliged to work in harmony with their news sources.

> *Edward L. Bernays, Propaganda*

Seems like a benign quote, this one. Harmony is good, Right?

It's good up until it implies that our media is nothing more than stenographers for those in positions of power in corporations and government. Poignantly, we can track a degradation in our national news media that exactly coincides with the rocket-like escalation of our greenhouse gas emissions from the 70s to today.

> Our opponents, the media and the whole world will soon see as we begin to take further actions, that the powers of the president to protect our country are very substantial and will not be questioned.

Stephen Miller, Trump
administration, Senior Policy
Advisor, On CBS, *Face The Nation.*
February 2017.

(American news and media) should keep its mouth shut and just
listen for a while.

Steve Bannon, Trump administration, chief
strategist, Post inauguration, January 2017.

We should start with the really low hanging fruit called, Fox News. Might as well
call this exactly what it is, the most blatant and powerful propaganda source that
has ever existed on the planet. I am asserting that the creation of this unmitigated
mouthpiece of neo-conservative, business-as-usual babel ranks high on the list of
influences that are leading to humanity's demise.

I know these are extreme words, but time and again I've found that there is very
little hyperbole when we are talking about the predicament we face— the eventual
crushing of our shared global habitat, the erosion of a once proud democracy and
even the bald-faced denial of world-class science and the warnings of extinction-
level events coming our way.

This might sound disturbing enough, but I actually am even more afraid of the
other mainstream news sources in the US market. At least with Fox you know
what you are getting and its obvious biases. With virtually every other major,
mainstream news source, there is an equally devastating lack of journalistic
integrity and full-throated compliance with business as usual as proscribed by their
corporate and government overseers.

Again, this topic has been covered at length by far more skilled journalists than
me. Suffice it to say that we need only look to the past twenty years or so to see
the abolition of speaking truth to power and the sycophantic-stenographer role all
major news outlets have taken on.

This is particularly true of the new Trump Administration. Trump has made his
intentions clear that he will favor only press that is sycophantic to him and he will
punish or marginalize any press that dares to criticize.

What I will spend some time with is the new, enhanced tool kit that the Trump camp has brought with them to this presidency.

In the first (pre Trump) draft of this book I focused only on the fantastic exposé mentioned above, *The Merchants of Doubt*. The uncovering of this cynical propaganda tool by corporate deniers was one of the most valuable contributions that has been made to-date in our global fight for truth and integrity in facing our predicament.

With the onset of the Trump Administration, the "Impossible" aspect of The Impossible Conversation has been expanded and intensified.

In a recent episode of On The Media, Cognitive Linguist, George Lakoff offered a brilliant layout of a considerable number of tools the Trump Administration has already been using in its dealings with the press, public announcements and interviews at the highest levels of the administration.

During the previous administrations, going back to Reagan or so, we were exposed to the basic tactics of the Merchants of Doubt – and the other (Bernays) methods being deployed subtly in the background.

Now there is no more need of fostering doubt among the voting populace. This administration has all but annihilated any consideration of climate impact mitigation and is well on its way to eliminating our own EPA, existing environmental regulation or enforcement and any small commitment we might now have to join with the rest of the world in the Paris COP21 accords.

The tools that Mr Lakoff describes for us are the tools of a team of bullies, liars and manipulators. They are clearly tools meant to shield the user from accountability, transparency or any unwanted interactions that might corner them into telling the truth about a given topic:

1. Preemptive Framing:

Frame an issue before someone else does. Example one… "This is fake news."

Example two… Trump's inauguration was very poorly attended, possibly the smallest ever. So, preemptively frame it as the largest in recorded history.

2. Diversion: Example… attacking Meryl Streep or the cast of Hamilton, so Trump's $25m settlement about his Trump University fraud might go unnoticed.

3. Trial Balloon: "The US must greatly strengthen and expand its nuclear capacity until such time as the world comes to its senses regarding nukes." He notices the reaction that this brings on, and files this info away for possible future use as a talking point.

(The barrage of red-hot, controversial cabinet appointments, policy projections, signing statements, tweets and press releases that has filled each day of Trump's first month in office, has been very deliberate and very consciously crafted. I assert that all of these issues are at best examples of Trial Balloons and at worst, a toxic smoke and mirror show to distract the public's and media's attention from far more substantive and damaging political activities going on behind closed doors.)

4. Deflection: Attack the messenger—CNN, Buzzfeed, any news agency that offends Trump. Their intention is to put the public attention on the "offending" news agency or reporter, hence eliminating the unpleasant focus of attention on a questionable administration policy or action.

An example of a public Trump statement (tweet) that involves all four of these tools.

"Intelligence agencies should not have allowed this fake news to leak into the public. One last shot at me, are we living in Nazi Germany?"

First: Preemptive Framing = This is Fake News.

Second: Diversion = It's going to be discussed, whether or not it's Fake News. So the original "leaked" news content won't get discussed, it is dismissed as fake news.

Third: Deflection = Attacking the messengers, e.g. calling their news, fake, and framing their delivery of the leaked information as an attack on him, rather than the agencies doing their job.

Fourth: the Trial Balloon = Will the intelligence agencies be stopped from doing this? Are they working like the agencies of Nazi Germany? (Both are useless rhetorical questions that can be tracked for whatever public reaction they prompt, and possibly used in future distracting tweets)

I am inclined to add one more important example of diversion or deflection. While all of the daily smoke and mirrors shenanigans rivets our attention on Trump and his crew, our collective attention has been completely disengaged from some of the core issues behind the surface outrage.

Given the central topic of this book, Abrupt Climate Change, I am primarily focused on how we, the US public, are raising our voices in various resistance actions around the country. These actions are aimed at issues that include: immigration, deportation and civil rights. There is precious little "resistance" to our new national policy of defunding and stripping power from agencies like the Department of State and the EPA and shutting down our involvement in COP21 agreements.

What Lakoff suggests for journalists covering the Trump administration:

"Instead of immediately parroting Trump's tweets and comments, offer an immediate analysis of which of these persuasion tools he is using. Reframe the tweet as a teachable moment in which your audience might learn about this type of deceptive persuasion. Keep going back to the actual substance and the truth."

For those of us that are not journalists, there is still good coaching here. Like it or not, these times require all of us to become facile at discerning fake news and discerning manipulative and deceptive tools as listed here. And, perhaps the most important advice of all—"Keep going back to the actual substance and the truth."

There are three more tools for deception and manipulation that I'd like to add here before we move on. These three tools have the potential to be far more devastating than any combination of the tools already described.

*　　*　　*

1. The first is, lies. We have been immersed in a culture of lies, untruths, truthiness, distortion, denial, BS and the like for so long that lying has become normalized. This normalization of lying will take constant vigilance to clear up. We all have our work cut out for us here.

For an example of this we need look no further than the Trump administration's first proclamation about the inauguration, via Press Secretary, Sean Spicer, who stated:

"This was the largest audience ever to witness an inauguration, period. These attempts to lessen the enthusiasm of the inauguration are shameful and wrong."

The next day, Trump senior advisor, Kelly Ann Conway, said that Spicer was merely stating "alternative facts."

Journalist, Dave Zirin points out that…

These are not alternative facts, these are lies.

> This is what is called, "gaslighting." It is unconscionable behavior
> for an Internet troll, let alone the press secretary of the President
> of the United States. It is one thing for a campaign to say things
> that are demonstrably untrue. That's been the reality for as long as
> we've had presidential campaigns. But it is chilling when people
> who hold the levers of power will look straight at a bank of
> cameras and lie.

2. The second tool of control and manipulation of both message and media is
access. It is already abundantly clear that the Trump administration intends
nothing less than complete control of all press contact.

While it could be said that US media has become sycophantic in order to stay
close to the cash cow that is American politics, no previous administration has
been so overt with its intentions to punish and marginalize any media outlet or
reporter that has the audacity to report anything other than the pre-processed,
toxic twitter rants that currently make up the bulk of the Trump communication
strategy.

In a recent public comment marking Black History Month, Trump interrupted
himself as he spoke of Frederick Douglass as if he were still alive. He spoke
directly to the press that was present at this event…about the press. "A lot of the
media is actually the opposition party— they're so biased." And, "So much of the
media is the opposition party and knowingly saying incorrect things."

With these comments and Trump's early refusal to call on CNN in a press
conference, because they are "fake news," Trump himself has clearly staked out
where he and his administration stand about journalists who actually have some
journalistic integrity as they report about this administration.

Trump's senior communications advisor, Kelly Ann Conway, also made the
administration's position clear about journalists who insist on seeking truthful
answers to important questions. In her January 2017 interview with Meet the
Press host, Chuck Todd, Conway stubbornly refused to say anything remotely
relevant to Todd's questions. And, to his credit, and perhaps for the first time in
his career, Todd stayed focused on Conway's avoidance and on Sean Spicer's lies,
and he actually asked follow up questions.

Kelly Ann Conway ultimately ended the cat and mouse interview by saying, "If we
are going to continue to refer to our press secretary in those types of terms, we're
going to have to rethink our relationship here. I want to have an open relationship

with our press, but look what happened the day before, speaking of falsehoods."

Conway then went on to barrage Todd with a flurry of deceptive smoke and mirrors that amounted to exactly zero cogent reply to Todd's repeated questions about why the press secretary was instructed to lie in his first public appearance in his job. It is from this interaction that Conway has coined the new term for lies— alternative facts.

My interpretation of the statements of Trump, Spicer and Conway is that they fully intend to lie, manipulate and gaslight (see the next "tool" description). Their language is saturated with psychological domination and manipulation designed to make the questioner look foolish and feel crazy.

3. The third tool is, Gaslighting. This tool is, in my judgment, the one that has been used longest and to greatest effect in our culture since the time of Edward Bernays and the rise of despotic, corporate and governmental influence through mass communication.

Particularly, I assert that the essential elements of gaslighting were at the center of the gruesome effectiveness of the denial/doubt, propaganda campaigns of the tobacco companies. I am also suggesting that this type of mass manipulation of public perception is also causal in the current denial/doubt, propaganda campaigns of the fossil fuel industry and our corporatist government representatives.

Further, as I highlighted above regarding Kelly Ann Conway's threat to terminate the Trump administration's relationship with NBC and Chuck Todd if he continues to ask probing and difficult questions, I am asserting that behind every instance of gaslighting, at every level, is an implied threat of psychological domination and or violence.

In a recent article in Psychology Today[10] Stephanie Sarkis Ph.D. articulates some of the dynamics of and indicators of gaslighting. Sarkis' article is obviously written to describe these dynamics on an interpersonal level. In The Impossible Conversation we will be looking into gaslighting and psychological manipulation on levels ranging from the interpersonal to the national and international:

> Gaslighting is a tactic in which a person or entity, in order to gain more power, makes a victim question their reality. It works much better than you may think. Anyone is susceptible to gaslighting, and it is a common technique of abusers, dictators, narcissists and cult leaders. It is done slowly, so the victim doesn't realize how much they've been brainwashed. For

example, in the movie *Gaslight* (1944), a man manipulates his wife to the point where she thinks she is losing her mind.

People who gaslight typically use the following techniques:

1. They tell blatant lies.

You know it's an outright lie. Yet they are telling you this lie with a straight face. Why are they so blatant? Because they're setting up a precedent. Once they tell you a huge lie, you're not sure if anything they say is true. Keeping you unsteady and off-kilter is the goal.

2. They deny they ever said something, even though you have proof.

You know they said they would do something; you know you heard it. But they out and out deny it. It makes you start questioning your reality—maybe they never said that thing. And the more they do this, the more you question your reality and start accepting theirs.

3. They use what is near and dear to you as ammunition.

They know how important your kids are to you, and they know how important your identity is to you. So those may be one of the first things they attack. If you have kids, they tell you that you should not have had those children. They will tell you that you'd be a worthy person if only you didn't have a long list of negative traits. They attack the foundation of your being.

4. They wear you down over time.

This is one of the insidious things about gaslighting—it is done gradually, over time. A lie here, a lie there, a snide comment every so often...and then it starts ramping up. Even the brightest, most self-aware people can be sucked into gaslighting—it is that effective. It's the "frog in the frying pan" analogy: The heat is turned up slowly, so the frog never realizes what's happening to it.

5. Their actions do not match their words.

When dealing with a person or entity that gaslights, look at what they are doing rather than what they are saying. What they are saying means nothing; it is just talk. What they are doing is the issue.

6. They throw in positive reinforcement to confuse you.

This person or entity that is cutting you down, telling you that you don't have value, is now praising you for something you did. This adds an additional sense of uneasiness. You think, "Well maybe they aren't so bad." Yes, they are. This is a calculated attempt to keep you off-kilter—and again, to question your reality. Also look at what you were praised for; it is probably something that served the gaslighter.

7. They know confusion weakens people.

Gaslighters know that people like having a sense of stability and normalcy. Their goal is to uproot this and make you constantly question everything. And your natural tendency is to look to the person or entity that will help you feel more stable—and that happens to be the gaslighter.

8. They project.

They are a drug user or a cheater, yet they are constantly accusing you of that. This is done so often that you start trying to defend yourself, and are distracted from the gaslighter's own behavior.

9. They try to align people against you.

Gaslighters are masters at manipulating and finding the people they know will stand by them no matter what—and they use these people against you. They will make comments such as, "This person knows that you're not right," or "This person knows you're useless too." Keep in mind it does not mean that these people actually said these things. A gaslighter is a constant liar. When the gaslighter uses this tactic, it makes you feel like you don't know who to trust or turn to—and that leads you right back to the gaslighter. And that's exactly what they want: Isolation gives them more control.

10. They tell you or others that you are crazy.

This is one of the most effective tools of the gaslighter, because it's dismissive. The gaslighter knows if they question your sanity, people will not believe you when you tell them the gaslighter is abusive or out-of-control. It's a master technique.

11. They tell you everyone else is a liar.

By telling you that everyone else (your family, the media) is a liar, it again makes you question your reality. You've never known someone with the audacity to do this, so they must be telling the truth, right? No. It's a manipulation technique. It makes people turn to the gaslighter for the "correct" information—which isn't correct information at all.

The more you are aware of these techniques, the quicker you can identify them and avoid falling into the gaslighter's trap.

Again, I hope this information is useful if you are experiencing any of these techniques in your personal relationships. My point, however, in going into such detail with gaslighting, is to say that gaslighting has been one of the powerful propaganda tools used in US corporate and government public relations (read, propaganda)—particularly since the ramping up of propaganda at scale in the 1980s to the present day.

Ironically, I had all of these distinctions in place for the writing of this book well before the advent of the election of Donald Trump. Needless to say what was already a worrisome background component of our national discourse—with Trump, has become a consciously created, constant parade of one disrupting and upsetting lie and test balloon after another.

Another place to look for the use of these manipulative tools is in the government and corporate responses to protest, activists or resistance from citizens. A useful practice for becoming more skilled at identifying these manipulations as they are happening, is to review the history of the enforcement measures taken against the Water Protectors and other activists. Listen to the public statements from the government and corporate spokes-people and from national and local media as they covered the story. This pipeline story is full of examples of every propaganda and public influence tool mentioned here, and graphically shows the violence that is always behind such tools.

*   *   *

What I am asserting here is, beginning with Bernays' profound foundation of propaganda at work at all levels of 20th century American business and government—and the supercharging effect of the largest propaganda machine the world has ever known, in the form of today's mainstream media—we have landed in a position of utter disempowerment of the electorate. And, as if that weren't enough, it seems as if the core tenets of this powerful influencing of the masses have been pushed to extremes not even dreamt of by Goebbels and the Third Reich.

*   *   *

I am asserting that this cynical program of mass deceit has grown so large as to be out of the control of its handlers. (a)

One of the core tenets of effective propaganda is to constantly repeat the desired message using trusted, familiar sources—the people become ultimately normalized to corporations, media and government speaking in unadulterated doublespeak.

Fox and all other corporate news outlets…check. (b)

Another: anchor those messages in an emotional tone of fear. Follow this with the assumption that with our invincible force, our police, military, intelligence services will keep us safe…check. (c)

And don't forget, we must always describe people who are not like us, whom we can fear and alienate, if not downright hate and ultimately kill, as "others" or "terrorists"… double check. (d)

Another—One grand aspect of our business-as-usual defining story, is that we must always pursue more. We must never stop our commitment to infinite growth on a finite planet. Our companies always find a way to produce the result, to extract that last bit of the gold in that vein; we always have the ingenuity to find the solutions to all the problems. The job of the people is always to just carry on, being consumers and compliant workers. (e)

All of these basic principles of propaganda and influence of mass populations appear to have been stretched to an extreme never seen before. Each of these over-blown principles appears to have a rather ironic, unexpected consequence.

*   *   *

(a) With the shock on the faces of even the Republicans at the outcome of the 2016 presidential elections, it is obvious that the decades-long disempowerment of America's middle class electorate had come full circle. We have elected a man

115

who, by his own admission, has no plans on building better lives for middle class Americans, as was promised while campaigning. We are mad as hell at the loss of our standard of living and the constant BS shoveled out by the politicians and corporate hucksters and banksters. Voting for someone who offers something, anything that might be different from choosing between the candidate—clones that we are presented with in every election.

(b) This is where the real muscle of the climate denial campaign lives. With the full-tilt propaganda doublespeak engine that is Fox News coupled with the meaningless parade of false equivalencies and faux-debates on all other networks, we have become a country that can easily justify its deep resistance to letting go of its very comfortable ways by referencing the non-stop barrage of vitriol, denial and doubt that is thrown at the very science that is attempting to save us from ultimate self destruction.

(c) This one is one of the most powerful because it cannot be questioned, ever. There was not one mention of reducing the military or intelligence budgets during the 2016 presidential election season. There likely will never be a mention of this possibility. We are too encased in fear to consider a draw down of our outsized military or intelligence services and, like the climate issue back at (b)… the money is too good. With a government completely owned and operated by corporate money, no "bleeding heart" voters' movement would ever compete against the maintenance of the status quo—of business as usual. What's that? Oh yeah, there is no voters' movement to reduce the military and intelligence budgets.

(d) This aspect of effective propaganda is the one that seems to bring on comparisons of the newly elected Trump administration with Hitler and the Third Reich. No matter how you slice this one, the message has been clear. Trump and his administration promises to bring a laser focus on any minority that fits this bill. He has already called out: Muslims, Mexicans, all illegal immigrants, people of color and many more. Members of his administration have significant histories of victimizing the LGBTQ community, women, low income workers, the press, and the list goes on. Good propaganda needs a good, long list of people to fear, hate and subjugate.

(e) This one has taken on truly storybook proportions. With Trump's nomination of Exxon CEO Rex Tillerson to Secretary of State we see an intensification of a commitment to more business as usual than has ever been. At a time when the countries of the world have their first ever global agreement on reducing CO_2 emissions and slowing climate change impacts, Trump is doubling down by inviting the world's most powerful fossil fuels extractor to be in charge of America's diplomacy, participation in future environmental summits and economic endeavors around the world.

That's not all for (e). As was mentioned in earlier chapters, Tillerson/Exxon are currently being investigated for what may well be the most cynical and destructive fraud in human history.

If at any point in that journey Exxon— largest oil company on Earth, most profitable enterprise in human history— had said: 'Our own research shows that these scientists are right and that we are in a dangerous place,' the faux debate would effectively have ended. That's all it would have taken; stripped of the cover provided by doubt, humanity would have gotten to work.

Instead, knowingly, Exxon helped organize the most consequential lie in human history.
Bill McKibben

So in the corporate pursuit of infinite growth on a finite planet—a company that knew full well that the continuation of business as usual would be massively destructive—generated and maintains to this day, a multi-billion dollar campaign of climate denial and vilification and threatening of climate scientists. And its CEO takes one of the most powerful jobs on the planet. What could possibly go wrong?

And, let's just put a bow on this last point. We have heard from a large number of spontaneously generated protest groups about a number of the issues listed above. This is a very good thing. As I mentioned before, I applaud any and all efforts to stand up, speak up, reclaim our collective, long-ago-forfeited agency in life!

We heard precious little about the disastrous team and policy platform regarding climate change mitigation and emissions reductions in the USA that has been assembled and now deployed by the Trump Administration.

*   *   *

In closing out this exploration of our collective shadow—again our shadow is an amalgam of aspects of ourselves we deny or refuse to own or be responsible for—

I invite us all to look at a particular current event in our world.

I invite us all to track with this example by continually checking to see where we position ourselves in terms of the political, the moral, the environmental, the social justice and finally the just plain human dimensions of this situation.

The example I offer is Standing Rock.

If we observe the actions through a lens of business as usual, we see a ragtag bunch of Native Americans, veterans and hippie environmentalists making a big fuss about how some oil pipeline is planned to go through some tribal sacred land.

If we are watching the mainstream news, first we will see almost no coverage whatsoever, and when we do hear about it, we hear about how the protesters are turning violent and costing the pipeline company millions by delaying the project.

If we observe the actions through a lens of reporting provided by sources that are *not* owned by massive corporate conglomerates we see and hear a very different story—better still, if we are informed by a media that founds its stories with the Sober Data as described in books or articles like this one.

We hear and see that these "protesters" are completely committed to honoring and protecting their sacred lands and to protecting the water in and on that land. In fact, we hear that they consider themselves to be "Water Protectors," not protesters at all. We see that thousands of people—other tribes, non tribal folks, people from all walks of life are getting themselves to the site of this faceoff in a gesture of alliance, of unity, of prayer, of protection of the sanctity of water, land and life.

If we keep watching, we can easily see that the other side of this situation was populated by a militarized police force and private security contractors. We can watch the painful videos that show police dogs savagely attacking the unarmed and peaceful protectors. We can watch as water cannons, rubber bullets and sound cannons are deployed against the thousands of people who have come to stand and say "No!"

We can see a government that was and is implicitly authorizing the use of rubber bullets at point blank range, ungodly amounts of tear gas again, sprayed in massive doses at arms-length. We can see a government that has no intention to protect the Water Protectors' rights to assemble and protest, as guaranteed in the Constitution. We can see a government that clearly is backing the profit-driven advances of the fossil fuel industry before any consideration is given to current land use and permitting requirements, long standing treaties or the ultimately ecocidal result of building more fossil fuel infrastructure in the face of our non-existent carbon budget.

I suppose one could stop here with the comparison between a business-as-usual view of a current hot-button issue in the US news and the view provided by the few alternative journalists that are brave enough to report from the scene.

But remember what book you are reading. Please remember my acknowledgement and warning at the beginning of this Impossible Conversation—called that because the data and projections of the first few chapters, even the most conservative of those projections, as they relate to our remaining global CO_2 emissions budget, imply that we must stop digging for more oil. We must stop building new fossil fuel infrastructure. We must begin the immediate reduction of our global CO_2 emissions.

The Impossible Conversation is the one in which we gather up the courage to tell the truth about our impact on the world and face down those in power who would have us stay in blissful ignorance in a business-as-usual world.

It is literally insane to propose even one more pipeline, added to the thousands that crisscross the US now. We must draw the era of doublespeak and propaganda to a close. We must wake up as a national and global citizenry and be responsible for our part in paying for this 150-years-long fossil fuel, "free-lunch" we've enjoyed.

*   *   *

It is more than a little ironic that we have stumbled onto a couple more strange and noteworthy benchmarks in our process of becoming a society fully immersed in propaganda.

It appears to me that in at least two ways, the powerful propaganda methods of Bernays and others hit a limit this year. These two covert ways of influencing masses of people actually turned around and seemed to shock and befuddle those who have been dishing out the propaganda for so long.

First… Is it possible that the propaganda-laced farce that our elections have become have so drained us of our sense of agency or hope or authentic democratic process that we have ended up with literally no choice but to elect the most outlandish of candidates in hopes of finding someone who is truly different?

In 2016, we saw a US presidential election season that lasted fully two years, netted the media billions in profits and covered sincere policy issues for a total of less than one hour of programming in 2016. That's sixty minutes total for all the major media news outlets combined.

The candidates' debates included exactly zero questions about Earth, environment or climate. The candidates mentioned precisely nothing about the more than trillion dollars the US spends each year on military and intelligence gathering, except when they proposed to increase that spending.

*　　*　　*

I see each of these to be blazing examples of how the national discourse has been tightly groomed into a parade of foregone conclusions about how the US operates, who our choices will be within elections, and who is going to be in power. Well done, Mr Bernays and all who followed in his footsteps.

It was stated in so many different ways at the conclusion of this election cycle— Trump was elected not because of his integrity or his alleged populist leanings; he was not elected because of his intricate knowledge of domestic and international policy making and diplomacy. Trump was elected by a deeply frustrated and disempowered electorate of Americans who knew only that they were angry and disappointed with the choices they had in front of them. They had felt their standard of living and trust in America slipping away for years; and Trump promised one thing: to be different.

I am suggesting that the US system of elections and of governing has been manipulated for decades to be a strictly corporate, biased arrangement behind a veneer of democracy. I am suggesting that the last thirty or so years have been so extravagantly and obviously choreographed to the tune dictated by the moneyed powers—who lost track of keeping up any veneer at all of America's once admirable democracy.

I'm suggesting that with the election of Trump even the most conservative Republicans and Ayn Rand influenced libertarians were shocked by the election of a complete foreigner to the inner sanctum of control. I just find their shock to be ironic.

*　　*　　*

This last item is really the capper for me. I'm sure that it has come as a surprise to those who have worked so long and so hard to craft our American defining story. It takes quite a bit of effort to get a country of 300 million-plus people to get used to being fed misinformation and doublespeak. It takes more effort, still, to convince the majority of the USA that what makes America "great" is for the electorate to vote solidly against its own best interests. What finer use for the powerful propaganda tools being used so powerfully for the past thirty-five years or so?

Of course, every American can list any number of examples of corporate or government doublespeak or just plain bullshit. But this season, this year, we've really had our share of incidents and trends that seem to indicate that the doublespeak and bullshit has finally gotten so thick that it has started to blow back into the faces of the propagandists.

If we just bring our attention back to the cynical control of media with a message of climate change denial, we recall the thousands of news shows we watched as a world-renowned climate scientist was paired with a well paid fossil fuel shill for yet another "debate" about climate science.

We all sat quietly and watched as the shill spewed his BS—that is, unless we just changed the channel. We all just ate it up, without a peep about how denial of climate change and of science isn't really a thing.

We all just sat and absorbed the doublespeak that claimed climate change is not real—or climate science is riddled by doubt and uncertainty. We even sat quietly while our elected representatives and despicable news media attacked and vilified the most talented climate scientists on the planet. We (the vast majority of us) seemed to breathe a sigh of relief when exactly zero climate -related questions were asked of the candidates in the presidential debates.

This "capper" item seems like the ultimate in ironic turn around for those who are interested in tracking the limits of propaganda. Just how much political obfuscation can people take? How many wars, justified with paper-thin slogans and barely concealed lies will we pay for and endure? How long will we keep believing that our representatives have any intention at all to truly represent people rather than corporate checkbooks?

This trend of having large-scale blow back in American culture is far from a healthy revolution. While at least it is a sign of some amount of frustration with aspects of business—as-usual culture, these ironic signs of giving the powers that be a taste of their own lies are proving to be just as problematic as the original propaganda and manipulation.

What I'm thinking of here is the relatively new upwelling of a global cottage industry, *fake news*. With the advent of fake news we are able to watch the frantic scrambling of those in power as their own powerful propaganda tools are put into the hands of indiscriminate fake news generators around the globe. This is truly the threshold of a new chapter in human communications.

It's hard not to make a comparison with Frankenstein's monster—with this new, chaotic beast called, fake news. If we stay with our primary focus on the billion dollar climate denial and doubt campaign we can see that that program, invented out of whole cloth to confuse and stop any public efforts to learn the truth about our planet and climate, was the ultimate inspiration for the creation of the world's latest, feral, media phenomenon.

While most Americans remained blissfully ignorant about the cynical biases in their mainstream news sources, profit hungry content creators around the world saw a grand money making opportunity.

Who could have guessed that internet hackers and shadowy entrepreneurs would see how much money and success was possible when even the most ridiculous "news" was broadcast to the general public? It clearly is very big business though, given our politically charged hunger for news that directly reflects only our personal, political worldview.

Again, this topic is far beyond the scope of this book. One can only imagine where this trend is headed and what effects it will have on our global efforts to improve our world in any way. Suffice it to say, our 21st century world appears to have far outpaced even the grandest hopes of those who planned to manipulate and propagandize and lie their way into ultimate power and control.

To refer, once again, to the remarkable work of another associate of Sigmund Freud, Carl Jung, we appear to have an out-of-control expression of our collective Shadow running wild in plain view.

While we have articulated a great many of the attributes of a collective or even global Shadow motivations and behaviors of our governments, corporations and even our cultures, we now must bring this exploration down to the very personal level, the level of everyday life. We can easily point fingers of well-deserved blame at those of great wealth and power. But the predicament we find ourselves in will change, not at all, if all we do is blame others for this challenging present and impossible future we are facing.

6 Choices to Make at the End of Business as Usual

We normalize the abnormal in order to maintain the status quo.

Deb Ozarko

*   *   *

In all of the previous chapters, particularly the last one, we have explored the historical context for how we Americans have ended up with this rather curious and tragic way of responding to the current circumstances in the world. More specifically I have described the evolution of our cultural, economic and environmental stance in the world using a very broad frame.

We've looked at how our shared cultural narrative, our way of defining ourselves, has been massively influenced by the manipulations and agendas of those at the highest levels of power in both government and corporate arenas. We've followed that up with a brief but important update about the escalation of those Shadow influences that has occurred in the short time since the Trump administration has taken office.

The focus of *The Impossible Conversation*, however, is actually not the daunting data and projections of the Abrupt Climate Change advocates. The focus is not even the long history of the wealthy and powerful manipulating mass consciousness. The focus here is to reacquaint ourselves with our own ability to discern the truth about life on Earth and— once we've oriented ourselves around that daunting truth— establish our personal responses to the question: "How will we live our lives together, as we face our challenges and predicaments?"

In this chapter we will take a more inward look at how our tightly controlled cultural narrative, or defining story, has instilled in each of us, not only the deep love for, but also an addiction to, our fossil-fuel-driven lifestyle. This has been the most privileged, productive and accelerated chapter of human history, providing lifestyles more advantaged than the royalty of history to billions of middle and "lower class" people around the world. (Not to mention the greatest concentration of wealth for the ultra wealthy that the world has ever seen. Currently, the top eight wealthiest people possess more wealth than the bottom 50% of people on Earth.)

We will also unpack some of the deep and tragic costs we each have incurred as we took our place in this remarkable parade of human expression, extraction and consumption. To be clear, this immensely privileged lifestyle has come at a price—hence the Sober Data section of this book. It has also come at a very deep and personal price for every person who has participated in it. As implied by the ground rules woven into Bernays' powerful propaganda, if you want to play this game, there are certain agreements (mostly unspoken) that one must make.

To get a more personal sense of how each of us has "paid the cost" of living a life fully immersed in our familiar, business-as -usual culture, we will start with a simple self-assessment tool similar to the Sober Data self-assessment offered in earlier chapters.

*   *   *

So this is the point at which many of the people I had asked to be informal, editorial advisors for this book, told me that I should shift gears to the "hope" part. This would be the spot where, after so much writing about the dismal data and projections and the voracious, cynical, capitalist systems, I should lay out the now ubiquitous sign-off for the average article about climate change.

It should go something like this: "...So, even though this is another depressing statistic about our climate and our global challenges, it's not too late for us to rally and take the immediate and significant action that is needed to shift us into a 'sustainable' future."

And, if I really want to toe the party line here, it would go further, something like this: "And by, 'Rally and take immediate action,' I mean there is really nothing that we Americans need to personally do to mitigate our situation. We all need to just keep on with life and business as usual, keep shopping, keep driving our cars, keep our diets the same as they ever were, keep up the greatest level of air travel the world has ever known. You know, sit back and wait for the experts and the corporations to fix our world with some form of 'sustainable development' and high-tech mitigation invention. "

Well, dear reader, I am here to share with you that, after all of this research on my "informed inquiry" project, I can't in good conscience go that way in this book. In the name of keeping it real, I just cannot wrap up all these findings with that incredibly cynical closing.

To quote the punch line from a very dry joke I've heard my friends from Maine tell: "You can't get there from here." Perhaps I could unpack this rather stark assertion by starting with the common use of two words in those last few paragraphs. *Hope* and *Sustainable*.

Hope: It appears to me that the use of hope, even by the most sober, climate/collapse aware environmental realists I know… has come to mean something like:

"I *hope* that the experts find solutions for all of these pesky problems, so we can finally get back to life and business as usual."

(I mean no offense here. If you, in particular, have a more empowered definition of hope, one that implies more human agency and more reality-based projections of what to hope for, I am thrilled to hear that. I am basing these redefinitions on my observations and hundreds of interviews, coaching sessions and conversations with people from all walks of life during this informed inquiry process.)

Sustainable: Again, the use of this word seems to have been not so subtly shifted. These days, when we are talking about sustainability we are talking about the relationship between Earth, our finite habitat and home, and our global Human Operating System, more pointedly, our infinite-growth-based, resource-extraction/consumption-based, economic systems.

Nowadays, when we use the word sustainable I assert we have intriguingly made the subject of the word— our global economic systems. What we are saying is, we are committed to *sustaining* our economic systems. This is where we focus our attention when we use this term. So I am saying that we are including the Earth habitat part of the concept of sustainability only as much as we absolutely have to—to figure out how we can keep all the features and privileges of our lifestyle in place and not do terminal damage to Earth.

This may sound a bit harsh, this redefinition of both hope and sustainable. But, I've got to say, as I'm looking back on the last paragraph on sustainable, I think I may have given us too much collective credit by saying we are somehow gauging sustainability by avoiding doing "terminal damage" to our habitat.

We need only look back to the data and projections (particularly those addressing species extinction) of the first four chapters of this book to be overwhelmed with evidence that we have virtually no collective will to "avoid doing terminal damage to our habitat."

Really this lack of will is not a big surprise. It is a natural outcome of the override and disconnection built into our system. This may be a good place to pause your reading and note in your own journal, what are the meanings you ascribe to the words, Hope and Sustainable?

Along with this brief snapshot of our collective view of hope and sustainability, I have also built out a list of some of the rules of the game. This is a list of some of the most pernicious memes or rules that have underpinned our human operating system for generations—keep your eyes open for the memes that have been around for millennia.

It has long been known that the most powerful influences on society are not its laws and overt traditions. The most powerful influences are the usually unspoken rules, memes and Shadow elements of a culture. These hold such power precisely because they are ever present in the background of our thinking, our relationships and our behavior. They do their mischief in the background, largely unhindered, because we have so little conscious awareness of them.

*   *   *

"Arrested personal growth serves industrial 'growth.' By suppressing the nature dimension of human development, industrial growth society engenders an immature citizenry unable to imagine a life beyond consumerism and soul-suppressing jobs.

Bill Plotkin, As quoted in:
"Collapsing Consciously,"
Carolyn Baker, 2013

＊　　＊　　＊

In order to participate in our global human operating system, a person must make a few agreements. (Largely these agreements are unspoken and even unconsciously adopted, this just becomes the, "water we swim in.")

- Blindly accept the core lie of our culture: "We will always have infinite growth on this finite planet."

- We must never question or challenge the full throttle realization of that illusion of limitless growth. Anyone who does challenge the primacy of the infinite growth model will be marginalized or worse.

- We must see everything—everything and everyone on Earth as either a potential profit source— or they have no meaning at all in the business-as-usual model. This includes the axiom that anyone who does not work is of no value. It also includes the notion that any waste or pollution or damage to the environment that can be done, without costing the corporation or producer to clean up or mitigate, is considered an unadulterated positive—an externality successfully transferred to the public sector or left to fester with Earth herself. This is clearly the result that fossil fuel companies have had in mind when they have lobbied for less regulation and less culpability for the damages caused by their business or by fossil fuel use itself.

- In order to live with ourselves and minimize the plague of cognitive dissonance (or discomfort, grief or regret, we commit to disconnecting from (numbing down) our built-in sensitivities with: our Deeper Selves, Others and Earth. We call this activity in life, disconnected from our own inter relatedness with all life—override.

- That disconnection— numbing or denying of our core sensitivities and sense of belonging within this miraculous interrelated web of life—created in each of us "a blind spot big enough to drive extinction through."

- Our disconnection will replace our sense of interrelatedness with the rich, immense diversity of life with one lone, remaining anchor for meaning in our lives—the business-as-usual paradigm itself. (Hence the redefinition of *hope* orients us not to a passionate stand for a healthy planet, but a return to our species-centric, comfortable and familiar lifestyle."

- By blindly accepting the core lie of infinite growth on a finite planet, by disconnecting from our birthright of interrelatedness with Deeper Self, Others and Earth, we have forfeited our agency in life. Our agency is our ability to accurately perceive the world around us, and our ability to find authentic meaning and purpose in life, and then harness that meaning and purpose in order to take meaningful action.

*　　*　　*

The capper to all of this is, no matter which Sober Data scenario you have chosen, we appear to be in a predicament, not just challenged by a set of problems. Problems imply solutions, fixes, and the inevitable targeting for a return to business as usual.

A predicament is defined as: "an unpleasantly difficult, perplexing, or dangerous situation." Vocabulary.com recommends thinking of a *predicament* as "an unpleasant state of being." Thesaurus.com offers a few synonyms that apply more pointedly to the definition I am wanting to focus on here—deadlock, crisis, dilemma, impasse, quagmire, pickle.

My emphasis is how essentially impossible it is to find *any* solution, no matter which perspective a person uses to view the predicament.

*　　*　　*

Another way of saying this is the now over-used quote attributed to Albert Einstein:

"We cannot solve problems by using the same
kind of thinking we used when we created them."

Notice even Einstein's quote slips back into the business-as-usual frame of problem/solution. We can still borrow the spirit of the quote—that the frame of our habitual thinking is insufficient to propel us through our massive challenges, and utterly useless when we face our shared predicament.

No matter how we slice it, we will not be generating the solutions for our global climate change and species extinction predicaments using the same thinking and methods that we used to get ourselves to this brink. If I haven't made it clear enough yet, all of my research in this project has yielded exactly zero proposed solutions or plans that offer both serious mitigation and a significant slow down of our global industrial systems. We are facing multiple predicaments.

This includes the utter failure of our brightest minds to create a scalable way to create "negative emissions." This means somehow sucking greenhouse gases out of the atmosphere at scale. It also means all other proposed geoengineering solutions to date have also proven to fall short of the needed scale and effectiveness, not to mention the immense risk involved with the implementation of these imagined solutions.

My recommendation for a quick and informative tour of the current state of geoengineering efforts around the world, is a recent interview [1b] with one of the premier experts on the subject, Ken Caldeira, of Stanford University's Department of Global Ecology and The Carnegie Institute for Science speaks very freely about his extreme reluctance to endorse any geoengineering efforts as they exist today.

Renewables.

I hate to say it, but this also points to the wishful thinking, nay, magical thinking that is involved with the whole notion that our global business-as-usual system could be rebooted and more robust than ever, if we just replaced all of our dirty fossil fuel power plants, cars and trucks with renewables. The prevailing sales pitch for this transition to renewables is that we will have all of the benefit of the old fossil-fuel-driven system, with none of the drawbacks.

The reader interested in getting a more sober outlook for a global transition to renewables might start with an insightful podcast interview between my favorite economics pundit, Chris Martenson and his guest, Gail Tverberg[2]. With a quick listen to this episode of the Peak Prosperity podcast, and a very few others on related topics, I think you will see that it is indeed magical thinking to hope for a grand return to the infinite growth model of business as usual by replacing fossil fuels with renewables.

I hope you will understand, in this chapter and the ones that follow, that I am in no way suggesting that we should stop implementing a strong renewables program around the world. What I *am* saying is that the corporate/government/mainstream media-driven narrative only slows down its complicity with the denial or minimizing of climate change long enough to minimally include the jazzy sales pitch that we can shift all of our global fossil fuel use to renewables and not only will the economy not falter in the process, it will grow and we'll experience a new wave of global prosperity. And, once again, the business-as-usual paradigm will be back, better than ever. Magical Thinking.

As you do some, informed inquiry, into this topic I believe you will find ample evidence that each of the now-popular, proposed strategies for 'saving our world' falls far short of substantial solutions. In fact, items like conservation efforts and geoengineering are laden with probable pitfalls and both invite fossil fuel users to ramp up their consumption – because of the very success they hope to provide.

*　　*　　*

As I started the writing and research for this book in mid 2015, I was deeply discouraged by the apparent lack of public enthusiasm or disinterest in any social justice cause— much less any kind of significant attention on climate change, except for the intrepid few who flew their activist flags at the occasional rally.

It just didn't seem like anything could wake the majority of the US from its climate denial and seeming indifference to issues of social, environmental or economic justice. This indifference was not due to the lack of strong articulation of the moral, economic and environmental benefits of attention on those issues.

In 2015, we saw the release of a powerful and clear encyclical by Pope Francis. In this document, *Laudato Si*[4] , Francis goes to great lengths to weave together the very dire climate issues that face our world and the issues of economic inequality and social and environmental injustice.

I have never in my nearly sixty years experienced such a bold, inspiring and clear calling for these vital issues to be addressed, and I frankly would never have guessed this kind of statement might come from the leader of one of the world's largest religions.

I strongly suggest you read *Laudato Si* in its entirety. But here, I am inclined to offer a quote from Pope Frances, delivered after the publication of his encyclical. In this quote he offers us a bold summary of our predicament and the consequences he predicts if we don't profoundly change the business as usual model.

> "Time, my brothers and sisters, is running out. We are tearing apart our common home. Today the scientific community realizes what the poor have long told us... Harm, perhaps irreversible harm, is being done to the ecosystem. The Earth, entire peoples and individual persons are being brutally punished. And behind all this pain, death and destruction there is a stench of what has been called, the Dung of the Devil, The unfettered pursuit of money rules. The service of the common good is left behind.
>
> Once capital becomes an idol and guides people's decisions, once greed for money presides over the entire socio-economic system, it ruins society. It condemns and enslaves men and women. It destroys human fraternity, it sets people against one another, and as we clearly see, it puts at risk our common home."

> *Pope Francis*
> Santa Cruz, Bolivia, 2015

*   *   *

It was about a year earlier a secular book was released with equal amounts of meticulous research and pointed rhetoric, *This Changes Everything: Capitalism vs the Climate*[3] was published by investigative journalist, Naomi Klein. I was deeply inspired by the integration that Klein did, showing us that it is virtually impossible to separate the long-standing global capitalist system (business as usual) from the issues of social, economic and environmental injustice.

> "Nothing but a full-on change in how humans relate to the Earth and to each other will save us now."

> *Naomi Klein*

Indeed both Francis and Klein made the point quite boldly, if we continue with our business-as-usual human operating system, we will be killing off a multitude of other species on Earth and quite possibly ourselves. And, on the dark business-as-usual road to that end, we will inevitably increase the suffering of the billions of people who reside at the bottom of our economic ladder, as the wealthiest jockey to reap the final bundles of wealth to be extracted from the world's resources.

Within months of the release of the Pope's encyclical similar (albeit smaller scale)[4] pronouncements were offered by top leaders in many other religious sects around the world. I have included links to all of the works mentioned here in chapter 11, Chapter References and Resources.

As clear and potent as the writings of Klein, Pope Francis and other spiritual leaders may sound they all seemed to do little in terms of influencing world corporate and governmental leaders to seriously engage with the cluster of issues the writings described. Now, more than two years later, it is hard to find any evidence that any of these writings have significantly shifted public opinion about climate change at all.

*   *   *

The COP21 Paris conference ended with a flurry of excitement about the generation of the first truly global agreement about reducing CO_2 emissions and reducing the inordinate amount of burden and cost assigned to developing countries. Before the ink was dry on the COP21 agreements, it was common knowledge that even full voluntary compliance with these agreements would fall woefully short of the 2°C temperature rise maximum at the center of the negotiations.

Specifically, the US had pushed for the voluntary nature of the agreements because it was common knowledge that the conservative Congress and, essentially "Republican" president, Obama, would never commit the US to any binding agreements about mitigating climate change, not to mention financially supporting poorer countries as they continue to grow their economies and, eventually, join in CO_2 mitigation efforts.

Far below the COP21 agreements were the social, economic and environmental justice issues that were so clearly detailed by Pope Francis and Naomi Klein. Our collective culture of privilege and denial promised to keep these issues out of the American discourse for decades, if not forever.

*   *   *

A strong example of the kind of minimizing or ignoring of vital issues, is the despicable treatment of and reporting about the Water Protectors involved with the protest against the Dakota Access Pipeline.

It broke my heart that there was not a single sitting government representative (that I was aware of) who would stand with and for the Water Protectors at Standing Rock. As you have read in previous chapters, it is clear that the US has no CO_2 "budget" that allows for even a speck of new fossil fuel infrastructure. If we were to sincerely join the rest of the COP21 countries in efforts to reduce greenhouse gas emissions, we would have to leave the transport of oil to the thousands of miles of pipeline that we already have in this country.

It was and is deeply inspiring that so many people from all walks of life, especially veterans, showed up to be of service to the Standing Rock Water Protectors.

However, it was also heartbreaking to see the militarized, corporate/government police forces pummel the Protectors with icy water canons, rubber bullets, tear gas, Tasers, dogs and god knows what else.

*　　*　　*

Let's pause here to ask you to consider another self-assessment.

I ask you to consider your reactions to or participation with activist actions like Occupy and Standing Rock.

Please add your responses to these questions to your Impossible Conversation journal:

Have you heard about the Occupy actions or Standing Rock?

Have you fully understood the motivations and purpose behind these actions?

Have you supported (or actively opposed) those actions?

Have you participated in those, or any other, protest actions?

If not, what would be important enough to motivate you to participate directly in any activist action?

Do you feel or think that this type of action makes a difference?

*　　*　　*

It was a particularly harsh challenge to write this chapter that has an anchor in our redefining of the word, hope. As 2016 approached fall and winter, I found myself searching for any sincere sign of a larger scale awakening of the American people at scale. More than the relative handful that was hanging tough at Standing Rock, I wanted to see parents of children from all walks of life start to stand up and make their voices heard.

I was hungry for some kind of affirmation that America still had a voice of any kind, other than the polarized voices of people arguing and spewing vitriol across party lines.

Then came the shocking result of the 2016 presidential election.

So, I must emphasize here that the spontaneous combustion of political resistance and activism that accompanied the insanity of Trump's first months in office is a massive breath of fresh air that inspired me deeply. I am beside myself with excitement as I learn about each new layer of resistance and activism that is showing up in virtually every city in America and around the world.

I am particularly impressed with the combination of the huge number of people joining in resistance activities who are doing so for their first time…ever… and, the integration of the Indivisible movement. Indivisible is the result of some very bright people who noticed that a few years back, the Tea Party in America, created a large amount of change with a relatively small number of people across the country.

Indivisible is committed to using the most effective pieces of Tea Party strategy and tactics, to forward a list of Progressive causes. It is clear that the Women's March groups are just getting started with their actions as well.

There was another march in April 2017 for scientists to come together and stand for not only the de-stigmatizing of science and scientists, but also an opportunity to express their deeply held, personal concerns for our planet and the health and wellbeing of all beings and Earth systems.

At this point in our story, however, I have significant concerns about, both the proto-fascist regime our country has just invited in, and the motivations, effectiveness and sustainability of any and all activist expressions that are currently showing up in the US and around the world.

I doubt that I need to explain much about my concerns about the Trump administration and its daily parade of insanity.

In this section of the book, I intend to make clear what I am meaning when I have mentioned the word, *Shadow*. In most of the previous chapters, and especially chapter 5, we have seen cynical and toxic examples of Shadow on the level of large groups, organizations, corporations, agencies, governments and whole cultures. It doesn't take a psychology professor to see these exemplars of Shadow as they bluster their way across the public stage, clearly motivated by a sinister, violent, rageful energy.

In this chapter we will begin to explore how that toxic Shadow shows up in our own personal lives.

Perhaps a reminder here, that the colleague of Sigmund Freud, Carl G. Jung, coined the term, Shadow, to describe psychological aspects of a person or group that are denied or resisted. When these, usually unattractive or uncomfortable, aspects are forced out of conscious, daily life, they tend to seek expression in some indirect way. To the person involved, it can appear to be as simple as emphatically denying that they have anything whatsoever to do with that aspect.

This indirect expression tends to cause great mischief in the person's life. A classic example is the fundamentalist preacher who preaches hellfire and brimstone shall befall anyone who is a homosexual—who later is exposed to have been gay himself, behind the veneer of his traditional, heterosexual life.

Our Shadow comes from the aspects of ourselves that we deny, repress or judge into hiding. To the degree that those aspects of ourselves remain hidden away, judged or repressed they become more and more powerful as motivators in our lives, all without the benefit of our conscious awareness.

What we keep out of our conscious awareness we can conveniently avoid confronting in our own behavior. One of the most common methods used to keep Shadow out of our conscious awareness is, projection. With projection I can redirect my Shadowy aspects away from myself and toward someone else. I can project these aspects onto another person and reinforce that projection by adding my judgment about *that* person and *their* flaws.

We have become masterful at avoiding our own Shadow in the good ol' US of A, and what do you know… we now have a country entirely run by Shadow.

I cannot pass up this prime opportunity to endorse and recommend a book literally written for this subject, at this time. My friend and colleague, Carolyn Baker, has written more than ten books, all having something to do with one central question:

"What are the qualities of relationship and being we will bring as we face our global predicaments?"

Her recent, deep exploration of human beings' collective and individual shadow, is detailed in *Dark Gold: The Human Shadow and the Global Crisis*. This elusive but very common aspect of being human beings is at the center of any, Impossible Conversation, and at the center of our global predicament.

As will be repeated in the remaining chapters, any human being who sincerely wishes to engage with the building and crossing of a "bridge" from our collapsing and ecocidal business-as-usual world, to a new, co-created world, must become knowledgeable of and facile with the individual and collective versions of, Shadow.

It is our collective ignorance of this whole topic of Shadow that has me so concerned about the sustainability of recent national efforts of resistance and protest. It is hard to over state the likelihood that even the most passionate and committed activist or protester will be quickly exhausted if they are driven by the unconscious motivation of their own Shadow and the Shadow of our culture.

There is no other book that so perfectly fleshes out the distinctions and dynamics of our individual and collective shadow as we face this world at this time as *Dark Gold*. The reader will also find many powerful exercises that help with the integration and embodiment of this vital material.

I cannot stress strongly enough this study of the Shadow and all of our collective weak-suits should be done, as much as possible, within a supportive community. It would also be wise to find a coach or counselor who has direct experience of this elusive but important work.

I know I speak for Carolyn Baker as well, when I say that the calling of life on Earth at this time, the calling of our deeply challenging problems and challenges, the calling of our shared predicaments, is a calling for a new level of personal awareness and reconnection with life.

We all have been immersed in the old business-as-usual paradigm which promoted isolation and individualism and an over riding of virtually every one of our built-in attributes for interrelating with other beings and Earth. That overriding has led to each of us having an immense blind spot regarding being alive on Earth. Our individual and collective Shadows have been more than happy to take up residence within those blind spots.

*　　*　　*

How does all of this fit with my aforementioned concern about our current flurry of anti-Trump protest?

Essentially I am concerned that in our present, collective, disempowered state the best we seem to muster is, resisting and protesting. Again, this is inspiring to see people get up off their couches and raise their voices together. But, in my estimation, resisting and protesting are both exhausting activities that require the subject of the resistance or protest, to continue to exist in order to validate the resistance and protest. A nasty cycle of disempowerment.

What I hope to steer us toward in later chapters here, is the generation of an entirely new and empowered vision, mission and purpose that could replace resistance and protest. This, I assert, would provide the resister and the protester with a far more energizing focus for their activism. A resounding YES for a clear purpose vs an exhausting NO to the insanity of political kabuki theatre and cynical destruction of our democracy.

I can't help but notice that all of the uproar and upset about the abominable behavior of President Trump, and, of course, all of that abominable behavior is occurring in that same context that we all know and love so well—the business-as-usual paradigm. Remember, this is the same paradigm we've been exploring in this Impossible Conversation.

This is the paradigm in which we have collectively chosen willful ignorance and been complicit with the creation of the deeply cynical denial of science with regards to human-caused climate change and habitat destruction.

This is the paradigm in which we (the majority of Americans) choose to exercise our privilege by staying "doubtful" about the veracity of climate change and disinterested in joining the rest of the world as they generate the first ever, international CO_2 emissions mitigation agreement.

This is the paradigm that demands that we comply completely with the perpetuation of our core cultural lie: We will always have infinite growth on this finite planet.

Will our protestations have enough heart, soul and spirit to prevail against the immensely powerful machine that our corporate/government overseers have become? Can we reclaim our sense of agency, of personal empowerment at a scale large enough to turn back the tide of destruction we now face? Indeed, *can* it be turned back?

If some number of us reclaim that power and agency, will we be able to find a way to reconnect our deeply fractured citizenry?

If we stay immersed in the ubiquitous water we swim in, called business-as-usual, the answers to all of the questions above is, no. If we continue on our well-worn path of disconnection from our own deeper wisdom, from others and from Earth, the answer will surely be, no.

If we continue to override all of our core sources for meaning in life, while constantly searching for "happiness," meaning and success in our business-as-usual hamster wheel, definitely not.

If by disconnecting so completely we have forfeited our agency in life, cursing us with a constant unquenchable thirst for happiness, authenticity, quick fixes and problem solving, material wealth, status, fame— what on Earth could reunite us with our own power and agency? What could possibly reconnect us with our own deeper selves, with other humans and beings and with Earth herself?

*　　*　　*

Sometimes you just need to stop talking. Sometimes the familiar way we communicate with one another is insufficient to convey the truth of the moment. And this is one hell of a moment. In moments like these, we can call on those special folks among us who seem to relate to life in a very different way. They seem somehow able to find meaning and light where the rest of us might see despair and darkness. Some of these special souls are poets.

In the poem, *The Dakini Speaks*, Jennifer Welwood speaks with the kind of sober, piercing honesty that seems to be called for now. Collectively we seem to have a lot of weak suits, many of which Welwood mentions in this poem. These weak suits keep us disconnected from the grace and power available to a human who is willing to "give everything for what cannot be lost." Let's sample one poet's suggestion for a path that promises to take us on the most challenging journey, from our current deeply disempowered state, to a new territory that is crackling with sobriety, intent and wild dancing.

THE DAKINI SPEAKS

Jennifer Welwood

My friends, let's grow up.
Let's stop pretending we don't know the deal here.
Or if we truly haven't noticed, let's wake up and notice.
Look: everything that can be lost, will be lost.
It's simple—how could we have missed it for so long?
Let's grieve our losses fully, like ripe human beings,
But please, let's not be so shocked by them.
Let's not act so betrayed,
As though life had broken her secret promise to us.
Impermanence is Life's only promise to us,
And she keeps it with ruthless impeccability.
To a child she seems cruel, but she is only wild,
And her compassion is exquisitely precise:
Brilliantly penetrating, luminous with truth,
She strips away the unreal to show us the real.
This is the true ride—let's give ourselves to it!
Let's stop making deals for a safe passage:
There isn't one anyway, and the cost is too high.
We are not children any more.
The true human adult gives everything for what cannot be lost.
Let's dance the wild dance of no hope!

http://jenniferwelwood.com/poetry/
Used with permission.

*   *   *

To me, this "Wild Dance of No Hope" is the full agency, sobriety and presence in the face of adversity that was originally intended in the use of the word, hope. This is the dance of a person who has fully reconnected: with their deeper self, with other people and with Earth herself.

This Wild Dancer has snapped out of the collective trance and come to the realization that life on Earth itself is at stake now and the only real expression for any of us in these times is to: "give ourselves to life and to dance this wild dance together."

This Wild Dancer is showing immense courage to name our global predicament for what it is—and to articulate what I agree is our calling as human beings in the face of that predicament.

We are called to see and speak the truth of our situation. We are called to be deeply honest about and accountable for the cost of our way of living. We are called to make the best of our lives from this moment forward, allowing the urgency of the Sober Data to shift us from primarily Takers in our lifestyles to consider a more humble stance of giving back and possibly a stance of stewardship or service. We are called to include ourselves in the web of interrelatedness of systems that is life on Earth.

*   *   *

I am compelled to add another vitally important piece to this Impossible Conversation.

That piece is… violence.

I have searched long and hard for a different context or frame in which to hold this Impossible Conversation, but the same word keeps coming up—violence.

I am asserting that every element of our Impossible Conversation has involved a background threat of violence to keep it in place. We have collectively normalized the largest scale of violence the world has ever seen.

Here I repeat the simple, powerful quote from Deb Ozarko from the beginning of this chapter: "We normalize the abnormal in order to maintain the status quo."

Yes, I am equating this Impossible Conversation about Abrupt Anthropogenic Climate Change and the imminent collapse of Earth and human systems that is associated with it, with violence. What other word could work? Certainly no other word has gotten our attention.

It is here I need to pause again and ask us all to take another series of long, centering breaths. When I began this research and writing process, I never could have imagined that so much of this book about anthropogenic, abrupt climate change, and the associated collapse of systems that goes with it, would end up speaking so much about the 20th Century history of propaganda and the Shadow backdrop of violence behind our familiar paradigm of business as usual.

I never thought that I'd have to put so much attention on our cultural and individual Shadows in order to make sense of our collective denial and apathy

140

toward our own well being and the well being of our glorious home, Earth.

This has been a long and demanding project but it has always been essentially driven by very simple questions:

- Is this Sober Data real? And, if it is, why isn't this the most important conversation on the planet today?
- Is this just a matter of reducing CO_2 emissions, or are there other critical metrics we might use to determine the health of our habitat?
- How much have our corporate and government leaders known and when did they know it?
- What is my part in all of this?
- How did we get to this brink?
- Now that we are aware of this brink, how will this awareness change me, change us?
- How can we best reconnect with the central sources for meaning in human life... connection: with Deeper Self...with Others...with Earth?

Behind many of those questions is a reply indicating our collective and/or individual Shadows have rushed in to fill the empty space where our sense of purposeful life and agency once dwelled.

That Shadow has compelled us to:

- ignore decades of world-class scientific reports of our condition.
- ridicule or shame anyone who attempts to point out a damaging aspect of our paradigm.
- malign speakers like, Al Gore as he presented, *An Inconvenient Truth*.
- yawn and change the channel when we heard from Pope Francis, other world religious leaders and authors like Naomi Klein inveigh that our deeply troubled environment is intimately interconnected with our deeply troubled human relations, including all manner of social, economic and environmental justice.
- collectively laugh and shrug when we heard that one of the most powerful steps each of us can take to reduce our greenhouse gas footprint was to reduce or discontinue our consumption of meat. (I will detail this point in a later chapter.)

Clearly, these times are calling for a complete reinvention of our collapsing human operating system. Also clear is the need for us to somehow reclaim our personal power and agency from the business-as-usual paradigm.

How will we do this? How will we find a way to set aside our automatic, habitual

141

mode of overriding every subtle, vital signal from our deeper selves, from others and from Earth herself? How can we join the sober, vibrantly alive, Dakini dance?

How can we fully awaken to the depth of Shadow danger we have invited upon ourselves and our home? How can we create a new way of communicating and relating that actively brings people closer—even people who think differently and come from different backgrounds?

How can we rally in the face of a breathtakingly cynical, corporatist world government that is boldly doubling down on a profits-before-life paradigm?

*　　*　　*

The rest of this book is intended to address, in some small way, this series of simple but perplexing questions. If you have lasted this long in your reading, I honor your stamina and courage. You have lasted through the many layers my writing coaches told me "no one would read."

I have asked a lot of you, dear reader. I've asked you to gain a minimal competence in understanding core elements of climate change and other life-critical predicaments on the planet now. I've asked you to assess your own relationship to the business-as usual paradigm: government, corporations, consumerism, media, politics and more. I've asked you to consider that we all have been swept up in a wave of contrived consumerism that is clearly at the center of the Anthropogenic Climate Disruption we are facing now.

We have also explored how the current wave of political domination, corruption and cynical manipulation of the populace is part of a continuous thread that started back with Edward Bernays and his government and corporate cronies.

Now we are here.

And, as if I haven't assaulted your sensibilities enough, I am now going to offer you my layout of an empowered, sober, more unified, potentially grace-filled path forward. We must start exactly where we are, which by any definition, is in the middle of a collapsing business-as-usual paradigm. If we are intending to be engaged, contributing members of this global community, or any smaller part of it, we must see ourselves with a foot in each of two worlds.

The first, of course, is this familiar, fossil-fuel driven, collapsing, business-as-usual, paradigm. The second, is a new and heretofore unimagined new paradigm for human life on Earth.

For those of us who wish to sincerely take part in bridging from a dying paradigm to one as yet unborn, we will need a newly expanded inner tool kit, with which we can build a bridge between our now collapsing world, and a new one. There will be a select few tools, methods and ways of being that may be salvaged from the old way of being. From the looks of things, their number will be relatively small.

We have brought ourselves to the brink of destroying ourselves and hundreds of thousands, if not millions, of other species on Earth. We have done so by overriding our innate sensitivities borne of our obvious, but long disconnected, inter relatedness with the miraculous web of life.

To build this evolutionary bridge between our dying paradigm and some new possibility, we will need to redeploy our attention and intent from its present exclusive fixation on the maintenance of business as usual, consumption and the extraction of profit from every available resource to some way of setting a foundation upon which a new way of human living on Earth may occur.

What I am suggesting is that fundamental shift—that redeployment of attention and intent—will be to reconnect with our deeper, wiser selves, with other beings (humans and non-human animals) and Earth herself.

*   *   *

It is my desire to share with you my own practices and insights that have helped me transform my own day to day living (and "bridge" building) from bouts of despair and rage, to embodying a grounded, deep appreciation of each moment of being alive.

In these last few chapters I will be offering far more clarity about this "bridge" we may wish to build. I will be describing the lives and bodies of work of people who are already well on their way across that bridge. I hope you will find as much grace and inspiration as I have as we learn how to expand our core life capacities and build up our inner tool kits, all in the name of reconnecting with the primary sources of meaning for human beings.

7. Bridge Building Tools

"A spirituality that is only private and self-absorbed, one devoid of an authentic political and social consciousness, does little to halt the suicidal juggernaut of history. On the other hand, an activism that is not purified by profound spiritual and psychological self-awareness and rooted in divine truth, wisdom, and compassion will only perpetuate the problem it is trying to solve, however righteous its intentions. When, however, the deepest and most grounded spiritual vision is married to a practical and pragmatic drive to transform all existing political, economic and social institutions, a holy force— the power of wisdom and love in action— is born. This force I define as Sacred Activism."

Andrew Harvey
The Hope: A Guide to Sacred Activism

"Don't apologize for the sorrow, grief and rage you feel. It is a measure of your humanity and your maturity. It is a measure of your open heart, and as your heart breaks open there will be room for the world to heal."

Joanna Macy

*　　*　　*

Unconditional

Willing to experience aloneness,
I discover connection everywhere;
Turning to face my fear,
I meet the warrior who lives within;
Opening to my loss,
I gain the embrace of the universe;
Surrendering into emptiness,
I find fullness without end.
Each condition I flee from pursues me,
Each condition I welcome transforms me
And becomes itself transformed
Into its radiant jewel-like essence.
I bow to the One who has made it so,
Who has crafted this Master Game;
To play it is purest delight;
To honor its form — true devotion.

© Jennifer Welwood
Used with permission.

We are shifting gears here. We're going to look together at how will we will let ourselves be changed by the Sober Data of the first six chapters and how we might grow, expand and prepare ourselves for lives that now must include immense challenges, problems to solve and, most importantly, predicaments to face.

Jennifer Welwood again helps us orient our attention and intent in a more empowered way than our default, denial-based ways in the business-as-usual world. Instead of the despair and depression that comes too easily to most of us, Welwood urges us to see this as a Master Game, in which just being able to play is "purest delight."

In this poem, *Unconditional*, Welwood has refined a core component of the Impossible Conversation to a luminous, clear instruction to the aspiring bridge builder. I might call this component of our work, naming, exploring and building our collective and individual weak suits. Welwood describes this process much more gracefully:

> "Each condition I flee from pursues me,
> Each condition I welcome transforms me
> And becomes itself transformed
> Into its radiant jewel-like essence."

For the rest of this book, this is the center of our inner work. This is the core notion of how we can even begin to imagine that we will have the strength to engage in The Impossible Conversation or more importantly, engage in our co creation of a new presence and way of being for human beings on Earth.

Jennifer Welwood, in this short, sweet poem, points to the deep well of grace that is available to each of us that is willing to face our weak suits, explore our own shadows, invite the intentional shattering of our hearts to feel the pain of Earth and the deep grief of our collapsing world.

In our grief-phobic, pain-phobic, loss-phobic, death-phobic business-as-usual culture, there is little as terrifying to the average American as turning to face and actually dive head first into those aspects of life we avoid at all cost.

But notice that Welwood doesn't leave us in a blubbering heap in the corner. She points us to the part of this global predicament that is far more mystery than science, far more art and beauty than hate and collapse.

> "Turning to face my fear,
> I meet the warrior who lives within;
> Opening to my loss,
> I gain the embrace of the universe;
> Surrendering into emptiness,
> I find fullness without end."

We will meet a number of thought leaders and pioneers in the next few chapters. Each of them, in their own distinct way, will share their own methods for thriving in the midst of chaos and loss. Each of them will offer practices that assist in the daunting work of facing our own weak suits, our own shadows and our own grief.

*   *   *

The challenges and predicaments of our world, as described here, constitute a collective challenge and existential threat larger than any humanity has seen in its relatively brief time on Earth. In a 2012 study[1] researchers estimate that as many as "200 million Americans will be exposed to serious psychological distress from climate-change-related events and incidents."

Indeed the stressors associated with the Sober Data and projections we have addressed in this book and the many more we haven't even touched, promise to demand a level of inner, psychological, spiritual and emotional capacity that few of us are currently prepared to muster.

In this chapter and the ones that follow, we will start to explore some of the most potent tools and abilities humanity has created to face the challenges of various past cultures and civilizations. We will hear from thought leaders, each of whom has built their own bridge from this rapidly collapsing business-as-usual world, toward a new, and as yet unrealized, world of our possible future.

What I can tell you is that there has been a remarkable consistency between all of the exemplars offered here. To the person, they each have spoken of an orientation of our attention, away from the comforting distractions and seductions of our familiar world. Each of them has taken the time to inquire deeply into the vetted data and projections of the topics closest to their hearts and getting a clear picture of what precisely is going on in our world. After that, you will see that they all point to the optimal focus of our attention being some form of what I've been calling *reconnection*.

They speak in their own unique way about reuniting ourselves with our own, innate, deeper wisdom, with other beings and with Earth. They also have a diverse number of methods of building up our "weak suits."

We will visit with a climate scientist who has developed a way of living for himself and his family that is at once aligned with reducing their impact on the Earth and amazingly effective at having them feel more connected to one another, to their community and to the Earth.

We will get some coaching from one of the world's most renowned scholars of spiritual, mystical traditions. How have the spiritual icons, contemplatives and sacred activists faced the immense challenges of their times?

Among others we will get to know a powerful life-activist and teacher who has created a body of work and training that has addressed the issues of this book, and far more, for decades. In facilitating this kind of inner work with thousands of people, she has brought untold thousands of participants to this important work of, bridging to a new reality.

Each of our exemplars shows us a way to have a foot in each of two worlds. Somehow we must all keep our heads above water, so to speak, in our familiar but collapsing world of daily life. And, we have the opportunity to imagine together, and build together, this notion of a bridge to a new world, or a new way for human beings to live on Earth.

This is no small task. In fact, I assert it is the greatest challenge and predicament humanity has ever faced.

*　　*　　*

The weak suit that I recommend we start with is Grief.

You may recall my earlier assertion that our collective skill at overriding our sensitivities, emotions and relatedness with life itself was instrumental in getting us to this brink of decimating our shared habitat and the extinction of species. This colossal exercise in overriding life has driven us to the brink of decimating our own, shared habitat and ourselves, and left us with an almost non-existent capacity to feel the essential, living emotion of grief.

I've always been kind of an odd bird. In college I put myself into a number of classes that were a bit morose and dark. Along with classes in suicide prevention counseling and conflict resolution I found a deep appreciation for the study of death, grief and loss. I also discovered a profound resonance with the work of hospice in our communities.

I am grateful to have this rather odd love and avocation. For the past forty years, I have seen that my curious appetite for this work is rare. Most people only come into contact with grief work because they are themselves grappling with loss in their own lives. And, perhaps this is as it should be—or as it was, not too long ago.

I am suggesting that the notion of becoming familiar with grief and loss is not just for people who have recently lost a person or pet or experienced a painful or traumatic loss in their lives. Consider the possibility that anyone who soberly considers the indicators and timelines projected in the first few chapters, will inevitably have to integrate grief and loss into their experience and their world view.

One of the most devastating aspects of this Impossible Conversation is that this becoming conversant with loss and grief is now a skill and capacity for every human on Earth to learn. At the center of the Impossible Conversation is the undeniable fact that the arrogant denial of our business-as-usual culture is making policy and lifestyle choices, right now, that are affecting not just our grandchildren or some foreign people in a far off land at the end of the century. Our choices are sealing the fate of our children alive now and even us older folks.

Grief and loss are no longer issues just for those who have lost someone close. They are issues for every person on Earth to incorporate into their daily lives and the inner, defining stories. These are the stories we use to make sense of our lives and our world.

*   *   *

What we have in grief is a universal gateway or access to our individual and collective feeling body.

Even the most hardened and inner-armored person is likely to find some small crack in their armor, and usually that can be found when that person is confronted with the loss of someone or something dear to them. The good news here is, what we love, we can grieve, and vice versa. This is another great place to refer to our lists of "loves in life" that was first suggested in the Introduction.

How strange that we've set up our culture to avoid feeling the all-too-human feelings of sadness and grief. We've set ourselves up for life-long pursuits of happiness, oddly unaware that our avoidance of our normal and healthy grief makes the experience of aliveness and authentic happiness more and more elusive as each year passes. Our relatively recent cultural fixation on constant happiness and avoidance of grief or sadness or any other uncomfortable emotion, has been at the center of what I'm calling override. It has also been the primary cause of our individual and collective blind spots in our experience of daily living.

For any reader who wishes to dive deeply into this arena of grief and loss and full presence in living and dying, I can point toward some of the most powerful and heartful leaders that have fueled my study and practices.

A reminder here that I'm about to layout some of the most potent teachings I've experienced in this field of grief and loss. It is likely that you, dear reader, are reading this book alone. If you are reading this with one or more other people, more power to you. To do the work contained in this book with others just may be the strongest step any of us could take to begin building our bridge to a new way of being.

If you are reading this alone, and grappling with either the direct experience of loss or grief in your life or struggling with the larger scale grief of facing our collapsing business-as-usual world, I recommend finding heartful allies for that journey. These allies may be family or trusted friends— or they may be a competent counselor or coach.

Somehow our culture has shoved this whole aspect of being human into a dark and distant corner. Mostly we assume that anyone experiencing any of our human weak suits is weak or inferior. And, with grief, we have given the lucky ones among us (the ones with any kind of benefits at our place of employ) a rousing two or three days off to handle that grief thing, and then back to work. Mostly, grief is a subject of great awkwardness and isolation for our culture.

There are cultures in which the thought of grieving alone, or for some day or two every few years, is considered deeply unhealthy. I am suggesting that the healthier human world we may build on the other side of this "bridge" would include many opportunities to share our grief—and share the aliveness that comes from our opening our hearts together.

It is for this reason that I recommend approaching these aspects of life first. Remember I am suggesting that we all will need to determine for ourselves (or hopefully with the help of a skilled counselor or coach) what practices we might take on, that assist us in the process of becoming more adept at integrating grief, and shared grief, into our direct experience.

To begin your journey in this work with the elements of grief, loss and pain, I predict a remarkable depth and breadth to the healing and growing you will do. There is no pressure; there is no way to push this river. If it is the right time for you to explore your relationship with grief, death and loss, then off you go. If not, undoubtedly you will find the right subject for your first practices in this, what is likely to be, life-long set of practices.

For the rest of us there are some essential tools, distinctions and practices that are important to keep close by. There are a few tools that we all will need to have with us virtually every day.

*   *   *

Self Assessment:

Have you made your list of "loves in life"?

Have you winnowed out that list for the aspects of life that are most precious in this moment?

Have you engaged yourself to learn more about these loves? Are you engaged in practices that have you deepen your connection, your inter relatedness with these loves?

Have you allowed your heart to break open with the life-giving grief that comes from full presence with the knowledge that all things will eventually be lost, even your own life?

This deep knowing is a prime example of a part of our inner wisdom we have forfeited in order to participate in the business as usual paradigm. In our ubiquitous use of override to justify our impacts, we lost contact with all of the emotional range beyond the minimal bandwidth that is allowed in our culture.

Have you taken a deep inventory to notice what emotions, sensitivities and relationships have been suppressed or diminished in the name of producing results, accomplishing, gathering wealth, succeeding in business, winning… ?

*   *   *

I know I've asked you to estimate for yourself what is coming in terms of climate changes, species extinction, habitat and species diversity decline and systems collapse. And, yes, I know it's a lot.

If you have done this estimate, what have been your reactions and emotions in response to that Sober Data? For many of us, we will have little or no emotional reaction to the Sober Data. One thing that is abundantly clear, we all must begin this journey exactly where we are, with the capacities that we have. Period.

Some of the wisest folks I know have created a few unique frames of reference for this experience we are all going through. One is that the world facing what is now called, "the Sixth Great Extinction," could be said to be in a global version of hospice.

Another, almost poetic, view of our changing world is to see our predicament as a world-scale rite of passage for humanity at large. This would mimic aspects of the

ritual rites of passage from some indigenous peoples. In these rituals, usually the
boys are sent out of the village to pursue an experience that crumbles their boyhood
world and demands of them an adult level of awareness and relatedness with the
world.

If we see ourselves in the first model, we can expect to stir up all of the denial,
negotiation and deep discomfort that is so common for those who are new to the
hospice environment. Being in the vicinity of death and dying can be a life altering,
no bullshit environment. It can transform a life - to be present with another who is
dying. In this model we could find ourselves breaking our own hearts open in
service to this essential human transition. We also could find ourselves ill-prepared
and terrified of feeling these grief-laden feelings.

In the rite of passage model it should be noted that many of these indigenous
rituals have a very real possibility that the boys may not make it back. There is also
a potentially, no-nonsense atmosphere to be had in this model. It could be said that
our global predicament, seen as a rite of passage, is already threatening to drive
millions of other species and humanity itself, to extinction.

This possibility of extinction shows the sheer insanity of continuing on with
business as usual. It calls to question any solution-based responses that return us to
business as usual. In an idealized rite of passage frame, our rite of passage appears to
shift us from disconnected beings extracting the life out of our world, to whole
beings, fully reconnected with life, peacefully coexisting in this miraculous web of
life. I find this idealized version of our collective rite of passage extremely attractive
and extremely naïve and chock full of magical thinking.

What our idealized process looks like to me is an ever expanding awareness of our
true impact on our shared habitat, and a growing willingness to surrender whatever
it takes to stop the destruction we are causing. Along with this awareness and
surrender we will need to engage our primary intent and creative attention on
reconnecting with self, others and Earth. We will need to reconnect with life.

One additional interpretive frame I have come to appreciate deeply, is the notion
that all of these daunting elements that make up our global predicament, even the
"extinction" elements, are elements of an entirely natural process of transformation.

In a recent posting, Julian Spalding (julianspalding.wordpress.com) wonders with
us, whether all of this destruction, chaos, extinction and deep disruption might be a
very natural and integral expression of Nature expressing itself quite intentionally

and deliberately. He asks if, perhaps, we are collectively experiencing something akin to the utter dissolution and transformation that is experienced by a caterpillar as it dissolves to become an entirely new being:

> It has often been postulated that humans are destroying our habitat because of our belief that we are separate from and superior to Nature. Yet we are in reality a part of Nature. We are not separate. May we not, then, be a part of Nature herself creating the Dream of the Planet? Is it possible that we are part of a great evolutionary process, in which the current state of planetary destruction is a necessary ingredient for a Great Transformation?
>
> The term dissipative structure was coined by Russian-Belgian physical chemist Ilya Prigogine. Out of that postulation came his Theory of Dissipative Structures which states that when a system is ready to move to a higher frequency, it disintegrates into a chaotic state. Out of chaos comes a new order, an order that would not have been possible had the previous order not devolved into chaos. What looks like chaos at one level, looks like a birthing in the new dispensation. One way of looking at this process is how a caterpillar voraciously devours everything in its path, until, sated, it stops eating and spins a cocoon. Inside the chrysalis, the body of the caterpillar turns to a mushy substance. Its cells disintegrate and new cells begin to grow called imaginal cells.
>
> At first the imaginal cells are experienced as foreign and the old caterpillar cells try to destroy them, but eventually the caterpillar surrenders to the process and the imaginal cells begin to build a new creature which eventually emerges as a butterfly, an entirely new creature.
>
> If the caterpillar cells had not dissipated into a chaotic mush, the imaginal cells could have not emerged out of chaos and the new creature could not have been born. Is it possible we are experiencing just this process on a world scale? Does Nature know what she is doing?

*   *   *

No matter how we frame our challenge of facing our global predicament, we are going to need the best inner tools and capacities we can get, in order to get through this Rubicon.

One such tool is one most of us have heard of, but precious few have really used.

Elizabeth Kubler Ross' (EKR) Stages of Grief/Dying.

EKR made it quite clear that these stages are not necessarily experienced in any particular order. In my experience, in hospice settings, not every person who is grieving experiences all of these stages and yet some stages get repeated. Additionally there are innumerable other dimensions of human life to experience that are not easily contained by this five stages list.

I am including this list because it is a valuable and easy to use starting point tool for a sincere beginner on this path. Much like the distinctions of Individual and Collective Shadow we have discussed, these five stages can be as useful for exploring our national issues of grief and loss as for our own individual exploring.

One way to get some early practice with using the five stages model, is to go back through the early chapters of this book—or even watch the news at the end of the day. A tremendous amount of insight is available to us as we view the events of our world through the lens of these very normal and human reactions to grief.

I have adjusted the more common, personal definitions here to fit a broader exploration of grief as it can be experienced with more global issues, like systems collapse or abrupt climate change.

> 1. Denial. In denial we believe the diagnosis is somehow mistaken, and we cling to a false, preferable reality. This is obviously the orientation of climate change deniers. Denial also has many subtler forms, combined with Bargaining, that are used by even dyed in the wool environmentalists.

> 2. Anger. When we start to realize that the denial can't continue, we may become frustrated especially with (but not limited to) people close to us. This anger can focus on the circumstances being unfair and also seek someone or something to blame (including Projection). This may sound a bit familiar given the current political atmosphere in the US. There is no shortage of rage and blame.

3. Bargaining. This appears to be the #1 favorite for people in the privileged positions of the more developed countries. Different from most hospice patients, the bargaining about climate change, species extinction and habitat loss can take the form of choosing not to be aware of global Sober Data or to focus on how solar and wind power or electric cars will save us and get us back to business as usual.

4. Depression. In this stage, the individual despairs at the recognition of their mortality. Advanced versions of this state can include comments like: "I'm so sad, why bother with anything?" or "We're all going to die, so what's the point?"

5. Acceptance. In this stage (often the last), there can be a remarkable calm and ease where before there may have been great pain or resistance. This state of being can range from an almost casual surrender to the inevitable, to a luminous and deeply inspiring grace and peace. While I can say that it has been a privilege to be with every dying person who has allowed me into their dying process, there is something truly transformational and infused with pure beingness and love in a person who contacts that grace and peace as they engage full presence in their own life and death.

Just in case it is still not clear why I'm including EK Ross's Stages of Grief, I repeat the invitation from above—recount your reactions, especially your emotions, as you've read the many lists in this book about what I call the Sober Data. (Projections re Abrupt Climate Change, Species Extinction and Systems Collapse.)

As simple as this Five Stages model may be, I find it useful on a daily basis. I am thankful for the clarity EKR's model has brought me. It can shed light on our individual reactions to our predicament and it can help us understand some of the reactions from our culture at large.

*   *   *

For the exploration of how essential grief is to a healthy human life, I recommend Frances Weller's most recent book, *The Wild Edge of Sorrow: Rituals of Renewal and the Sacred Work of Grief*:

> "Grief and love are sisters, woven together from the beginning. Their kinship reminds us that there is no love that does not contain loss and no loss that is not a reminder of the love we

carry for what we once held close. Alone and together, death and loss affect us all.

"Every one of us must undertake an apprenticeship with sorrow. We must learn the art and craft of grief, discover the profound ways it ripens and deepens us. While grief is an intense emotion, it is also a skill we develop through a prolonged walk with loss. Facing grief is hard work. It takes 'the outrageous courage of the bodhi heart,' as Pema Chödrön calls it.

It takes outrageous courage to face outrageous loss. This is precisely what we are being called to do. Any loss, whether deeply personal or one of those that swirl around us in the wider world, calls us to full-heartedness, for that is the meaning of courage."

Weller is so very gifted in the art of making the dark and scary world of grief a secret garden in which a deep and sweet love of being alive can grow. I have found myself breathing much easier through trying times as I've pursued the exercises in Frances' wonderful book.

*   *   *

Another robust leader, teacher and performance artist who focuses on the qualities we bring to living, as informed by the eternal presence of our eventual demise, is Stephen Jenkinson who brings his love of the mystical together with his long history of working with people who are dying. In his book, and especially in his live presentations/performances, he weaves a magical web for all who attend. This web is full of the bittersweet human experience, some humor and plenty of a poetic, musical, mystery that is actually a part of some hospice or near death moments for all involved. Jenkinson helps us see how pale, fearful and shallow the experience of dying tends to be in our death-phobic culture.

"Someone looks up into the night sky and says, 'You see that star right there? Could be it isn't there anymore.'
All conviction is sent reeling.
Nothing is truer than this.
The mysteries roll.

You are welcome. If that didn't quite happen in your earlier days, it has now. If it did, then it's happened again.

"You need witnesses for wonder.

Some things in life are too hard to see by yourself because they take up the whole sky, or because they happen every day, unwinding above your busyness, or because you thought you knew them already. Wonder takes a willingness to be uncertain, to be thrown."

Stephen Jenkinson
Die Wise: A Manifesto for Sanity and Soul

Jenkinson, like virtually every one of the exemplars in this book, has a special place in his life for gratitude. There is perhaps no more powerful key to shifting a human being from being a business-as-usual drone, with no apparent connection with life, to a being immersed in the beauty and grace of the simplest moment in a day.

But Jenkinson speaks here of a heartier, more robust form of gratitude. It is this grittier version of gratitude that I believe we will all need to practice. It is easy to generate gratitude for the many blessings made available to us (especially in the developed world) each day.

It is another story altogether to find gratefulness for a life that includes deep suffering and loss. Jenkinson challenges us to find gratitude in exactly the opposite direction of our business-as-usual preferences:

"Gratitude needs practice—gratitude for the things that don't seem to help, that aren't sought out or welcome— that's a demanding kind, and it is needed in hard times. A book about dying should have that kind of gratitude in it, bleeding through from the other side of sorrow."

*   *   *

Another master of gratitude, is Brother David Steindl-Rast.
http://gratefulness.org/explore/new-to-gratefulness/

There are few people who have so brilliantly articulated the essential power of gratitude as Brother David. One dive into his website or his TED talk and you will be awash with the potency and deep healing that is gratitude.

To put it into terms of our business-as-usual disconnected lives, we are constantly overriding our experience of authentic life in each moment. We are trained from infancy that we are never enough and there is never enough of the things that our paradigm has us pursue. We always want more of that which brings us no core satisfaction.

With the constant presence of that core dissatisfaction, we find ourselves starved for fulfillment. We all really know that this hole inside cannot be filled with money or things. But, the business-as-usual world offers no authentic alternatives. In fact, to attempt to disengage from the business-as-usual world is most often seen as threatening behavior. Those who try to step away from the rat race life are rarely admired or honored.

With the introduction of even a few moments of gratitude, the experience of core dissatisfaction can quickly start to diminish.

It is clear that anyone who sincerely wishes to disentangle from our collapsing paradigm, while activating presence and resilience, will have gratitude in their inner tool kit.

Perhaps the simplest practice we can use to deepen our experience of gratitude is to keep a gratitude journal. You might be seeing a trend here. So far I am asking you to track a number of your inner ways of relating with your world.

We started with the "What You Love List." We further refined that list to deepen our relatedness with a select few subjects and really learn about them. (Under the assumption that it is far more difficult to kill off something with which you have familiarity, love and relationship.)

In the next few chapters, there will be more journaling, if you are willing. Some of this next episode of journaling will be challenging for us all. There will be no more enlivening and empowering addition to the journaling of *The Impossible Conversation* than the ongoing tracking of your Loves in Life and your Gratitude.

"Gratitude arises from paying attention,
from being awake in the presence of everything
that lives within us and without us."

David Whyte

*　　*　　*

This is a good place to give a bit of context for this chapter. It is about expanding our inner tool kit and core, life capacities as we face our daunting future, challenges and predicaments.

In the course of the past three years of what I've come to call my informed inquiry into Abrupt Climate Change and the parallel collapse of Earth and human systems, I've had the pleasure of meeting many folks who are living normal lives and doing their best to build some kind of bridge between this troubled world and whatever might be next in human and Earth history.

I've met a number of scientists and particularly been impressed by the climate scientists I've met. They are truly on the front lines of this cynical human melodrama that includes the arch villain, the denial of science. More often than I'd like to count, I've sat with experts in this field and paused for long moments as we both feel the waves of grief and rage waft through our conversation.

I've also been blessed to meet a handful of the journalists and authors who are brave enough to cover these Abrupt Climate Change and Systems Collapse topics. These brave souls have a special brand of integrity and courage. With all of the shadowy, aggressive and vitriolic reactions from the denial-based business-as-usual world, these fine reporters are sent out to the margins of our society, ostracized for being "the messenger."

One such courageous soul is Carolyn Baker. I've mentioned Carolyn already as the author of more than ten books, most of which address some version of the questions, "Who will we be together in the face of our global predicaments?" And, "What will be the qualities of our presence as we are called to live, create and relate in these impossible times?"

As I mentioned before, Carolyn has produced a Daily News Digest (see http://carolynbaker.net) for years, that is focused on providing vetted news and updates about Sober Data, Systems Collapse and a healthy dose of how we can stay connected and inspired in the midst of it all.

I am recommending, whole-heartedly, that anyone proposing to face our daunting predicament-laden future would be wise to subscribe to Carolyn's Daily News Digest service. In these times of fake news and alternative facts Carolyn's synthesis of the events of the day is essential.

It has been a joy to produce a few online symposia with Carolyn, intended to bring the wisdom of thought leaders, authors and heartful bridge builders to an audience seeking incisive and inspiring content.

As we finished up the most recent of those symposia, we both commented on how all of us involved in the symposium—the participants, the guest speakers and we who were hosting— talked about how important it is to have this kind of safe container where people can learn about the state of the planet, feel the associated raft of feelings and have the opportunity to bond with some number of kindred spirits.

We decided at that moment to start a new level of this work, going beyond writing books and articles, beyond the occasional online symposium and podcast episode to offer a consistently safe environment in which people can grapple with what amounts to reinventing their lives.

Between us we have worked with thousands of participants in transformational coaching and workshop environments and literally written the book(s) on the topic of how to face our shared predicament with grace, beauty and deep reconnection with our inner wisdom, with other beings and with Earth. It is our intention to provide a crafted menu of powerful offerings, all designed to serve aspiring bridge builders. We are offering in-depth tutorials, workshops, webinars, books, articles, interviews with thought leaders, life-resilience coaching and so much more than could possibly be contained in a primer book like, *The Impossible Conversation*.

To finish this chapter, I am compelled to cover just a few more dimensions of the human psyche and dynamic before launching us into the sharing and bodies of work of the exemplars.

Shadow

First, with Shadow, I am drawn back to the work of Carolyn's recent book, **Dark Gold**: *The Human Shadow and the Global Crisis*. Baker provides us a clear and deep roadmap into the least visible and often least attractive aspects of our lives. Within the insights and exercises of *Dark Gold*, Carolyn guides us into vivid clarity about the collapsing world we are experiencing right now. *Dark Gold* will leave readers with a stunning understanding of both the raw, destructive power of our individual and collective Shadows when left in the unconscious realm, and the grace-filled power of a unified presence in a person who has integrated their Shadow. Baker quotes social commentator, Andrew Bard Schmookler:

"Evil in the human psyche comes from a failure to bring together, to reconcile, the pieces of our experience. When we embrace all that we are, even the evil, the evil in us is transformed. When the diverse living energies of the human system are harmonized, the present bloody face of the world will be transformed into an image of the face of God."

Carolyn Baker has a remarkably grounded and realistic perspective about what can and cannot be hoped for if a person does their Shadow work.

"We commit to Shadow work not only to reach a holy place, but to transform our relationships with all beings and all things, and that transformation is the dark gold that results from wrestling with the personal and collective Shadows.

"If we are to transcend the illusion of separation from the Earth community and members of our own species— if we are to cease 'Othering' and experience profound psycho-spiritual union with creation— the personal and collective Shadows must be engaged and healed.

"While it is humanly impossible to heal every aspect of the Shadow, and while the collective Shadow is monumental, we can begin the journey of withdrawing our projections and thereby cease contributing our personal shadow material to the larger whole."

There is no more powerful personal work that an aspiring bridge builder could take on than to deepen their competence and knowledge of personal Shadow. There has never been a time when the common ground of the human experience has been so Shadow laden and literally insane. While we have seen, in human history, examples of immense cruelty and despotism, we have never seen this fully global threat to the existence of millions of species and of humanity itself.

Shadow work starts when we commit to learning about the dynamics of the Shadow and to owning how those dynamics show up in our lives. One prime (mentioned in the previous chapter) example of this kind of Shadow dynamic is projection. When we resist owning an aspect of ourselves, we can easily slip into the Shadow habit of projection. We project that denied aspect, and our judgments about it, onto other people.

This one Shadow dynamic could be said to be the very water we all are swimming in—especially at the level of politics. We no longer have civil discourse, we have frothing, polarizing battles of projection. This leads to an endless spiral of blame, judgment, vilification and polarization. There can be little debate that our entire political process has become an exercise in Shadow dynamics.

For us to start our Shadow work on the individual level, it could be good to start another section of our journals. A powerfully informative list or personal inventory to add is: What are my projections onto the world at large, politicians, local people or agencies, family, coworkers, friends?

> "Refusing to feel pain, and becoming incapable of feeling pain—which is actually the root meaning of apathy, refusal to suffer—makes us stupid and half alive. It causes us to become blind to see what is really out there. We have a sense of something being wrong, so we find another target and project our anxiety onto the nearest thing handy.
>
> *Joanna Macy*

Carolyn Baker includes many useful exercises in *Dark Gold*, exercises that give us a direct experience of the pain and damage that can result from unresolved Shadow dynamics and the freedom and authenticity that can result from discontinuing harmful Shadow habits in being:

> "Authentically valuing the positive aspects of another person, as well as being able to be present with their negative qualities, is only possible as a result of taking back all of our projections on them."

I'd go so far as to say that the amazing resistance and activist movements that have sprung up in these first few months of the Trump administration run a very high risk of collapsing if they do not include some in-depth Shadow work within their membership ranks. In terms of projection, Trump is all too easy to blame and vilify. Rightly so, but, if we stop with just our passionate outrage and projection, we will miss the ripe opportunity to see something about ourselves as a nation that brings forth a Shadow leader like Trump.

If it seems too optimistic that we will ever be that collectively committed to learning from our own mistakes and Shadows, perhaps we could just focus on the individual, family and neighborhood level of being responsible for our own Shadow dynamics. Without these efforts, what will slow down or stop the polarization of our families, neighborhoods, states, nation?

From the viewpoint of The Impossible Conversation, the person who aspires to somehow contribute to a human transition to a more wholesome way of being on Earth, has their work cut out for them.

We can readily see that we should reduce our volume of consumption and extraction on the planet and reduce our greenhouse gas emissions in a ridiculously short period of time. We can see that our political, economic, environmental and social systems are all teetering on the edge of collapse. And, all of this at a time when our media is packed with trust corroding elements like lying and corrupt politicians, cynical business leaders, alternative facts and fake news.

Challenges and predicaments of this scale will take work to address. And, any sincere bridge builder will have vetted the Sober Data and reinvented their sense of purpose and direction in life to accommodate their new, sober view of our world. This whole situation is going to take work and focus and, I suggest, a whole new way of engaging with life.

These coming chapters are basically suggestions for how to engage in a new way. We will be talking about people who are fully aware of the Sober Data and still live full, gorgeous lives. This is not the usual smattering of life-hacks and listicles with "the five ways all really cool people avoid extinction," or, "Twelve ways to be happy even when the oceans are dying."

This is the sharing of people who have taken the hard road of leaning into their weak suits. Each has chosen to dig deep into their own Shadow and grief and other darker aspects. They do these difficult things not only to come to terms with the core truth about human life on Earth today, but also to tap into the peace, love and grace that awaited them when they made their inner journey and intentionally broke open their own heart, to feel the pain of this world.

*   *   *

Resilience

This kind of story of transforming a devastating tragedy and trauma into a flood of blessing and grace is the center of the zone mental health professionals call, resilience— the ability to shift one's orientation from victimhood, deep wounding and crushing loss to an experience of lessons learned or gratitude for basic elements of life. To release our fearful grip on the illusion of a life of constant security and stability and expand to include the reality that uncertainty, mystery and even chaos are also normal aspects of life, is resilience.

There are not many people who have dived as deeply into this Impossible Conversation as you have by reading this far. There are even fewer people in the helping professions that have shifted their attention to include the massive scale stressors to the human psyche that are implied in the Sober Data and projections that we have explored.

I've had the pleasure of meeting many of the professionals in various agencies and helping professions that are, in fact, addressing these oncoming stressors. In December of 2016, I had the opportunity to attend the first conference of a new association, the International Transformational Resilience Coalition.

This association is led by the author of the seminal book on the subject, conveniently titled, *Transformational Resilience*. Bob Doppelt has created a remarkable body of work and a vibrant association, and produced a truly inspiring conference in 2016. There were people from every level of agency and private practice in the helping professions.

I was particularly impressed in meeting representatives of the US Department of Homeland Security and the Rand Foundation. These two formidable and notoriously conservative organizations sent absolutely brilliant representatives to this conference. With the remarkable presentations of these and many other presenters, I was able to piece together a picture of an America that was actually looking ahead, anticipating the waves of stressors to come.

Bob Doppelt and the growing number of practitioners who utilize, Transformational Resilience, are committed to equipping as many people as possible with strong tools and capacities with which they may face our present and imminent challenges. These tools are remarkably well suited to this Impossible Conversation, even the constant return to the core practices aimed at reconnecting with self, others and Earth.

They might use different jargon for some elements of their books or exercises but the fit between the methods and practices described here, and those in Transformational Resilience, is hand in glove.

One central exercise in Doppelt's book is to explore and clarify a person's values. First, Doppelt helps us understand the difference between values and opinions, thoughts or emotions. Once the reader has landed on a clear and personally integral set of values, they are empowered to use those values as a source of ongoing inspiration and course-truing in challenging times.

Doppelt does a great job of helping the reader understand how, in stressful times, we can lose our inner compass or sense of direction. Indeed stress can knock us off track and leave us vulnerable to that ever present Shadow element.

We will spend some time with the importance of a clear, personal mission or purpose statement in chapter nine. Here, let's take note of a few of Doppelt's suggestions for clarifying our own values. These values are the cornerstones of any life purpose statement we might want to generate.

Surfacing you core values (Transformational Resilience)

Step One: Ask yourself what truly matters, deep in your heart.

In the list of values that follows, mark each value with:

"V" for any value in the list that is <u>V</u>ery important.

"S" for any value that is <u>S</u>omewhat important.

"N" for any value that is <u>N</u>ot important.

Values List:

Personal responsibility	Honesty	Fairness
Patience Compassion	Simplicity	Protection of nature/ climate
Generosity	Gratitude	Independence
Family	Community	Professional achievement
Reverence for human life	God	Honor
Loyalty	Social justice	Respect for authority
Humility	Self-sufficiency	Kindness
Personal safety	Rank and power	Self-awareness

Diligence	Public recognition	Love
Social equity	Integrity	Charity
Mercy	Respect for others	Status
Brotherhood	Selflessness	Wealth
Forgiveness	Open-mindedness	Success
Insert your own…		

Step Two:
"Look at all of the items that now have a "V" or "S" next to them and separate values from goals. The difference is that values are how you want to act in all circumstances, while goals are something you want to attain or achieve. Take a moment to scratch off your list anything that from your perspective is actually a goal rather than a value."

Step Three:
Identify your most important values. Notice which values are Very important to you. Circle the ten values which are most important to you. This may take some time.

Doppelt advises us that, by becoming aware of the values that are most important to you personally, you will have a "greater sense of who you are and how you want to live your life. Events or situations that violate your top ten values are more likely to trigger your 'Fear and Alarm Center' and cause you to become dysregulated." (Dysregulated is a term Bob Doppelt uses to describe when a person is knocked off-center by stressors in life, when we are triggered into stress behavior.)

List your top ten values in your Impossible Conversation journal or workbook.

Step Four:
Prioritize your values. 1 to 10. 1 being most important.

> "I want to emphasize that it is not always helpful to live by only a few values because your flexibility and openness to new experiences can become limited. But when push comes to shove, your top "1" or "2" values are likely be the ones that have the most influence over how you act. Your top "1" or "2" values are also likely to be the ones that are most sensitive to violation, and thus to dysregulation when they are breached.
>
> Increasing your awareness of the values that are most significant to you

offers guidance on when and how to devote extra effort to regulating your reactions so you can live your values. "

Step 5.

Reevaluate your top values.

It is this step that sold me on using Bob Doppelt's Values exercise here in *The Impossible Conversation*. In what I judge to be a gutsy move, Bob Doppelt challenges us to see that what we have just articulated is a list of values that has been true for us in life, up to this time. He dares us to reevaluate our list of top values by asking ourselves if we are completely satisfied with that list. He asks us to notice that that list is what has created the life we are now living.

The reevaluation is a looking to see if we have anything gnawing at us. To see if we have any thought that a different value might have us feel better about ourselves or achieve different outcomes.

Doppelt offers us a few questions that we can ask ourselves to determine if our current values help us to be the person we want to be.

(I am very impressed by this variant of a very common personal growth exercise. What a perfect opportunity to reinvent ourselves at the level of values, motivated by our recent exposure to the daunting Sober Data of our world.)

How do you ideally want to treat other people?

How do you ideally want to treat the natural environment?

What personal qualities do you want to cultivate?

How do you want to be remembered after your time on the planet ends?

In sum, what type of person do you really want to be?

The gist of this exercise is to go to the center of who you are and what you value. Then articulate the values that you have assembled in your life. Then revisit them, even reevaluate them to be sure they are still a profound fit for you and your life now. If they are not... change them so they are.

This is a stunningly simple and powerful exercise. Those who take it on are showing a level of personal courage that few human beings have had to show.

It will take the kind of in-depth self examination that is prompted by this last exercise for each of us to discover what new values may need to be adopted, and which of our long-held values may no longer serve us so well.

One traditional American value is rugged or extreme individualism. While it is easy to see this value in everything from books and films to laws and cultural customs, it may be worth reevaluating this iconic image of the rugged individual forging a life on the wild frontier. First, we haven't had any more frontier to conquer for generations now. And, second, It appears that one of the boldest callings of our predicament-laden era, is the calling to come together as groups, tribes, families, neighborhoods, communities. The courageous "bridge builders" of these times, who are called to contribute to the betterment of this world, no matter the outcome or density of the predicament, will obviously fare better and realize greater grace in their efforts, if they join together with kindred spirits in that presence and expression.

*   *   *

In all of the previous chapters we have explored the breadth and depth of our shared predicaments and the many Shadow filled customs and practices we have mastered in the personal, political, cultural, economic aspects of our world. These are the same customs and practices that have brought us to the brink of those predicaments.

For the next three chapters we will, with new tools in hand, explore the remarkable lives and bodies of work of people who have been bridge builders for some time now. In the expression and presence of these exemplars we can start to imagine ourselves as able to not only endure the coming stressors and challenges promised in our future – but to possibly learn and grow and even thrive in the midst of chaos, challenge and uncertainty. We will explore what it is like to approach our shared, global predicaments with an inner tool kit filled with resilience.

8. Reconnecting With Earth

"Real change will only happen when we fall in love with our planet. Only love can show us how to live in harmony with nature and with each other and save us from the devastating effects of environmental destruction and climate change."

Thich Nhat Hanh

"To leave the matrix entirely, to enter places not yet too ground up by the machine, is to remember what it is to be alive. The world smells different in a living forest. Time changes meaning. Sounds change texture. To listen to the hollow booming of a pileated woodpecker is to be reminded that we do not inhabit a world ruled by computers and two-cycle engines, that these minor artifacts are peripheral to our lives, that our real home is the wild, that we ourselves are wild.

I do not need a heaven, either technological or religious.

This life is good enough."

Derrick Jensen
Welcome to the Machine…Humanity

"Never, never be afraid to do what's right, especially if the well-being of a person or animal is at stake. Society's punishments are small compared to the wounds we inflict on our soul when we look the other way."

Martin Luther King

As negotiators headed to Copenhagen in December 2009 to forge a global climate pact, concerned U.S. business leaders and liberal luminaries took out a full-page ad in the New York Times calling for aggressive climate action. In an open letter to President Obama and the U.S. Congress, they declared:

"If we fail to act now, it is scientifically irrefutable that there will be catastrophic and irreversible consequences for humanity and our planet."

One of the signatories of that letter: Donald Trump.

*   *   *

"This we know:
All things are connected
Like the blood
That unites one family…
Whatever befalls the earth,
Befalls the sons and daughters of the earth.
Man did not weave the web of life;
He is merely a strand in it.
Whatever he does to the web,
He does to himself."

Chief Seattle

"What we are doing to the forests of the world is but a mirror reflection of what we are doing to ourselves and to one another."

Chris Maser
Forest Primeval:
The Natural History of an Ancient Forest

"For decades experts in climate change have been telling us that we're in trouble. Rachel Carson wrote *Silent Spring* in 1962, illuminating the devastating effects of pesticides on the environment. Yet, in 2007, we used about 6 billion pounds of them.

"How could intelligent beings seek to control a few unwanted species by a method that contaminated the entire environment and brought the threat of disease and death even to their own kind? Yet this is precisely what we have done. We have done it, moreover, for reasons that collapse the moment we examine them.

"The reasons may collapse when we talk about them, but nothing changes when we just talk about them. Change, real change, requires more than 'tell and agree.' This takes more than 'scream and protest.' What works is 'experience and action.' And that, I fervently believe, begins in nature."

Laura Sewall

"The obvious choice, then, is to extend our notions of self-interest. For example, it would not occur to me to plead with you, 'Don't saw off your leg. That would be an act of violence.' It wouldn't occur to me (or to you) because your leg is part of your body. Well, so are the trees in the Amazon rain basin. They are our external lungs. We are beginning to realize that the world is our body."

Joanna Macy, *Greening of the Self*

*   *   *

Throughout The Impossible Conversation I have used the term, reconnect, to describe the essential healing process that we must invite if we are to heal from the deep damage and disconnection that has occurred in our business-as-usual world.

We are now in the three chapters aimed at articulating the costs of that disconnection and some of the practices that may be useful for the aspiring bridge builder. To more fully define reconnection let's review some of aspects of our business-as-usual culture and how we have ended up at this brink.

In the 20th Century ramp up of the business-as-usual model, human beings refined their skills at extracting resources from Earth and depositing the waste products of that production process back onto Earth without regard for their actual impact on any Earth or human systems.

In order to be "successful" in this business-as-usual model, indeed to be loved and revered, a person had to be substantially better at some part of this extraction/dumping process than his competitors. With this competition-fueled model of accessing wealth, the acceleration and intensification of our global extraction and free-for-all dumping of waste became an international orgy of resource consumption, without a lick of self-consciousness.

That absence of self-consciousness, or perception of subtler warning signs of harm to vital Earth and human systems, has been a natural outcome of our cultural agreement to override. By choosing and using this tool of intentionally disregarding our once-innate connection with the web of life, we could proceed apace with our mad dash to extract and dump at an ever-growing (infinite growth) scale.

With this powerful tool of overriding at the helm of the business-as-usual model we would, by definition, create a massive collective blind spot in our perception of ourselves, other people and Earth. We have a blind spot big enough to drive extinction through.

I am asserting that whatever or whoever ends up in our blind spot becomes something or someone we intentionally don't "see." We cannot love, or even care about, what we cannot or will not see. Within that blind spot are all of the aspects of our world, ourselves and of our business-as-usual impacts that we have denied or preferred to not see. Outside of that blind spot, we have chosen to see everything— everything and everyone, as resources to be fed into the business-as-usual model. Objects to be used. Objects that only hold value to the degree that they are worth something as a commodity in the business-as-usual marketplace.

Within that blind spot we do not feel, acknowledge or perceive the existence of the beings there. Outside that blind spot we only feel, acknowledge or perceive the existence of, or the importance of, the beings that we have determined support our worldview and are somehow useful or of sufficient value to us to deserve our attention. As we will see in these chapters, anything and anyone who is deemed to be "undeserving of our attention", is often seen through a lens of contempt.

This way of divvying up the world by either deserving our attention or not deserving our attention, is common to *all* of our relationships, even our relationship with ourselves.

*   *   *

I have chosen to break down our sources for meaning and beauty and inspiration in life into the three I've mentioned time and again in this *Impossible Conversation*: our connection with our innate, deeper and wiser self; our connection with other beings (humans, non human animals and other living beings); our connection with Earth.

*   *   *

I am making another rather bold assertion here. I am asserting that any human being who is attempting to co-create some sort of bridge between our dying, business-as-usual paradigm and a new way of living on the planet will need a few key elements in place to have any chance of realizing that bridge.

They will need:

- Massive courage and stamina.

- A solid commitment to clearly seeing the Sober Truth of our life on Earth.

- A cadre of supportive, loving allies with whom they can walk the path.

- A willingness to do the profound inner work entailed in any truly transformational venture.

- A willingness to reinvent themselves, discarding the destructive ways of doing and being learned in business-as-usual and to learn and co create new ways of doing and being.

- Powerful practices. This level of personal, inner work will take a special depth of personal practices. This is not the realm of a few life hacks and reading a few articles about: "The 8 habits that will keep you happy as we face the Sixth Great Extinction." This chapter of evolution for humanity demands that we lean directly into our weakest suits, intentionally reaching for the aspects of life that our business-as-usual paradigm has taught us are to be avoided at all cost.

The last part of this assertion is that the aspiring, bridge-building human need look no further than their commitment to reconnection with Deeper Self, Others and Earth to discover and formulate the set of practices that will propel them and protect them through these dark and challenging times.

PRACTICES:

With this chapter we begin the translation of the work you have been doing while reading this book, the lists and self assessments, into a foundation from which you can develop a set of personal practices.

Any insights that might be gleaned in the process of engaging in this Impossible Conversation, will quickly be lost if they are not soon crystalized into practices that allow us to embody some of these realizations and clarifications of purpose.

We will each need to craft personal practices with which we might slowly but surely reconnect with vital aspects of the miraculous web of life we call home. The majority of those reconnecting practices will come from a sober inquiry about our blind spots and our points of disconnection from our deeper selves, other beings and Earth.

Passionate, Sacred Activist, Spiritual Scholar and author, Andrew Harvey, when speaking about the importance of having personal, spiritual practices in our lives, often mentions a quote from Jungian analyst and author, Marion Woodman:

> "Continuing to do pioneering sacred work in a world as crazy and painful as ours without constantly grounding yourself in sacred practice would be like running into a forest fire dressed only in a paper tutu."

And, the Dalai Lama:

> "I once asked the Dalai Lama what gave him the strength to keep on working for the freedom of Tibet, and he replied, 'I begin each day with three hours of meditation and visualization practices. It is they that give me what little calm and wisdom and persistence I have'."

Andrew Harvey . The Hope.

*   *   *

In this and the next two chapters I will be asking us to do a ruthless inventory of our relatedness with Self, Others and Earth. I will also be asking that we inventory the costs of our long-standing modus operandi of overriding and disconnecting.

I am asking that we do some deep looking into the massive blind spots we all have— as we've forfeited our deeper senses and awareness in almost every domain. I am asking that we take a full frontal look at how our own, individual Shadows have gleefully filled the spaces we have left unattended in our frenzy of override, disconnection and distraction.

*   *   *

I am deliberately choosing to start my detailing of these three gateways to meaningful life, with Reconnection With Earth. I am starting here because we have already done quite a bit of exploration of our many and varied ways of impacting and damaging our planet and habitat.

Before we get going with our process of steering ourselves back toward a reconnection with our miraculous home, let's take a few moments to self assess regarding just how disconnected we have become.

*   *   *

Self Assessment: Disconnection From Earth.

I am suggesting that we make a detailed inventory here of, how we have disconnected from the web of life—and the costs of that disconnection.

So, please take a few minutes now to set down this book and pick up your workbook or journal. Start a new page and write the questions:

How has humanity disconnected from Earth?

In what ways have we overridden important signs and symptoms that we are off track from sustainable living on Earth?

What have been the costs of our overriding and disconnection?

How have I disconnected from Earth?

In what ways have I overridden important signs and symptoms that I am off track from sustainable living on Earth?

What have been the costs of my overriding and disconnection?

*   *   *

One brief example from my own responses to this exercise: I shared quite early in *The Impossible Conversation* about my deep respect and appreciation for one of my heroes, Jacques Yves Cousteau. I mentioned that his remarkable footage and descriptions of the destructive impact of human systems on the world's oceans, made a profound impression on me. This impression inspired me to learn to dive and to spend countless hours in oceans around the world.

Where does the cost of my disconnection from Earth, and specifically the oceans of Earth, come in? It starts as I leave college to enter the business world. If I am honest here, I would say that I knew that the results I would be producing as a corporate training professional, would primarily be feeding the insatiable corporate hunger for more consumption, more production, more devastation of our environment, more disempowerment of more people at the lower end of the economic ladder… more disconnection.

That, after all, is the name of the game in the corporate world.

So, this is just one small example of the kind of personal review I am asking of you, in response to the questions above. If you are in need of more potent prompts to get you going here, please review the extinction and habitat loss Sober Data back in chapter three. Again, I suggest that you set up these self assessment exercises and lists to be living documents, easy to add to in the coming weeks and months.

*   *   *

It is here we would be well served by a review of Elizabeth Kubler Ross' Stages of Grief and Dying. (Chapter 7)

Denial.

Anger.

Bargaining.

Depression.

Acceptance.

I have been amazed at how many layers of denial and negotiation or bargaining I have uncovered in myself as I've pursued a truer path in the face of our predicament.

What stages of Elizabeth Kubler Ross' model do you tend to gravitate toward?

What aspects of the Sober Data here in The Impossible Conversation do you find yourself resisting or trying to renegotiate somehow?

What data or projections have spurred you to a sense of despair or anger?

*   *   *

It has been remarkable for me to see how reluctant we humans can be to make this kind of inventory or self assessment. This kind of looking and exploration, by its nature, compels us to acknowledge hard truths about ourselves and to feel that which we have overridden for a lifetime.

Like the first self-assessment or inventory I asked of you back in the introduction (What do you love about living this life?), I suggest you keep these questions handy, and keep growing your list as you become more aware of our dramatic impact on our shared habitat.

Your responses and lists will also be wonderful sources for informed inquiries you may want to take on in the future.

Reconnecting With Earth:

Probably the simplest practice one can adopt when desiring to see, feel, experience, blend with the natural world, is to be in it.

Yes, many of these practices are going to be just this basic.

Countless spiritual traditions and meditation, mindfulness and wellness practices throughout the ages have pointed us toward a deeper intimacy with the natural world. Only problem is, our business-as-usual paradigm has exactly zero appreciation of that natural world. In fact, it has no option but to see Earth as a mass of resources to be exploited, profits to be reaped, receptacle for waste. If anything, our business-as-usual frame for seeing the world appears to be one of contempt.

As I have pursued this more extensive research into the state of Earth and our impacts upon her, it is hard not to end up with an even more chilling conclusion as to the business-as-usual view of our miraculous home. A quick review of the Sober Data and a reminder that most of that Sober Data has been common knowledge for decades, points to a willful ignorance built into our ubiquitous overriding and, even further, an aggression, a conquering, a domination, a violence is implied in our relationship with our Mother Earth.

So, here we land. In the first suggested practice we are stopped in our tracks by the subversive act of just *being in nature*.

We can imagine together some of our resistant inner voices and their freak out as they consider spending hours, many hours, just being in nature:

"Oh, I couldn't do that. I'm so damn busy I couldn't think of spending even one hour in the woods, much less three, five, eight hours a week out there. What are you, nuts? Besides, I went on a vacation to Hawaii last year and we went snorkeling and hiking and surfing. That has to count for something, right?"

What have been the costs of our overriding and disconnection from Earth?

Another, very different way of asking this question is: What Earth symptom would be necessary to have you take notice? What Earth symptom would be necessary to have you take action in your life, business, family, community?

We have, in this *Impossible Conversation*, addressed a number of astounding projections about Anthropogenic Climate Disruption and about the massive losses to our global habitat, biodiversity and to the reduction and full-loss of innumerable species within the last fifty years.

This is a good moment to do a bit of a reality check, to breathe while we recount a few of the most stunning projections and data.

- 150-200 (now over 300) species per day going extinct every day.

- All global fisheries in full collapse by 2040.

- The loss of 50% of Earth's wild animals since the 1970s.

- Dozens of references to global temperature rise of 4°C to 6°C or higher by 2050 or sooner. Recall the most accelerated projection was: 4°C to 10°C by 2016.

- The unliveability of Earth for humans and millions of other species at a temperature of 4°C and above.

- The imminent demise of the world's coral reefs by 2050, including the Great Barrier Reef by 2030.

- The loss of 40% of the oceans' phytoplankton within the last fifty years.

And two more reports that have arrived just before publishing this book:

- The Rusty Patch Bumble Bee has been placed on the Endangered Species list in the US. This, as glyphosate is banned in a number of EU countries and suspected of being carcinogenic to humans and disastrous to Earth habitat and species far beyond the pests originally intended to kill. Why I am including this bee, is because we are steadily losing this kind of essential pollinator around the world. Lose pollinators = lose agriculture. Lastly, as if on cue, Trump's administration has recently attempted to suspend the rule that was used to place the Rusty Patch Bumble Bee on the Endangered Species List. This smacks of the East Coast jurisdictions that have prohibited the use of the words, 'climate change', in any land use or planning agency deliberations. If you don't say the words, then it doesn't exist, right?

- Climate scientist, David Barber, in a 2017 *Real News* interview, relayed recent findings that in addition to the obvious acceleration of every type of land and sea ice on the planet, the Greenland Ice Sheet is melting 600% faster than even recent modeling was predicting.

With Sober Data from vetted sources with this level of severity, we need to ask ourselves in all seriousness, "What Earth symptoms will need to be present to motivate us to become more engaged in our own version of an Impossible Conversation with ourselves and with other people?" "What amount of loss of Earth habitat and species would inspire you into a different way of living or behaving in this world?"

What amount of Sober Data will we need to hear to wake us from our collective dream of returning to infinite growth on a finite planet? Perhaps on the day we've installed enough solar panels or purchased enough Teslas and Priuses?

What level of Shadow and willful ignorance will we tolerate and even encourage from our fellow citizens and from our political, corporate and media leaders, and from ourselves?

What I believe we will need to do to have any chance of standing up for life on Earth, is to ask ourselves questions of this caliber and beyond. We will need to pierce through our arrogance and species-level entitlement and superiority and tell the truth about what we are doing. We will need to pop the bubble that the vast majority of us are in, the bubble of resistance, denial and distraction we use to avoid all of the uncomfortable emotions and realizations we have spent decades overriding and suppressing.

"I believe we are a species with amnesia, I think we have forgotten our roots and our origins. I think we are quite lost in many ways. And we live in a society that invests huge amounts of money and vast quantities of energy in ensuring that we all stay lost. A society that invests in creating unconsciousness, which invests in keeping people asleep so that we are just passive consumers of products, is clearly not interested in asking any of the truly important questions."

Graham Hancock

We must find a sincere love of life on Earth. Collectively, we have disconnected from life on Earth. We identify with the perpetual motion and distraction and consumption of the human operating system at the expense of our innate birthright of being just one of millions of species that each hold a unique place in the web of life.

To transform our relationship with Earth and with life, we will need to deploy our attention and intent in a very different way. The depth of this transformation, this potential collective rite of passage, is most profound. The scale of the challenge of bridging between our current, ecocidal way of living in business-as-usual and some more life affirming way of being, is daunting indeed.

In the small space we have here to introduce the whole notion I must defer to one of the most inspiring authors and Earth loving activists I've ever met. Derrick Jensen is one of the most prolific authors in the field of Earth Activism and presents a sober view of the costs of humans disconnecting from the web of life.

Jensen is asking us to conduct yet another version of a self-assessment exercise or perhaps a deeper exploration that I'm calling, an Informed Inquiry. He is asking us to lean in to one of our weak suits—our reluctance to fully be present to the impact we are having on our planet, our reluctance to feel our impact on our shared biosphere, our home and our neighbors:

> ..."Here is what I want you to do: I want you to go outside. I want you to listen to the (disappearing) frogs, to watch the (disappearing) fireflies. Even if you're in a city—especially if you're in a city—I want you to picture the land as it was before the land was built over. I want you to research who lived there. I want you to feel how it was then, feel how it wants to be. I want you to begin keeping a calendar of who you see and when—the first day each year you see buttercups, the first day frogs start singing, the last day you see robins in the fall, the first day for grasshoppers. In short, I want you to pay attention.
>
> If you do this, your baseline will stop declining, because you'll have a record of what's being lost.
>
> Do not go numb in the face of this data. Do not turn away. I want you to feel the pain. Keep it like a coal inside your coat, a coal that burns and burns. I want all of us to do this, because we

should all want the pain of injustice to stop. We should want this pain to stop, not because we get used to it and it just doesn't bother us anymore, but because we stop the injustices and destruction that are causing the pain in the first place. I want us to feel how awful the destruction is, and then act from this feeling.

And, I promise you two things. One: Feeling this pain won't kill you. And, two: Not feeling this pain, continuing to go numb and avoid it... will."

*　　*　　*

The process of reconnecting with deeper self, other beings and Earth is full of practices as relatively simple but deeply transformational as Jensen's suggestion. The deceptive simplicity of any exercise we might use to connect with Earth hides the immensity of the importance of that reconnection and the difficulty of changing ourselves in this way.

We now see our world as an endless source for all the cool things we buy, sell and consume and a bottomless pit to receive the waste products that come from that consumption. Derrick Jensen often tells a story of an Oregon logger who says that when he looks at a forest, he sees dollar bills.

Seeing the world through business-as-usual eyes, we can only see that which can be consumed, extracted, profited from, we only see "dollar bills." We literally can't and won't see our world in any other way. Remember the "agreements" I mentioned that we all made when we got on board with the business-as-usual paradigm?

What may have been an obvious and inborn sense for some early, indigenous tribes, is now strange and foreign to us in our disconnected culture. Specifically, I am pointing to the sense or ability to see the world in terms of the inter-relatedness of all life.

I am clear that not all early, indigenous cultures were particularly successful at living in balance and harmony with other people or their environment. But there are formidable examples of whole regions of Earth in which large numbers of tribes lived peacefully and sustainably for upwards of ten thousand years or more.

Just this fact alone could inspire some serious consideration of alternative human operating systems. I found it fascinating, while doing this research, that we seem to have an utter failure of imagination regarding human beings living on planet Earth.

For those of us who do have this kind of imagination and will to reconnect themselves with Earth and the web of life, we must remember first and foremost how to love this life and this miraculous, ridiculously rare planet and biosphere upon which we live.

Another, simpler practice that we might use in our efforts to reconnect with Earth is to walk out in nature with an intention to be aware of what we might call, non-ordinary perception. Perhaps the simplest of these excursions into nature is currently called, Forest Bathing. While, of course, there are those who will make a more complicated process of it, it is remarkably easy to calm and ground yourself and allow the forest to clear our personal space of the many anxieties and tensions we tend to collect in our busy day of override.

Another variation of this is to carry a current, personal inquiry or question with you into the forest. This could be done by just writing the question on a small piece of paper and putting in your pocket. A perfect example of a strong personal question could be your consideration of any of the values that are mentioned in Bob Doppelt's values reevaluation exercise here in *The Impossible Conversation.*

The challenge is to soften your focus and intent while taking this time in the forest. The value of this kind of reconnection with Earth only comes when we allow ourselves to slow down to match the natural pace of the forest. We need to shed our constantly chattering "monkey mind", slow down our rapid fire, business-as-usual pace and release the whole notion of accomplishing any sort of goal or outcome in our forest time. In this released state, there is some possibility of gaining some non-ordinary perception or experience.

*　　*　　*

There are those who assert that this time in human history is a kind of rite of passage for all of humanity. If we see ourselves collectively as an adolescent, it could be said that this massive predicament we face, is our threshold experience that, if successfully completed, could have us "return" as full fledged adults, full interbeing members of the tribe, and of the web of life itself.

I personally am very familiar with the tradition and mythology that is the rite of passage from adolescence to adulthood. I had the privilege to work with many young men and a few young women in guided rite of passage programs in my work history.

I am a bit reluctant, for a number of reasons, to frame our collective process in terms of a rite of passage. Perhaps my greatest reluctance is that we are not consciously staging this process for ourselves and we have no wise elders holding the tradition or the safety of the container for this process. And, as you may recall, my conclusions in vetting the Sober Data landed squarely in the range of massive destruction of our global habitat and massive, extinction-level loss of species, diversity and habitat by sooner than 2050, perhaps as soon as 2026.

The whole notion of humanity at large sharing a global rite of passage experience is compelling and interesting and, I'm afraid, a bit naïve. I tend to agree with a remarkable author and futurist, Charles Eisenstein, when he proposes that we are between two stories. Starting with the premise that all cultures have defining narratives or stories that they use to make sense of the world and how they fit in that world. It is obvious that all cultures rise and fall. It is perhaps a bit less obvious, but important to note, that the fall of a culture is precipitated by the collapse and eventual death of its defining story or stories. We are now in the middle of the collapse of our defining stories.

We are in for a long stretch of extreme discomfort, even suffering, as we watch our core defining stories die—and we scramble to create some kind of new, defining story or stories to take their place. This is another, more direct, way of saying "we are building a bridge." Perhaps this way of describing our global predicament makes it a little clearer why I introduced our weak suits around death, loss, dying and grief.

There is an immense scale of loss and grief that is built into the collapse of our business-as-usual paradigm and our core stories.

*   *   *

To come anywhere near the notion of reconnecting ourselves with life on Earth, we will need to start with a few very basic preparations for the process.

Meditation / Mindfulness

There are a few practices that will show up in all three of these Reconnecting chapters. One of those universally valuable practices is *meditation*. There are many kinds of meditation and I trust any reader who does not yet have a meditation practice, will be able to take one on in a relatively short time.

What matters here is a bit more context, a few more of the reasons why we should take on a practice like meditation. What we've seen so far in *The Impossible Conversation* is that the business-as-usual world is hitting the brick wall at the end of a fossil fuel-driven rocket ride. The entire run of this rocket ride has been conducted with a couple of guiding principles: more is always better and more-faster is better still. We have fully integrated that addiction to speed into the fabric of our lives.

As we have started to see in the Sober Data, the combination of constant, breakneck acceleration and our mastery at the skill of override, has left us completely disinterested in any kind of signal from Earth, or from our own inner faculties, when anything is out of balance or not right in the web of life.

Even with this ubiquitous and deceptively simple practice of meditation or mindfulness, our challenging times and predicaments will strain even the calm and grace of well practiced meditators.

Gratitude

We've already begun this one. The first self-assessment exercise in the Introduction section of this book involved our listing our loves in this life—the people, non human animals, places on Earth, arts, activities et al. that we love, appreciate or are grateful for. To repeat, this is recommended as an ongoing practice for the rest of our lives.

This simple activity powerfully shifts our attention and thinking from the business-as-usual mindset of disconnection, judgment, competition, consumption and scarcity to a direct experience of interrelatedness, compassion, cooperation and sufficiency. This shift to gratitude is perhaps the simplest and most powerful of the tools of reconnection.

A powerful combination is to blend your meditation practice with your focus on gratitude. A sincere practitioner can replace the common, draining habit of ruminating or worrying in life, with a meditative focus on gratitude. One visit to the website of Brother David Stendl-Rast, as mentioned in an earlier chapter, will provide abundant suggestion for building this practice.

Slow down

Next the aspiring bridge builder would do well to slow the heck down. Notice Jensen's suggested exercise implied not just one visit with nature, but many, over years. He also was clear about how curious and clear the person's attention would need to be in order to really see at a new level.

These particular qualities of attention and perception were the focus of years of my professional training. While only small portions of my years of training in advanced seeing were actually useable in the corporate or youth-at-risk workshop programs I led, I don't regret a moment of those remarkable years of non-ordinary perception training.

Ironically, the demands of our global predicament and of people who are desiring coaching and assistance in building their inner, predicament tool kits, are showing more appetite for this Seeing training than any other generation of participants I've known.

So, a person building their practice here will engage a mindset of gratitude and open curiosity, then orient themselves to a much slower pace of movement, thought and breath. They then could include some of their meditation or mindfulness practice to bring more of their fluid attention and presence to the session of time spent in nature.

Spoiler alert, this series of suggested elements inviting deeper perception and presence, will show up frequently as we move between the three dimensions of intentional reconnection: with deeper self, with others and here, with Earth.

The basic set of elements that make up this practice will undoubtedly be familiar, in one form or another, to those who have practiced any of the many different contemplative traditions that have existed for millennia.

We won't have the time or space for fully detailing these practices here in this one book. My allies and I are offering coaching, training, live workshops, workbooks and online tutorials with the intention of assisting aspirants in building their inner skills, capacities and tool kits.

"All the while, there is an unformed awareness in the background that our world could be extensively damaged at any moment. Awesome and unprecedented in the history of humanity, the awareness lurks there, with an anguish beyond naming. Until we find ways of acknowledging and integrating that level of anguished awareness, we repress it; and with that repression we are drained of the energy we need for action and clear thinking."

Joanna Macy, Working Through Despair

In this quote, Joanna Macy points to one cost of repressing or denying essential inner aspects of ourselves. I am in full agreement with her assertion that repression of this awareness and anguish is draining, even exhausting. I would only add that by repressing aspects of ourselves we are also growing our Shadows.

In this one paragraph, Joanna Macy has summed up our cultural practice of overriding, and begun the articulation of how that overriding depletes our life energy and invites our shadows to fill the void left by our denial of our anguished awareness.

I suggest revisiting the works, mentioned before, of Frances Weller and Stephen Jenkinson. They both speak to this odd cultural habit we all have, of repressing the most valuable practices we could be including in our lives. Both have poetic gifts for reminding us of the beauty, grace and even core joy of consciously experiencing these darker, often anguish-filled aspects of life.

*   *   *

Informed Inquiry

In the middle of this now years-long research project to vet the Sober Data in that original presentation, I realized that there was another benefit to all of this research. Beyond the validation of deeply disturbing data and projections there was the warm and reassuring realization that as I learned about an aspect of our world or about a particular species, I would automatically find myself more in love with it or them.

It seems obvious now, but it was a pretty exciting realization. A particularly strong example of this is when I looked through my list of loves in life and found the first mention of the ocean. I had written it down in memory of watching Jacques Cousteau on TV, becoming a diver myself and recounting the hundreds of times I had sought out the immense healing presence of the sea during the troubled years of my youth.

I decided to take on a side project of articulating more than this vague, overarching concept called, the ocean. I committed to put a few hours in, here and there, to research specific aspects of the ocean world. This is how I ran into the daunting figures about our collapsing fish populations and the decline of phytoplankton and coral reefs around the world.

In one Informed Inquiry, I discovered the immense damage that the US military does to ocean species and habitat, in the course of its daily operations and especially during its war games and exercises around the world.[1]

The notion of an informed inquiry is to choose a subject that is already dear to you. In the process of deepening your knowledge about that subject, it is likely that your love and appreciation of those beings or that place, will grow. The logic is pretty simple—it is all too easy to ignore the diminishment or killing of a being about whom we are ignorant. Or, it is far more difficult to destroy someone or something we appreciate, are aware of, and know something about.

Again, this simple practice is one that can be repeated endlessly. In our data-filled lives, it is ridiculously easy to choose a new subject and dive into their world for only a few hours—and come out a bit more connected with those beings, other beings with whom we share this miraculous planet.

This informed inquiry process is particularly helpful in having us feel more and more of our healthy emotional body. With an expansion of the experience of love and appreciation, and perhaps of grief, we start to expand beyond the relatively flat and compressed emotional range that is "acceptable" within business-as-usual culture. Frances Weller calls our compressed emotional range, the Flat Line Culture.

*   *   *

In the transformational training world, we are always looking for catchy ways to amplify a particular learning piece or technique. We had one particular phrase that was intended to help students broaden their learning from one insight about one lesson, to possibly applying that same insight to many other areas of their lives.

"How you do one thing is how you do everything."

Looking back, it is more than a little presumptuous, even arrogant, but it did the job of expanding the teachable moment to include far more of the participants' lives and a deeper integration of what was often a valuable tool or technique of personal transformation.

What I'm inclined to do is to request that we each take this rather rough, assertive phrase and carry it with us into the next two chapters. It seems to me that we actually have global circumstances that could justify the use of this phrase.

The more I've done the research for *The Impossible Conversation*, the more I've seen just how dead-on accurate some of the authors and thought leaders described here, have been. I had no idea that I would find myself embracing the cultural analysis of Naomi Klein as she drew the connections between our collapsing global habitat and the environmental ravages of the capitalist model of infinite growth, production and consumption.

It has knocked me to my knees to see how Naomi Klein and Pope Francis, and other religious leaders, then broadened the web of connection between Earth and human systems by beautifully detailing the interrelatedness of all life. They repeatedly moved me to tears by showing how damage to beings on one side of the planet meant equal damage to us all.

We are all indeed, one life.

What I am asking here, is for each of us to hold open the possibility that the massive blind spot we share regarding the destruction of our precious shared habitat on this Earth, promises to be equaled by blind spots in our awareness of ourselves and each other.

An example: in the midst of my Impossible Conversation research I cornered myself into a deep remembering of my younger self loving the oceans of the Earth through the profoundly beautiful story telling of Jacques Cousteau. I then had to confront how I had abandoned the proud, activist stand taken by my twelve year old self – as he absorbed the Cousteau stories. I had to hold myself to account for "forgetting" the Sober Truth of our damage to our oceans, as I forged ahead in my adult/career years. What a deep well of remembering, forgetting, beauty, shame…and so much more.

A reminder here—a resounding cheer for those of you who are reading this book and completing its exercises or workbook with other people. There are many ways in which The Impossible Conversation is deepened by engagement with others. With the notion of exploring your own blind spots and Shadows, by definition, you will not be able to complete that work alone. Indeed much of what created our Shadows and blind spots was created by our robust mythology of the rugged individual standing alone and creating their life alone.

It appears to be remarkably difficult for us to imagine any other way of being. In the aloofness of our overriding, we seem uninterested in sober observation of the state of our shared habitat, reconnecting with our inner sensitivities and perceptions or collectively taking on the figurative bridge building to a new way of being.

* * *

9 Reconnecting With Deeper Self

"Hate is just a bodyguard for grief.
When people lose the hate, they are forced
to deal with the pain underneath."

Sarah Fields

"As my sufferings mounted, I soon realized that there were two
ways that I could respond to my situation: either to react with
bitterness or seek to transform the suffering into a creative force.

I decided to follow the latter course."

Martin Luther King Jr.

"We either operate from the fears of the ego or
the love of the soul."

Richard Barrett

"I am saying, as one grown up to another in a troubled time, you
have an obligation to be able to proceed minus any assurance
that anything good will come from it."

Stephen Jenkinson

"Confront the dark parts of yourself, and work to banish them
with illumination and forgiveness. Your willingness to wrestle
with your demons will cause your angels to sing. Use the pain as
fuel, as a reminder of your strength."

August Wilson

"It's the action, not the fruit of the action, that's important.

You have to do the right thing.
It may not be in your power,
May not be in your time,
that there'll be any fruit.

But that doesn't mean you stop doing the right thing.

You may never know what results
come from your action.

But if you do nothing, there will be no result."

Mohandas K. Gandhi

"I have learned things in the dark that I could never have learned
in the light, things that have saved my life over and over again, so
that there is really only one logical conclusion.
I need the darkness as much as I need the light."

Barbara Brown Taylor

"The heart that breaks open can contain the whole universe.

In the face of impermanence and death, it takes courage to love
the things of this world and to believe that praising them is our
noblest calling."

Joanna Macy

*   *   *

It is with this long chain of powerful quotes that we begin our chapter about reconnecting with our deeper, wiser selves. As with the last chapter about reconnecting with Earth, the actual practices we will consider are deceptively simple. It is cracking open the tightly sealed box that surrounds our collective and individual hearts, where the process gets more complicated.

In the last chapter I mentioned how Carolyn Baker is perhaps the most potent and prolific author addressing the question: "Who will we be together, in the face of humanity's predicament?" or "What will the quality of our relationships be in the turbulent times to come?" The same could easily be said for the many books and especially the thousands of workshops led by Joanna Macy and her teams of facilitators.

Macy's work, called The Work That Reconnects, is a gentle and safe space in which participants can express their deep loves and concerns, feel the world's pain and ultimately conjure a new, more encouraged future together. Sound familiar?

The workshops, coaching and online offerings that support *The Impossible Conversation* are all designed to honor and include core components of The Work That Reconnects. Readers who wish to explore more would do well to start with a comprehensive sharing of the inner workings of TWTR and to read, *Coming Back To Life*, written by Joanna Macy and Molly Young Brown. This book generously offers people the full TWTR tool kit for use in any family, organization or support group setting.

What we will cover here is a deepening of the notion that to make a difference in these extraordinary times, we must turn to face the aspects of life (our weak suits) that the business-as-usual culture has compelled us to avoid. This is at least as true in this chapter as it was in the last. We will need to become far more facile with the aspects mentioned before: Shadow (both cultural and individual) grief, and access to our full emotional range, re-membering our love for others and for Earth.

And, here, we will focus on our reconnection with our deeper, wiser selves. This includes a reclaiming of our personal empowerment and agency that have been forfeited in our life-long habit of overriding within the business-as-usual culture.

"It is no longer appropriate to think only in terms of even my nation or my country, let alone my village. If we are to overcome the problems we face, we need what I have called a sense of universal responsibility rooted in love and kindness for our human brothers and sisters. In our present state of affairs, the very survival of humankind depends on people developing concern for the whole of humanity, not just their own community or nation. The reality of our situation impels us to act and think more clearly. Narrow-mindedness and self-centered thinking may have served us well in the past, but today will only lead to disaster. We can overcome such attitudes through the combination of education and training."

> Joanna Macy
> *Coming Back to Life:*
> *The Updated Guide to the Work that Reconnects*

In any TWTR workshop, we begin in step one of the "spiral" of Macy's work, the step of acknowledging what we love about our lives, what we are grateful for. Now it might be clearer why I asked us to start that personal inventory of gratitude and loves in life back in the Introduction.

The next step is to feel together the pain of the world. Again, as I mentioned last chapter, this is not meant to be an endless wallowing in the depressing doom and gloom of our world. It is meant to be a powerful transformative movement that frees up immense amounts of life energy. This is the life energy we all use to keep us from feeling the darker, more intense emotions that are with us every day. This is the skill of being able to break our own hearts open, intentionally, to reconnect us with our deeper selves.

"For me, the price of admission into that present is allowing my heart to break. To be completely with the grief and despair I feel for the world, for those suffering and for the future of my children. Just to be with that grief and despair and hold it as tenderly as I would a young child.

And, when fully felt, despair transforms, in the face of overwhelming social and ecological crises, into a clarity of vision, then into constructive, collaborative action."

Justine Corrie
Being With My Grief For The World.
Uplift. December, 2016.

"I've been asking myself: How can I be honest and not spread fear? How do I say 'game over' when we mustn't give up? Maybe the game that's over is the pretense of normalcy. Maybe what's over is the delusion that with millions of souls already in prison, with millions of undocumented already deported, with over half of America already in poverty, the rest of us can stay so preoccupied with our personal pursuits. Perhaps what's finished is the fantasy that we can find ourselves without taking our suffering seriously."

Joanna Macy

Joanna Macy got her start as a course designer and facilitator and activist when the dangers of nuclear weapons and nuclear power were more in the public eye than they are now. While obviously those dangers are as present as they've ever been, there are so many more global issues of equal or greater concern its hard to know where to start.

Throughout the decades that I've followed Macy's teachings, she has not wavered from the graceful blend of Buddhism and Systems thinking that has always underpinned her work.

In fact it was one of her core tenets that boosted my research of Abrupt Anthropogenic Climate Change from a brief, due-diligence project to a global scale, Informed Inquiry that has transformed my life.

Joanna has often mentioned a couple of core components of what she sees as most needed as people attempt to make a difference in the world. One, an ever-growing sense of compassion for life and for humanity. The other, to continuously expand our awareness of the interrelatedness of all things. It was her repeated suggestion to experience the intricately interwoven web of life and the systems within it that woke me up to the immense scale of what I now call, The Impossible Conversation and our global predicament.

PURPOSE, VISION, MISSION

"Many people who are going through the early stages of the awakening process are no longer certain what their outer purpose is. What drives the world no longer drives them. Seeing the madness of our civilization so clearly, they may feel somewhat alienated from the culture around them. Some feel that they inhabit a no-man's-land between two worlds. They are no longer run by the ego, yet the arising awareness has not yet become fully integrated into their lives.

Eckhart Tolle

As I've mentioned a few times here, people who sincerely engage with this Impossible Conversation, can be said to live two lives, or have a foot in two worlds. I've also been saying it as if, "crossing a bridge while building it."

Having been in the training, coaching and personal-growth-workshop world for more than thirty years, I am fully aware that there is perhaps no topic more articulated, coached, promoted, espoused, encouraged, demanded and sought after than, purpose. Of course we have to include purpose's cousins: goals, vision, mission, dreams, aspirations, and on the list goes.

What I'm asserting here is that every stitch of that now ubiquitous body of work on success in life, utilizing the power of clear purpose, has been created in a world saturated in businessas-usual. I am part of a team that is reinventing this entire body of work, so it has some amount of relevance here at the end of business as usual. I invite you, dear reader, to proceed through these final chapters of TIC and consider deeply how this Sober Data and projections of *The Impossible Conversation* might change you. How might your vetting of the Sober Data transform your own sense of purpose or mission in life? How might this predicament inspire a new defining story or narrative for your life?

How might you live your life differently if you were to gradually shift your attention from a singular focus on scratching out a living in our familiar, collapsing, business-as-usual paradigm, to a focus on reconnecting with deep sources of meaning: self, others and Earth?

"The real magic is turning pain into beauty and more love through emotional transformation. When we don't know how to do this, or don't want to, we disembody and seek these deeply fulfilling qualities in addiction and magical thinking. Embracing the dark we make it fertile. Ignoring it we make it lethal."

Jack Adam Weber

I am asserting that there is no larger, or more over-analyzed aspect of the personal and professional growth-training world, than vision, mission, purpose. In our business-as-usual world, this core notion of "powerful, clear, vision, mission, purpose yields better results, more achievement and better life"... has been the backbone of inspiring and motivating workers, executives and entrepreneurs since early in the 20th Century.

What I'm asserting here is that the calling of life on Earth at this time is for a complete reinvention of how we as human beings generate a vision, mission and purpose. I am saying that the old, business-as-usual model that we've all used to bring ourselves to higher levels of clarity, productivity and attainment, no longer enjoys its solo position at center stage for our attention and intention.

It could be said that with the collapse of the business-as-usual paradigm comes the collapse of our shared, defining stories—the stories that were based on premises like: We will always enjoy infinite growth on this finite planet. There are so many rich resources on Earth, we never have to pay attention to running out. The Earth is so vast that we never have to account for the impacts of the waste products that our business-as-usual processes create.

While the thrust of *The Impossible Conversation* is personal exploration and growth, there is an obvious parallel track to be walked in a later book – The now bankrupt model of corporate structure and governance in which short term profit takes precedence over any and all other possible motives. This includes that pesky little motive called survival of our species and of life on Earth.

If we are aligned that we are currently immersed in the collapse of our business-as-usual world and the defining stories that underpin it— and we know our current visions, missions, purposes are directly tied to those core, defining stories— we would do well to begin crafting new defining stories in anticipation of bridging to a new way for humanity to live on this planet.

It may be a very long time before large numbers of people, much less entire nations or regions, generate new defining stories at scale. Given that, a core practice at the individual level is to create or reinvent your own vision, mission and or purpose.

We will include a less detailed, shorter version of this vision, mission, purpose process here. Readers who desire a far richer, more detailed process outline can find it in *The Impossible Conversation Workbook* or contact us personally via the links at the end of this book.

We call this process, ***Recreating Purpose.***

We have taken many of the preliminary steps to recreating purpose in the chapters of this book. We have listed our loves in life, the aspects of life for which we are deeply grateful. We've taken an unflinching look at some of the Sober Data of our world so we can be more present to what is actually going on and less affected by other, distracting or deceitful influences of our world. We have assessed ourselves regarding how vulnerable we are to the cynical, disempowering influences of our corporate-government-media state.

And, now we are at the level of exploring practices that will reconnect us with our core sense of empowerment and agency. We are looking forward to how we might reignite the passion that comes from opening our hearts together, reuniting with other people and reconnecting ourselves with the miraculous web of life.

This progression, above, could be said to reflect the process of generating a new vision, mission and purpose. If I've taken the steps above, I could be on the edge of generating a vision, mission, purpose that draws me into a positive and intentionally declared future for me and the dear ones in my circle of influence.

Perhaps the greatest challenges in generating this new, re-created purpose… are:

- Our life-long immersion in our business-as-usual world. The tools, methods and even the way that we see and experience our world within business-as-usual, are universally ill-suited for the generation of this, re-created purpose. Starting with the central focus of business as usual being extraction of profit driven by override— a new vision calls for vision, mission, purpose that are founded in the interrelatedness of all life and human systems.

- Our individual and cultural habits of Denial and Negotiation. (Remember the stages of Dying and Grief of Elizabeth Kubler

Ross?) To the degree we are unwilling to face our weak suits and soberly face our troubled Earth and human systems, we will be hamstrung by our resistance to be truly present to life on Earth, life in our disconnected relationships and life in our bodies— disconnected from our core experience of purposeful living and interrelatedness with life. We will have no choice but to keep perpetuating business-as-usual.

This is not the end of this introduction to re-created purpose, this is actually only one third of this proposed tool for 21st Century bridge builders. Because we find ourselves still neck-deep in our collapsing business-as-usual paradigm, we must also create a current, powerful, sober vision, mission, purpose with which to hold our day-to-day life…now.

As we've seen, *The Impossible Conversation* includes some extraordinarily disruptive Sober Data and projections. It also points to imminent immense stress and collapse for essential Earth and human systems. Basically, the whole point of going through the Sober Data in the first few chapters of *The Impossible Conversation,* was to empower you to establish your own baseline understanding of the state of our world.

Without this kind of self-generated, vetted, foundation of understanding, we all are essentially vulnerable to any change in the wind, not to mention any change imposed by powerful cultural, financial and political forces.

So, I am suggesting the generation of another re-created purpose; this one focused on our current, daily lives. While many of your existing goals, plans, vision, mission, purpose and even dreams may stay in place and be as valid or aligned as ever, you may well discover that large swaths of these elements in your life are wanting to morph or change to accommodate your new Sober Data-informed life view. It is extremely likely that each of us will find portions of our day-to-day and long-term priorities shifting as we integrate our own, vetted estimates of the Sober Data into our life plans.

If you will recall the Transformational Resilience exercise of reevaluating our values, this could be considered to be the next stage of that reevaluation process.

I know a number of parents with older teen children who have taken on a very serious re-looking at their plan for their child's future. I have had hundreds of conversations with people who are consciously rebuilding and retooling their investment and retirement strategies as they attempt to include Sober Data and imminent human and Earth systems collapse elements into their future view.

I must again mention the fine work of Chris Martenson and his website, Peak Prosperity. For years, Chris has offered his Crash Course at no charge to the public at large. Martenson and his crew not only offer a long and a short version of the Crash Course online webinar, but also a fine series of very informative podcasts and website articles. Of particular importance is Martenson's articulation of exponential growth and its shocking progression, especially in the last few moments on the exponential growth curve.

By now you may have made the connection between the non-linear or exponential acceleration that was mentioned by many of the Sober Data points in the early chapters, and the utter unsustainability of the infinite economic growth model articulated by Chris Martenson in his Crash Course. These two dynamics are inextricably related.

I obviously recommend Peak Prosperity's many and powerful offerings. Of all the practices and tools recommended here in *The Impossible Conversation*, this commitment to strengthen your knowledge, awareness and skill of managing your financial affairs is one of the most essential if you intend to minimize the crushing stress that comes from being caught off guard when markets tumble.

And they do promise to tumble.

Remember I mentioned that we are suggesting three versions of vision, mission, purpose?

We have already touched briefly on generating a re-created purpose to bolster our view of a new world, a new culture, a new way of being during and after the collapse of our business-as-usual paradigm.

We then suggested the creation of a new, sober vision, mission, purpose framework with which you could hold your current, daily life. It should be mentioned here that the center point of all three purpose, vision, mission statements need to be created with a core focus on the state of being one aspires to— rather than the more common central focus of attainment, achievement or other business-as-usual metrics. Each of these three revised purpose statements will have some amount of articulation of the state of being to which one aspires.

The statement addressing the creation of a new world obviously will have the most emphasis here. The recreated statement addressing our life in this collapsing business-as-usual paradigm may still have less emphasis on being and more on the traditional doing.

And, lastly, the Shadow purpose, vision, mission statement will involve the articulation of our Shadow's aspirations in the creation of a new world. Whenever I get to that step in this process, it is daunting to admit that I have such cynical and destructive impulses anywhere in my inner world, but indeed I do. I assert that we all do.

I've jumped ahead of myself a bit here. I've assumed you know what I'm talking about with this notion of a Shadow purpose, vision or mission. It may be instructive to expand the earlier mentions of Shadow (both cultural and individual) to imagine what a Shadow version of a purpose statement might be, but let's step back and give you some supporting description.

*   *   *

The third version of a mission, vision or purpose statement has been used by a number of personal and executive development providers over the years but by far the most powerful version I've seen is used in a remarkable training program for men that has established itself around the world. The Mankind Project (MKP) has been offering a version of a rite of passage for adult men for decades. This powerful and empowering program, the New Warrior Training Adventure, is teaching men extraordinarily important tools for being responsible, authentic, powerful contributions to their families, workplaces and communities. This mysterious third vision, mission, purpose component is called, in MKP lingo, The Shadow Mission.

The idea here is to surface some of the Shadow influences that we all carry, and articulate those influences in the presence of a safe circle of men. If we are successful at that articulation, and have the commitment of our supportive friends or counselor or life coach, we stand some chance of reducing the massive impacts of unconscious Shadow dynamics in our personal lives.

It should also be said that this awareness at the individual level is a huge help in our being able to perceive and understand the Shadow expressions going on at the regional, national and global levels as well.

The drafting of a Shadow vision, mission, purpose statement is a bit trickier than the other two: our business as usual version of purpose, and our purpose generated to keep us on course while creating a new way of being.

By definition our Shadow is made up of aspects of ourselves that we dislike, deny or disown. In its most unconscious form, the Shadow is only expressed through the person's Shadow projections onto others. This is usually accompanied by a large helping of judgment and emotional charge, also projected onto the "other."

As has become almost an American tradition (yes, I'm aware that this is global) the person who is unconscious of their Shadow dynamics will often make a big show of how "not-that" that they are, for instance a Congressman who lectures and legislates for years against the evils of homosexuality and for traditional family values, who is discovered to be a closeted gay and living a lie in his political life and marriage with his wife.

Similarly, we all have the experience (albeit at a less grand scale) of having less success than we might like with regard to our goals, plans, vision, mission, purpose. We may even find ourselves sabotaging our own integrity or success, and not know why. We may experience the repetition of painful patterns in relationship or other life endeavors, and again, not know why these negative outcomes keep showing up.

I have seen immense growth and wisdom, and even significant improvement in various metrics for success, when a person takes on the challenge of mapping their own inner, Shadow dimensions and dynamics. I predict the very near future will bring with it large scale stressors that will affect every person you know—and, yes, you. With the advent of those stressors, the average person who is unaware of this thing called Shadow, will be run ragged by the unbridled exploits of their Shadow and the Shadow dynamics of their family, community, workplace and nation.

If I take the time and effort to create a Shadow Mission, it is likely some of my blind spot, regarding my own Shadow, will be reduced. If I generate all three of these purpose/mission/vision statements in the presence of trusted allies I will expand my clarity and field of view greatly. If I invite their feedback regarding my progress in realizing those states of being I will have the extra fuel source of their support, coaching and frequent reality checks.

To give you a sense of how these three re-created purpose statements can look, let's take a look at mine at the time of this writing:

For life in day to day, business-as-usual living …

My mission is to deepen authentic connection in the world by living and teaching conscious, courageous and compassionate transformation.

For life in a co-created, new paradigm for human life on Earth…

With each breath I am more connected to the web of life.

Shadow vision, mission, purpose…

My Shadow mission is to survive and successfully compete by promoting: disconnection, separation and polarization in others, wherever I go, through the use of fear, privilege and disregard for presence or awareness in myself and others.

*   *   *

I'm inclined to say a few words about this notion of a shadow vision, mission, purpose.

It might seem like an almost silly or confusing add-on to the Re-Creation of Purpose process. What I've found: Shadow awareness is as priceless as it is slippery and elusive.

The more reminders and cues we can have in place to remind us of Shadow's pungent, behind-the-scenes influence, the better our chances to eventually integrate that shadow, consciously, back into our daily lives. This releases much of its background influence on the integrity and quality of our lives.

Some indicators that we are on track with our aspirational purpose or vision: We will have access to surprising amounts of energy, core joy and inspiration for our daily life activities. We are likely to experience considerable alignment or synergy with others in our safe circle. It is likely to involve a spirit of service to others and to the life around you.

A few of the attributes of the Shadow Mission: It is founded the murkier aspects of ourselves including: insecurity, guilt, self importance. It can result in us feeling: exhaustion, alone, resentment and, as mentioned before, contempt for life, others and Earth.

As we have seen in the earlier chapters, there is no shortage of Shadow influence on the global level today. Shadow appears to be running the show in almost every aspect of our world. Similarly, we will see that Shadow is plenty active for all of us on the individual level as well.

*   *   *

This notion of a three-part vision, mission, purpose statement may seem a bit much, especially if the whole notion of a purpose statement is new to you. Have no fear—this is meant to be a useful tool in our shared adventure of "bridge building" in these bizarre times.

And these are bizarre times.

You will find the right timing to address your particular challenges and weak suits. I am not suggesting that anyone take on all of the practices and exercises in this book or the workbook at one time. Indeed one of the core lessons for us as we seek to transition to a new way of being, is to discontinue that oh-so-familiar habit of overriding and taking on too much in life. I am suggesting that you take on the basic exercises and self assessments in *The Impossible Conversation*, and consider beginning your first practice or two in the next couple of weeks. Be kind to yourself and honor your authentic timing for each step of this daunting journey.

There are many resources available in this alliance of authors, coaches, therapists and thought leaders that are co-creating the body of work that supports *The Impossible Conversation.*

We all are painfully aware that facing our shared challenges and predicaments will not be easy. We are also aware that, while there are certain pieces of this work that can only be done alone, the majority of these practices are best done in the company of others, kindred spirits. We are committed to offering the most potent and valuable workshops, webinars, coaching and resources for embodied learning and transformation.

We all send our warmest blessings to any folks who are newly stepping onto this bridge. It is our hope that we all find, "our people" —kindred spirits with whom we can bravely co-create and reconnect.

*　　*　　*

EMBODIMENT

To reconnect with deeper self is first and foremost a reconnection with our body.

"Let the soft animal of your body love what it loves."

Mary Oliver from *Wild Geese*

No attempt at reconnection with our inborn sensitivities and wisdom can be done without a deepening of our understanding experience of our bodies, and the cost to those bodies, of living a life of override.

Here the costs run easily as high as the costs have been for our overriding the warning signs of Earth. This is an immense topic, the many impacts that overriding has inflicted upon our bodies, psyches and souls can and do fill hundreds of books beyond this.

Given the minimal amount of space here, let me just breeze over a few aspects of our human corporal arrangement that can easily be explored with a couple of hours and a web browser.

By now we all know that a moderate amount of exercise is a very good thing for almost everybody. Most folks don't exercise enough to maintain good body tone and function.

Mostly we work too much and don't have the energy or will to keep ourselves fit.

Most of us know that a basic meditation or mindfulness practice is one of the easiest and least expensive practices we can include in our daily lives. Again, precious few of us actually maintain this type of practice.

Along with that contemplative practice I can strongly recommend a breathing practice. This can often be found with yet another practice that is universally available and valuable—yoga.

So, ok, we know all of that. How is it that we all continue to do way too much of what we know we shouldn't do, and not nearly enough of what would serve us so well?

When we want to get to a more core or root level of awareness with our body, we must go beneath those more surface practices and habits. We must peel back the lifetime of layers of override that have oriented us to food and activity that numb us to the brilliant truth and wisdom innate in our bodies. We have all been suckered into shaming and overriding the subtle insights, sensations and impressions that come from within. We've all been well trained to override our natural rhythm and pace in life. We have learned to numb and distract ourselves with any number of substances: food, sugar, alcohol, drugs and activities: sex, work, , exercise, video games, and states of being: lethargy, judgment, mood. (add more addictions and distractions here)

This subtle inner truth of the "soft animal of your body" can only be heard when we quiet the chorus of addictive inner voices that squeal for the next fix of an addictive input.

For a remarkable dive right to this core or root level of our relationships with our bodies, I recommend starting with a life-changing essay from Philip Shepherd.[3] In Shepherd's *Embodiment Manifesto* we find a remarkably clear and detailed layout of an inner terrain most of us avoid with a vengeance. Shepherd articulates masterfully how our relationships with our bodies are direct reflections of how we, humanity, are relating with life on Earth. Here, in the opening lines, Shepherd uses familiar words and phrases to describe our multi-dimensional predicament.

> "I believe that humanity can survive the crises that are mounting around us—but that our ability to make it will depend on us forging a new kind of clarity.

Specifically, we need to shed light on the story we tell ourselves about what it means to be human. It's a story almost too familiar to question, yet it provokes fantasies of limitless growth and power, and puts us on a collision course with the realities of our world.

I believe this story is the single greatest danger to our survival.

I also believe that the single most dangerous effect of this story is the way it estranges us from our own bodies, and makes that feel normal.

It is clear to most people that the way we are living is not sustainable. It is clear in the damage we are inflicting on the ecosystem that sustains us; in the cataclysmic rate of species extinction; in the pressures of a growing human population on the earth's finite resources; and even in the stress we carry in our bodies day in, day out. We try to lessen our impact by changing our behavior, and such changes are important—but their effect is dwarfed by the sheer scale and momentum of what we face. Our instinct to seek more control over our situation is the familiar reflex that created it in the first place.

The real challenge we face is to surrender our agendas of control, and turn our hearts instead to the task of coming into harmony with our world.

Control and harmony are not different degrees of the same impulse— they are opposites.

If we are to come into harmony with the world, we need more than adjustments to our way of living— we need a revolution in our understanding of ourselves. To make matters even more challenging, the revolution that is needed sits firmly in our culture's blind spot. This has always been the nature of revolutions. In our case, that blind spot involves our relationship with our bodies."

As you will recall, I am asserting that our blind spots are equally distributed among the core relationships we have long separated from our deeper selves, others and Earth.

Shepherd offers up his take on one of the great mistakes of our now familiar way of relating with our bodies. His strong research and experience agrees with a number of ancient traditions that propose that the center of the body is found in our lower abdomen. This is a profound disruption to our cultural notion that the center of our experience is our head.

> Today it is similarly understood that the head is the center of the psyche, and that every aspect of the self— our thoughts, our emotions, our desires and senses—is set in orbit by what lies within our cranium. In this case, though, *our knowledge supports our flawed experience:* that is, we learn from our culture that the head is our center, and that knowledge orients our entire experience. This socially-ingrained, head-centric way of being, which we take for granted, is a desperate anomaly. It is at odds with a host of ancient cultures that experience the center of their thinking in the belly— Chinese, Mayan, Incan and Japanese, to name a few; it discounts facts of our own physiology— that we have an independent, second brain in the belly, for instance, that perceives, thinks, acts and remembers without any input from the cranial brain; and it turns a blind eye to history and the roots of language, which show that eight thousand years ago, Europeans too experienced their center in the belly, and that it took millennia for that center to migrate up through the body to where it resides today.

> Living in the head and experiencing all our thinking there distorts and impoverishes our sense of being and belonging, because when thinking cuts itself off from the body, it cuts its lifeline to reality. The body holds the deepest currents of our being, and is our bridge to the life of the world around us— the being of the world. By separating the center of our thinking from all that, we enter a kind of alienation that makes us feel like spectators on the events that surround us.

This is an uncanny description of the experiences I was having as I researched the question, "How can we be sitting quietly by as we are warned of human-caused, extinction-level impacts? How can we remain silent as we are bombarded with the message that denial of science is a valid and worthy debate?" We all seem to be content to watch whatever moves across the screen, with no actual embodied experience of the subject—just watching.

> Furthermore, we start managing from on high what we cannot experience, because head-centric thinking is keen to create structures of control, systemization, judgment and acquisition. But being out of touch and off balance ourselves, we can only seed more imbalance with every willful, managerial impulse— even when our impulses spring from an agenda that seeks to improve things.

> "The desire to behave ethically, if coming from a place of disconnected reason, will necessarily focus on fixing how our behavior affects the material world; because disconnected reason tacitly expresses a **contempt** for the body, it will overlook the problem of how our relationship with the body affects our behavior. This is our blind spot— and it is a towering liability, because *our relationship with the world can only mirror and express the relationship we have with our own bodies."*

Time and again I have found myself whispering two words to myself—contempt and violence. As I would come across another article blatantly stating the wonton destruction of some precious aspect of life on Earth—say the Great Barrier Reef, for instance—I would find myself mumbling the words, contempt and violence.

I strongly recommend reading Shepherd's *Embodiment Manifesto* in its entirety. I am amazed at how he expands the interconnected web of life from the innermost reaches of our bodies out to their global analogues in humanity at large.

Like Pope Frances, Joanna Macy and Naomi Klein, Shepherd helps us to expand our view of whole systems and the interbeing of systems at every level of this Earthly life. I am particularly struck by his way of articulating our need for a truly revolutionary change in how we see and experience this world and which essential influences we might engage to replace our fixation on the head as body center and world center.

> What is asked of us is a revolution as radical as the one that brought to light the true center of the solar system. We need a revolution that will challenge the rule of the head and bring us home to the hub of our being— a hub that lies deep in the pelvic bowl, and is associated with both our second brain and the

209

female aspect of our consciousness. We need a revolution that is
at once deeply personal, and as boldly political in its implications
as were the insights of Copernicus. And just as Copernicus
helped to disclose the harmony of the heavenly bodies, the
emerging revolution will disclose the true harmony of our life on
this heavenly body we call earth.

I applaud Philip Shepherd for his exquisite articulation of this reflection of our
relationships with our bodies, in our relationships with other humans and with
Earth. This is as clear as can be stated—the interbeing, the interrelatedness of all
life at every level and how vitally important it is to reconnect ourselves with our
deeper selves (starting with our bodies) with other human beings and with our
miraculous home, Earth.

Please visit Philip Shepherd's website[3] to read the full text of his *Embodiment
Manifesto* and to find information about his recent book, *New Self New World*,
and his workshop schedule.

*   *   *

WHERE OUR SHADOW REALLY RUNS THE SHOW:

WHAT WE EAT.

There is no more dangerous minefield to cross than to talk with people about
what they eat. I've had far more heated conversations with people about food
choices and preferences than I have about their religion or their opinions about
climate change!

People like what they like regarding their diet and they don't like what they don't
like. And they really, really don't like to be told what they can or cannot eat or
should or should not eat. This is really a core issue for folks, especially in the
privileged, developed world where the average diet is more rich and bountiful than
even that of royalty of past ages.

The next exemplars of leadership, in a portion of *The Impossible Conversation*, is
one that blindsided me. I did not see this coming. Here I was researching

greenhouse gas emissions and species extinction and out of nowhere comes a documentary that changed me.

This film hit me right square in my daily choices—right in the middle of how I spend my money shopping and what foods I choose to consume at every meal. It even brought issues of corporate domination and even assassination to my consciousness, where before I could sit back in blissful, willful, ignorance and just not think about the impacts of my food choices.

This source appeared in the middle of my Informed Inquiry research and proceeded to blow away an already staggering set of indicators about Earth's existential, Anthropogenic challenges. This source is a well-done, simple documentary made by a couple of guys from the San Francisco Bay Area.

I have been involved in video and film production for upwards of twenty years. I have always loved documentaries. I have long desired to find just the right topic to focus on and to make my own doc. And, I've always known that the best documentaries show us a part of the human story that no one knows about—the ultimate hook.

This documentary has that ultimate hook. The filmmakers focus our attention on something that is right under our collective nose. They discovered an aspect of our world so common place, so universal (especially in developed countries) as to be invisible as an issue. This invisible issue turns out to be a far larger source of CO2 than any other human-caused source— far more than the CO2 emissions of every type of transportation we use on the planet—by almost three times. The UN's Food and Agriculture Organization estimates that this source emits 44 percent of the globe's human-caused methane. It accounts for more than one-third of all the planet's fresh water consumption. It is the cause of 90% of Amazon forest destruction. It is the leading cause of species extinction and habitat destruction globally and the leading cause of ocean dead zones.

Many people have been distressed by the industrial and agricultural use of water in these times of critical drought (2015), e.g. California, Oregon, Washington to name a few drought stricken agricultural centers.

Who hasn't at least heard of the public outcry of water-thirsty residents of California cities as they complain about their water rationing while California almond growers keep raking in the big bucks producing almonds that require a gallon to produce each almond? That adds up to approximately eleven gallons of water to produce an ounce of almonds.

The agricultural item that is the subject of this documentary is often served in four ounce servings. It is estimated that it takes 660 gallons of water to produce that four ounce serving. Remember, the almonds that have folks so up in arms take 44 gallons of water to produce a four ounce serving. Well, the subject of this documentary just flat out dominates the water use conversation.

Or, it would if anybody was talking about it.

So what is this mystery food source?

Animal agriculture—of course led by beef and pork and including poultry and fish.

So, then, a four ounce hamburger patty takes an estimated 660 gallons of water to produce!

The documentary is called, *Cowspiracy.*[4] I truly love-hate this documentary. These guys, Kip Andersen and Keegan Kuhn, have found what appears to be the single largest contributor to Anthropogenic Climate Disruption, habitat destruction and water use.

After picking up my jaw off the ground, I started to explore how deeply I am entwined in consuming animal agriculture products in almost every meal I eat. And I am now on a very intentional phase-out and phase-down program for every meat and dairy product in my diet.

Rest assured, dear reader, I am not here to pass judgment on you regarding your choices, dietary or otherwise. My only commitment here is to offer you information, data and projections that impacted me greatly and helped me to complete my Informed Inquiry into this topic. While I freely share with you my own choices as inspired by *Cowspiracy* and related sources, I imply no judgment toward other people and the choices they make.

I am, however, going to make full use of this opportunity to point out how our dietary choices are remarkably strong indicators of our conscious and unconscious motivators and how much Shadow is expressed, on the individual, corporate and cultural level, as we hold tightly to our food preferences.

*   *   *

I had whined for so long that I wanted some way to make a difference in the face of our daunting circumstances. Well, here, in my lap, were easily the most powerful and impactful choices I could make in that direction.

Here was my first introduction to the difficulty of confronting my own complicity with our global, self-destructive and ecocidal Human Operating System. This one wasn't conceptual. It wasn't indirect or obscure— like the slave wages and conditions behind my favorite smart phone, pair of jeans or cheap, big-box trinket… this is right there, going into my mouth at every meal.

Why I love/hate this film is that it leaves me with a very clear choice— a choice, of course, that I would much rather not have to make— or even be aware of. Yes, the choice is whether or not to continue to eat meat and dairy products in the same amounts as I have for my lifetime, or continue to eat them at all.

Lastly, with *Cowspiracy* I have another vivid, visual and emotional exposé and mapping of many of the layers of inter-connectedness to be experienced in the world— a brilliant detailing of the overlapping Earth and human systems we rely on but stay willfully ignorant of— in order to reap the many rewards, without accounting for the real costs and real impacts of our choices.

I am particularly impressed by the producers' commitment to expose the Shadow aspects of our global animal agriculture industry and the global environmental activist organizations that are so renowned for their efforts to save particular species or particular aspects of our environment.

An inspired bridge builder could deepen their knowledge base about the Shadow side of our business-as-usual culture, by watching *Cowspiracy* and the aforementioned, *The Merchants of Doubt*. Both of these films are profound examples of speaking truth to power. Both expose aspects of our individual and collective Shadows. Both clearly detail the immense influence that is wielded by the moneyed, power interests of the world and the cynical results of their influence on virtually every aspect of our lives.

Cowspiracy is available to view on Netflix and available, along with mountains of supporting data and activist support materials, on their *Cowspiracy* website.[4]

With all this new data and information, I am able to make far more potent choices about where and how to put my attention. Equally important, I am able to make more powerful choices about my actions and behaviors. Seems to me that that is the challenge for all of us from this day forward—to make the best choices possible from a foundation of the best information we can gather.

Sometimes the gathering of that important information takes the form of an Informed Inquiry. And, as you might join me in concluding, any Informed Inquiry that is intended to inspire change must result in the integration of personal practices that promote: reconnection with Self, Others and Earth.

*   *   *

Self Assessment.

The powerful impacts of our daily choices and our Shadow's control over those choices.

Please take some time to journal about what you have read in this chapter.

Are there pieces of this chapter that inspired you to think, feel, see or act differently?

If not, what do you notice about your inner thoughts and feelings about the subjects we've covered here?

Are you aware of any topics here that prompt you to dig in and say, 'NO!'?

Would you consider making any changes to your diet?

Please note your reactions to the *Cowspiracy* detailing of habitat destruction, assassination of activists, Ag-Gag laws here in the USA, greenhouse gas production— all from animal agriculture. These issues will only grow in importance as we continue to add to the population of the planet and billions more humans desire more meat in their diets.

What amount of data would you need in order to make changes in your own diet to reflect healthier, personal lifestyle choices and/or global food production choices?

Are you present to the amount of privilege involved in our dietary and other lifestyle choices? Please start another page in your Impossible Conversation journal or workbook and start a list of examples of how the privilege of your economic status, race, nationality, class, gender (and others) affects your life and lifestyle choices.

*   *   *

JOY AT THE ROOT OF IT ALL.

In earlier chapters we have examined some of the cynical underbelly of the US and of the business-as-usual paradigm at large. We got to see just how long various governmental and corporate leaders have known about the Sober Data— and how far they have gone to suppress that knowledge from the public and create an atmosphere of doubt about vetted science.

We also can easily listen to the news today to find out just how far our culture, our government, our corporate leaders and even ourselves, have gone to seal our fate with regard to worst case scenarios in so many different prickly problems and predicaments that we face. These updates would have all the qualities needed for a tragic comedy, if it weren't for the fact that our very existence is at stake...

I want to mention the work of two very dear allies and friends in this remarkable, Impossible Conversation. The two allies are Carolyn Baker and Andrew Harvey.

Carolyn Baker, whom we've met before, particularly addressing issues of Shadow, is perhaps the most prolific and powerful author addressing the question, "Who will we be together in the face of our global predicament?" I know of no other person who has so artfully articulated the human challenges entailed in facing our daunting future. After years as a therapist, college professor and author, Carolyn shifted her attention and intent toward supporting others in our collapsing world. She has become a speaker, thought leader and life coach. Carolyn has also been hosting a podcast on this topic for years now, "The New Lifeboat Hour." As if that weren't enough, Carolyn Baker leads juicy and heartful grief rituals in the style of West African scholar, Malidoma Somé, and is currently offering workshops and life coaching to audiences, live and online, with yours truly.

Andrew Harvey is himself a scholar of great renown. Harvey was a child prodigy regarding the deep study of the world's religious and spiritual traditions. He is an expert in the translation and transmission of the beauty and mystery that is the work of the Persian poet, Rumi. Please do not pass up an opportunity to experience Andrew Harvey's immense passion and mastery of the world's mystical traditions.

Together Baker and Harvey are both powerful and mischievous. When they write together they bring that power and mischievous energy to focus on topics that fit right into the Impossible Conversation. They have a knack for articulating the content, context and experiential exercises that a sincere bridge builder needs to face the daunting Shadows and stressors of this path.

In their most recent book, *Return to Joy*[5], Carolyn and Andrew offer a clear and concise layout of the terrain that awaits the aspiring bridge builder. They both are intimately aware of the Sober Data. They both know that, while no one knows exactly when we will pass the immense and devastating tipping points in our Earth and human systems, we are rapidly approaching those points, and have clearly already passed numerous other critical thresholds.

But, like all the exemplars in this Conversation, they are also well versed in how to create a life that has perpetual access to grace and beauty no matter what the circumstances. They each draw on a different body of study and expertise to assemble their inner tool kit as they look into our shared future. Carolyn pulls from her long experience in the psychological, emotional and relationship realms. Andrew draws upon his immense body of knowledge about the spiritual mystics, saints and icons who have similarly had to face the impossible— and somehow flourished.

I mention Harvey and Baker here because in this short, sweet book they fiercely coach the reader to establish a robust set of life practices that will sustain the person through all of the purifying fire that life will throw at us. They also make abundantly clear that the joy they refer to is not the narcissistic, spiritual distraction and bypass that is plastered on every self-help website. The joy that Andrew and Carolyn refer to is the joy of hearts intentionally broken open, time and again, as we walk head long into our shared predicament.

The only way to experience this joy, or to use the term that fits for me, this grace, we must take on sincere and potent practices that are aimed at reconnecting us with the primary sources of aliveness and meaning—reconnection with our deeper selves, with others and with Earth.

If we intend to stay awake and engage with life in this ultimately challenging time, we must be aware of the Sober Data. We must be engaged in life practices of reconnection with our sources of aliveness and grace. And lastly, we must become knowledgeable of the dimensions of ourselves and our culture that constitute the largest obstacles to sustainable human life on Earth.

Harvey and Baker have their own unique ways of articulating the process one must engage in to contact their core joy. They invite us to do the hard work of leaning into our weak suits and Shadows in life in order to access the precious birthright of core joy that lies within. They also shake us loose from the delusion from the "happiness" that our culture seeks breathlessly at every turn. Core joy is a deep and steady state that is not altered by circumstance or addictive whim. Core joy is, as they point out here, the ultimate nature of reality.

> "Joy is the ultimate nature of reality. Happiness is circumstantial; it is a state that as everyone knows, comes and goes. The joy of which we speak is not conditioned by shifts of fate or the play of emotions. Knowing this makes clear to everyone that the true task of life is to uncover this primordial joy in oneself and then live from its peace, energy, radiant purpose, and embodied passion."

*   *   *

It has been quite a while since I last invited us to take a collective, long and grounding, breath. Hopefully you have been slowing down and breathing as needed as you have progressed through *The Impossible Conversation.* I am very clear that the subject matter of this book is, by its nature, extremely disturbing and disrupting at the very core of how we see and experience our lives.

For some, the data, projections and conclusions are just validations of their own projections, conclusions and intuitions about the state of our world. For others, this material may be nothing short of devastating to the core, defining stories that make up our culture and much of the history of humanity on Earth.

I again wish to slow us down as we consider this *Impossible Conversation* and the Sober Data contained within. I ask that we all take some time to let the implications of these projections sink in.

Starting at the most conservative point on the Sober Data timeline, let's recall some of the apparent fallout of humanity staying on a business-as-usual track.

Please recall that the IPCC (the ultra conservative scientific body that establishes the metrics and the language we use to set policy regarding all things "climate.") has stated that if we stay on a business-as-usual track, we are projected to reach 3°C to 5°C by 2100.

Now, recall back in chapter two when the World Bank and others described a 4°C world as "catastrophic" and "to be avoided at all cost." Now, recall just how much substantive action you are aware of that is actually reducing our business-as-usual emissions. There is not much substantive action going on. As we look ahead to the most conservative projections it is likely that we see the collapse of many Earth and human systems and indeed, the collapse of our defining stories.

I recommend we use this time to do some deep contemplation and, hopefully, some journaling in preparation for the drafting of a new core, defining story. This will be a story, first and foremost, of how each of us, and our families, will expand our capacities and skills at being present in the face of world-scale stressors and predicaments.

Please, dear reader, take some time to contemplate, how you will let the Sober Data of our shared world affect you. How will you let yourself be changed? How will you build your inner tool kit to prepare for dramatic changes in our world? How will you retool your sense of purpose or vision or mission in life, given the implications of continuing on our business-as-usual track?

For now, we are about to step into perhaps the greatest challenge in this triad of reconnection chapters. Next we will be addressing reconnecting with others.

Fasten your seat belts, this final chapter may well be a bumpy ride.

* * *

10   Reconnecting With Others

At the time of the writing of The Impossible Conversation, early 2017, Oxfam reports that the eight wealthiest people on Earth have the same amount of wealth as the bottom 50% of humanity.

> "The technology we need most badly is the technology of community – the knowledge about how to cooperate to get things done. Our sense of community is in disrepair."
>
> Bill McKibben

> People don't talk to each other. You're alone with your television set or internet. But you can't have a functioning democracy without what sociologists call, "secondary organizations," places where people can get together, plan, talk, and develop ideas.
>
> You don't do it alone.
>
> Noam Chomsky

As we arrive here in the last of three Reconnection chapters, we land in what I judge to be ground zero of humanity's predicament.

In chapter nine, we explored the costs of our disconnection from our inner wisdom and sensibilities and proposed some primary steps to reconnect with our own sense of agency and purpose, unleashed from the business-as-usual paradigm we call home.

In chapter eight, our focus was our relatedness with Earth. Again, we reviewed the costs of our disconnection from our ultimate Mother. Those costs were easy to remember as we had detailed so many in the first few chapters, particularly chapter three regarding species extinction and habitat degradation.

Each of these Reconnection chapters is intended to articulate the costs of our essential disconnection from the primary sources of meaning in human life. Each is, indeed, essential.

I am calling this chapter, Reconnecting with Others, ground zero for our predicament, because it appears to me that our disconnection from other people is both the locus of our darkest Shadows, and the aspect of human life that holds the most possibility for positive change, healing and transformation—no matter how dire our predicament may be.

Please don't get me wrong. I still hold strong to the notions that we must reconnect with Earth and the web of life. Without this, we will have no option but to build craftier and craftier on-ramps back onto the business-as-usual superhighway. Only letting our hearts break open, time and again, expressing our love and grief for our collapsing home, will reduce our immense, ecocidal hubris. We must find our way back to an interbeing within the web of life so fully experienced by every other species on the planet.

And, yes, we also must follow a path like the one described by Philip Shepherd—a path that reconnects each of us with the powerful, miraculous, animal, magical, wise, wild presence that is within each of us, within our own bodies.

And, here we are in the center of the most vexing, challenging, possibility-filled, scream-at-the-top-of-your-lungs, frustration aspect of our human operating system. This is how we communicate with one another, how we speak, listen, belittle, condescend, honor, cherish, teach, insult one another.

This aspect of being human beings is subject to the same fatal flaws that we have explored in chapters eight and nine—Earth and self. We have caused great harm in our over use of override with each other. In our global love affair with weapons and war, we have normalized the anonymous, sanitized killing of people around the globe. We have normalized a conversation that allows for a toggling off and on of our belief in science, fairness, ethics, treaties and agreements. We have normalized an economic system that takes no account of Earth life, other than how much profit can be extracted and how much destruction can be "externalized."

*   *   *

Self Assessment: Reconnecting With Other Human Beings.

Set aside a few empty journal pages for the creation of another living document. This one will be a list, similar to the list of Loves in Life, that we started in the Introduction.

Give yourself plenty of room to articulate:

"How has humanity at-large disconnected from other people?"

"What have been the costs of that disconnection?"

"How have I disconnected from other people?"

"What have been the costs of my disconnection?"

A couple of sample responses to prime the pump of your exploration: I have written pages about the obvious and deep rifts between peoples of different races, nations, classes, to name just a few. One particularly bold example from my years of living near the US / Mexican border, the creation of the "Free Trade Agreement" NAFTA, created manufacturing plants just over the border in Mexico, two of the effects of NAFTA that appear to show our complete disregard for the people most affected by this policy, One, the complete destruction of small scale Mexican farming and Two, the lack of regulation for wage and benefits and working conditions for the Mexican factory workers, leaving them with jobs that pay consistently below a "living wage" level. Readers who are interested in this topic could also follow this thread to its impact on the massive growth of the drug trade in the same areas, over the same years of NAFTA existence.

A huge number of similar examples can be found in Naomi Klein's, *This Changes Everything*.

Two more of our fatal flaws are even more pungent in this chapter than in the last two: Contempt and Violence. Here we will see the pinnacle of our expression of toxic projection, Shadow, Contempt and Violence. We will also be reminded of the deep love and stand for life, that can be called on in the human experience. This chapter is chock full of this immense paradox of the deep beauty of human love, living right beside our utter contempt for life itself.

One last time, let me explain why I keep mentioning contempt and violence. We are living in a time like no other in history. It is a time of great polarization of people on Earth. While it is more complicated than this, it serves to summarize our situation in terms of Naomi Klein's book title: *This Changes Everything: Capitalism vs the Climate.* How we include violence and contempt here is by understanding that our human experience is not occurring on a level playing field upon which all the players have an equal opportunity to win, if they play by the rules and play fair and play harder than those on the opposing team.

We are a world beset by, and run by, our own Shadows. To think that changing our light bulbs and buying electric cars is going to "save the planet", is flat-out crazy.

In this chapter about reconnecting with other people we will explore some of the sweeter practices, of reaching out to sincerely connect with both the people in our own families and neighborhoods and people who are not like us. These simple practices will be at the core of any sincere effort to create a more functional, sustainable, new world on the other side of our metaphorical bridge.

But also in this chapter is some rough truth telling about, Capitalism vs the Climate. The important term here is, vs. Versus. A bout, a duel, a fight, a war, versus means one party against another. And this is not a light-weight little backyard play game with squirt guns and curse words. This is as savage and serious a battle as humanity has ever known.

Those who choose to stand tall and proud for life on Earth, pick up picket signs and dive into the political arena, will be facing off with the largest, most aligned, best funded, wall of status-quo, business-as-usual, that has ever presided over life on Earth. I am asserting that the predominant tone of that aligned wall of status quo is one saturated with contempt and backed with a constant threat of violence.

When we combine that massive wall of business-as-usual with our cultural tendency to settle into the cozy familiarity of how our human operating system works, we end up with the very annoyance and apathy that we explored in the first few chapters. We don't want to hear about all of this stuff, and more importantly, none of us wants to be "that guy" who brings up the difficult topics of conversation.

It is here I'd like to offer the notion that we actually *are* our conversations. So if you and I are average Americans, seventy-plus percent of us never talk with friends or family…or anyone for that matter… about any of the Sober Data that is discussed here in *The Impossible Conversation.* So, if more than seven in ten of us never talk about these important topics, much less engage in any sort of political action, is there any question why most of us are completely resigned about the state of our world and particularly the state of our political system?

A brief recap: In order to participate in this business-as-usual system we all made a silent agreement to disconnect from our inner wisdom, from others and from Earth. That disconnection created in each of us a massive blind spot regarding the miraculous world within and around us. That disconnection has left us disempowered, with a sense of no personal agency in life. When we then turn to face the massive, business-as-usual wall – we are loathe to speak up or speak truth to power. We end up with that default definition of hope from earlier chapters: "I hope the experts hurry up and find the answers to all of these pesky problems, so we can get back to business-as-usual." …And, we, quite intentionally, have no conversations of any significance with anyone else.

Here, having named our situation, we can start to look with a bit more depth at how our individual and collective Shadows affect our lives in ways we may never have imagined. It is here we can start to reclaim an empowered definition of hope.

> "Active Hope is not wishful thinking.
> Active Hope is not waiting to be rescued . . .
> by some savior.
>
> Active Hope is waking up to the beauty of life
> on whose behalf we can act.
>
> We belong to this world.
> The web of life is calling us forth at this time.
> We've come a long way and are here to play our part.
>
> With Active Hope we realize that there are adventures in store,
> strengths to discover, and comrades to link arms with.
>
> Active Hope is a readiness to discover the strengths
> in ourselves and in others;
> a readiness to discover the reasons for hope
> and the occasions for love.
>
> A readiness to discover the size and strength of our hearts,
> our quickness of mind, our steadiness of purpose,

our own authority, our love for life,
the liveliness of our curiosity,
the unsuspected deep well of patience and diligence,
the keenness of our senses, and our capacity to lead.

None of these can be discovered in an armchair or without risk.

Joanna Macy

*　　*　　*

Let's start with the simplest level of communication. First within ourselves individually, then out to our conversations and relationships with loved ones, co-workers, neighbors, and beyond.

If you have done a few of the basic exercises offered in this book, you will have plenty to work with here. This brief exploration can also be done with no preparation. You may find it useful to have some writing materials with you to keep track of your work. Those of you who have been using a journal or *The Impossible Conversation Workbook*, know what to do.

I will be offering you some of my responses to the questions here, to give you some idea of how the responses can fit together and clarify the internal elements you use as the foundation for your most important conversations.

First, recall your self-assessment regarding the Sober Data of chapters one through three. Recall what symptoms of Abrupt Climate Change, species extinction and habitat destruction really struck you, what concerned you, what got your attention.

Next, recall the most conservative scientific body on the planet—the group of climate scientists that give us the language and metrics we all use to even speak about climate issues—the IPCC. The IPCC offers us a business-as-usual estimate for their favorite year for projections—2100—of global temperatures 3°C to 6°C above pre-industrial temperature levels.

Now, if you've already done this exercise, you have positioned yourself somewhere on a timeline between now and 2100. You have already read the Sober Data offered in the first few chapters and combined that with your own conclusions and estimates. After my year of interviewing experts, intensive study and research, I have estimated that we will see the dreaded 4°C and above within a range of time between 2026 and 2050.

As I detailed in chapter two, life on Earth at 4°C is nothing short of a horror show. So, this is the time to notice your own timeline of estimated climate impacts. Perhaps you have chosen to align with the most conservative view of 3°C to 6°C by 2100, perhaps you have landed somewhere closer to my conclusions. Good, now that part of the exercise is done.

With *your* Sober Data, take a moment to see, to imagine the effects on Earth and humanity brought on by these Abrupt Climate Change events. Allow yourself to imagine what life will be like on Earth, perhaps you can imagine someone who is now quite young… and what their adulthood has in store for them. Invite your own internal waves of emotion or reaction to these projected events. Let your heart break open.

This pause, this invitation for us to feel the waves of healthy, human emotion, is something very rare, even threatening, in our business-as-usual culture.

The mental calculations part of this exercise is also rarely overtly or consciously done in public conversations. Strange that we so rarely take the time to make this kind of estimate. Yet, I assert that we all are making some kind of rough estimate in our heads.

In one of my first jobs in transformational training, we had a great bit of jargon for this unconscious estimating—we called it, "making shit up."

It is in this largely unconscious realm of piecing together select factoids, opinions and stuff we've heard on our favorite social media or news sources, that the entire conversation about climate denial occurs. We all are shaped, to a ridiculous degree, by the custom designed echo chamber we have crafted around ourselves.

Add to that our deepest need and fear— our need to belong. We all have a deeply rooted need to be accepted by our group, our family, our tribe, our class, our political party, etc.

As we have all seen, in the past couple of years in particular, we are so committed to staying aligned with our tribe or group, we will sacrifice virtually anything to stay in the good graces of that group. One significant example that has become far more visible in just the past year is our collective acceptance of the notion of Alternative Facts. We should also mention the media version of Alternative Facts—Fake News.

In the past thirty or so years, we have seen our public and political discourse decline from a challenging but functional system of maintaining our democracy, to a deeply polarized populace being essentially herded into a small number of warring opinion silos.

It is within this now twisted atmosphere of lies, alternative facts, propaganda, fake news and corporate and government double-speak, that we all are trying to live our lives and make good decisions about our own and our families' futures.

My assertion here is: without taking on sincere practices at reconnection and utilization of vetted Sober Data, as described in these pages, even the most outraged activist doesn't stand a chance against the massive tsunami that is our cynical, corporatized paradigm.

> Continuing to do pioneering sacred work in a world as crazy and painful as ours, without constantly grounding yourself in sacred practice, would be like running into a forest fire dressed only in a paper tutu.

> Andrew Harvey, *The Hope*

It is very important to mention one other thing about our choices once we have discerned for ourselves "the state of our world", via the Sober Data. Even though I tend to mention activism, political action and heightened community engagement quite a bit in the examples here, I have no agenda or attachment whatsoever regarding what any awakened person does with their "one precious life." Yes, the majority of people that I've encountered in this process, do find some "love" in their life that calls out for action of some kind. But this is by no means the end of the choices, nor is this the "right" choice to make.

Indeed, as we face our shared predicaments, there is no more personal or essential a question to ask ourselves, "What shall I do with my one precious life?"

What may not be intuitive here is that there is as much need for the grounding and deepening practices mentioned so often here whether you dive into sacred activism or you choose to spend the rest of your life perfecting your watercolor painting or teaching children about gardening. This process of awakening requires the firm foundation of physical, psychological and spiritual practices.

What appears to matter most to people awake and aware of having a foot in each of two worlds… is that they adopt a set of practices that is founded in their core reconnection with the web of life. This is the only realm of which I am aware in which we can access the core joy, the strength, the grace we will need to face our predicaments.

I have seen one particular "choice" being made by the vast majority of folks engaged in the Impossible Conversation. This choice is an orientation toward service. It appears that one of the side benefits of intentionally breaking open our hearts, is an innate desire to be of service in some way, to our loved ones, our community or even to Earth herself.

So, the practices I am suggesting are very few in number. In fact, here, I will offer only two, following my assumption that you are engaged sincerely with the practices of reconnection with self and Earth.

The first is, start to have more heartfelt conversations.

This starts with polishing up your new articulation of purpose, mission and vision. Review your list of loves in life and hold close your current favorite cause; mine is a small handful of Sober Data points about the decline of the world's oceans. Armed with these powerful gems of the heart, start to have conversations about what concerns you in the world. Start to share about the things in life you love and the grief you carry about the state of those things and about the world at large. Combine this sharing with a sincere curiosity about the life and loves of the person with whom you are speaking.

Notice I'm not suggesting that you rush to your Sober Data Timeline conclusions. What I can tell you is that the whole conversation about CO_2 emissions and any attempts to mitigate them, are like a slab of fresh meat on the sidewalk on a sunny day. For the metaphorically hyper-carnivorous climate deniers, your conclusions will be seen as tasty morsels to be shredded in an exhausting feeding frenzy, which will yield absolutely no positive results for you and will benefit the denier by wearing down another opponent.

For almost everyone else (other than your own personal "choir"), those conclusions will very quickly turn them off.

What I'm suggesting is to refine your ability to share your heart, your ability to share what is important to you. Add to that your increased ability to generate sincere curiosity about the concerns and values of others and you soon have the beginning of a real conversation.

> People fail to get along because they fear each other; they fear each
> other because they don't know each other; they don't know each
> other because they have not communicated with each other.

Martin Luther King Jr.

The second practice I am suggesting is to establish a set of efficient, vetted sources for information about those subjects you love and about the most significant issues occurring in our world. This includes establishing a filtering system to keep the flow of information well below your tolerance level.

I am suggesting this practice because we are in a Post-Truth world and a world in which massive campaigns of business as usual: sales, political manipulation and propaganda are constantly at play. Ours is not a world of common sense or civil discourse. We live in a world in which facts are entirely disregarded if not disdained. We are constantly bombarded with corporate and governmental communications that are both cynical and deeply jaded in the direction of sustaining the status quo and contempt for any suggestion of alternatives.

To stay informed in these times takes a refined focus on only vetted sources and a trained nose for following the money to determine the motives for mainstream news and information.

Again, my examples for this practice. I have a half dozen or so news and research aggregators, all set to retrieve topics related to *The Impossible Conversation*. I rarely have all six engaged at any one time. Usually I am limiting my consumption of this challenging material to a maximum of three to four hours per week.

While I do have weeks when I have to dive in more deeply and for longer stretches of time, I make a concerted effort to disengage from these select sources. I have been pretty successful at avoiding contact with mainstream news sources for two years now. If you haven't guessed by now, I am asserting that the entirety of the mainstream press is saturated in and committed to the maintenance of the business-as-usual paradigm.

I included a few suggestions of quality sources for Sober Data in earlier chapters. I will always include an updated list of sources, authors and aggregators for vetted Sober Data, on *The Impossible Conversation* website. Bottom line on this notion of staying current about the issues that matter to you: find your limit to the quantity of Sober Data that you consume and stay beneath that level. This, hopefully, will include taking the occasional break from news of all kinds. While there have always been many important issues to track in our human operating system and on Earth, these times and these problems and predicaments produce enough stressors to crush even the sturdiest sacred activist. Take frequent breaks.

In nearly every chapter, I have included numerous references for further information, validation or study about a particular Sober Data point. I have included these references at the end of this book. If you are wanting more sources for a particular subject of Sober Data or recommendations for quality journalism or vetted data sources, you can find more on our websites:
www.LivingResilience.Earth

www.ImpossibleConversation.net

or by signing up for Carolyn Baker's Daily News Digest at, www.CarolynBaker.net.

Lastly, about this notion of doing, Informed Inquiries about the subjects that are significant to you. Again, there are resources to assist you in formulating those inquiries, on the Impossible Conversation page of our Living Resilience website. What I must caution you about, is the red-hot temptation for most of us, to use this Informed Inquiry to further validate or confirm your already rigidified opinions about a particular topic. This is the way of the world these days.

To be of any real value an informed inquiry must be done in an atmosphere of real curiosity and openness. There are very few topics that make it into a sincere informed inquiry process, that don't have some amount of paradox to them. There will always be some amount of Sober Data about a particular topic that will confound even the most open minded of us.

A few of the most challenging topics I have seen folks take on: Abortion, Vaccines, Religion, Chem Trails. You may want to start on smaller, less volatile topics before taking on any of these.

*   *   *

Now that you've read the two central practices I am recommending for this very important aspect of reconnection, you may be wondering about action. I mean, once we get into these practices of reconnection what about doing something about all of this Shadow mess going on in our world?

Before we talk about action, I just want to deepen my assertions about what it means to be living in a collapsing world and attempting to bridge into a world that has not yet been created. It may sound odd but if we move too quickly into doing, we may find ourselves bringing the same motivations, actions and patterns of override that got us into our predicament— taking the steering wheel again, this time driving a Prius, faster and faster toward the cliff edge. I am not saying that I endorse inaction or giving up…

There is no better antidote for despair than action.

Edward Abbey.

I am saying that the simple looking practices that are suggested in these pages are essential if we are to truly intend to reconnect with our deeper selves, other people and Earth. I am also saying that if we don't do some substantial healing, growing and learning with regard to our cultural and individual weak suits, we are destined to bring those blind spots and under-developed skills and capacities with us into our daunting future.

Remember those weak suits—full emotional range and literacy, grief, shame, judgment, compassion, presence, listening, receptivity, curiosity. Add your additional weak suits here.

I am saying that if you are clear about your purpose in life and what you love enough to stand for in life, you will have no shortage of things to share about as you have conversations with others. Again, if you couple that with an authentic curiosity about what they hold dear and what concerns them, you are well on your way to having a meaningful conversation with another person.

I don't mean to sound condescending here, but it really is that simple to start a connection with someone very different from you. I have also been amazed by how this simple layout of basic conversational connection has brought great joy and connection to my conversations with friends and family.

As these conversations mature over time, we find ourselves talking about subjects we otherwise never would have covered. While not all conversations promise a deep connection or relationship, you will unquestionably have better conversational outcomes if you share what is important to you personally and offer sincere interest and curiosity about the concerns and values of the other person.

We are living in very strange and challenging times. While I have, indeed, had hundreds of very positive and encouraging Impossible Conversations with people from across the political and philosophical spectrum, I have also been confronted daily with instances of individual and collective Shadow running our day-to-day human operating system. Those Shadow influences on our culture have grown in strength and ferocity over the past forty years or so, with the greatest jump in the past ten to twenty years. They currently have control of power in all branches of US Government and are stripping any and all vestiges of climate change mitigation and research from public-facing agencies and websites.

These recent actions follow the years-long practice of vilifying and threatening climate scientists from the highest levels of corporate and government leadership. As I mentioned in earlier chapters, there is a long list of climate scientists who have had their lives turned upside down by verbal attacks and Congressional investigations, not to mention actual threats on their lives by rabid climate deniers.

I have already spent some time acknowledging and praising the stamina and professional demeanor of Michael Mann[1]. Mann has taken more of this abuse than most other climate scientists and yet he carries on, writing more books aimed at keeping the public informed about the most recent updates to the Sober Data on both the cultural and research fronts.

There is another climate scientist I'd like to introduce you to. He has not been subjected to nearly the abuse that Michael Mann has had to endure. But, like virtually all the climate scientists who are active in the field, he is painfully aware of the Sober Data. The difference with this particular scientist is that he has consciously designed a way of living, for himself and his family, that reflects their deep care and concern for the health of Earth and humanity. Peter Kalmus, makes it very clear that his personal lifestyle choices, and non-work related writings, are all his own and not intended to speak for NASA, CalTech or JPL (Jet Propulsion Laboratories), all of which he works for.

I am introducing Kalmus because he exemplifies a person who is fully steeped in the Sober Data of our time, as relates to Anthropogenic Climate Disruption. He has engaged in or invented practices that invite a full reconnection with deeper self, other people and Earth. He has designed a lifestyle template for his own family that can be used and adapted by any other person or family. Kalmus' lifestyle suggestions reflect his (and his family's) deep love for and care for their home, their community and Earth herself.

Peter Kalmus also exemplifies a scientist who has shed the stereotypical, Sceintist as Awkward Communicator role. If it can be said that we are the conversations we have in the world, then Peter Kalmus could be described as: clear, generous, caring about life on Earth, logical and heartful.

You will see a huge overlap between the suggested practices and context described in *The Impossible Conversation* and Kalmus' offerings. Please enjoy as you get a sense of what is possible when a person chooses a life direction in which hope is described as, Activated Presence, vs. the business-as-usual definition of hope: "I hope the experts invent solutions to the world's problems, so we can quickly get back to my comfortable business-as-usual lifestyle."

What Peter Kalmus has done is combine his first hand knowledge of the Sober Data with his extraordinarily creative mind, crafting a lifestyle and a context for right living for his young family. In his recent book, *Being the Change: How to live well and spark a climate revolution*[2] , Kalmus generously shares about the steps that he and his family are taking to make their participation in our great transition to a more sustainable world as joyful and empowering as possible.

In a few brief excerpts, we can follow Kalmus' path from his obvious strong suit of linear systems and scientific thinking to other, equally important aspects of human life. The elements he describes may sound familiar.

> I've ... reduced my personal CO_2 emissions from twenty tons per year (near the U.S. average) to well under two tons per year. Far from being a sacrifice, the changes that have allowed me to do this have made me happier.

> The path I'm on can be understood in terms of three parts. One is intellectual understanding: the head. The head allows me to prioritize. It helps me navigate to my goals, although it's not good at choosing the goals.

> One of the lessons I've learned on this path is to accept that I have limitations. If I'm to make any progress, I need to choose my path wisely so as to make best use of my limited time, energy and abilities. This means asking the right questions, gathering information about reality as it is (which is often different than

how it appears to be, or how I want it to be), and drawing conclusions objectively. The head is a scientist.

Another part of my path is practical action—the hands. Society's business-as-usual trajectory is carrying us towards disaster. If we wish to avoid disaster, we must take action.

Since I can't change the entire global trajectory by myself, I perform practical and local actions, changing myself and how I live right here and right now. Direct practical action is empowering; it brings measurable, tangible change. It's fun, and therefore it's sustainable. It also provides its own guidance. Often only doing something can reveal the next step. I find that all the planning and intellectualizing in the world can't substitute for just doing something. There is wisdom in doing.

A third part of my path is like seeing from the heart, so it's like the eyes. You could call this part spirituality, although that term carries perhaps too much baggage. This third part is what connects. The head is objectively detached, and action can easily become robotic without a deeper reason for acting.

This is why connection is so important— connection to myself, to other people, and to nature. Connection brings purpose and meaning. (Emphasis mine.)

I have a specific and concrete practice for this third part: I meditate by observing my body and mind in a particular way. When I'm not sitting, I try to continue this awareness. This brings mindfulness, and allows me to be joyful (most of the time), even while studying global warming every day at work. Meditation helps me connect to the sea of everyday miracles around me— the plants growing, the sun shining, my older son lovingly putting his arm around his brother's shoulders, and to take strength from them.

These three parts support and balance each other. No one part is sufficient by itself. Each is necessary in the face of our predicament.

Kalmus has called his way of living, "Be-cycling." This reflected his emphasis on

Being in a new way in our troubled times.

I find great comfort and inspiration in Kalmus' generous writing. He has a particularly strong ability to make logical and heartful connections between the pragmatic elements of our world and the elusive inner world of the heart:

> Be-cycling is a straightforward path. Be-cycling says that if fossil fuels cause global warming, and I don't want global warming, then I should reduce my fossil fuel use. This seems straightforward and obvious to me, but the behavior of the majority of individuals and of society as a whole indicates that this isn't obvious to most people.

> Be-cycling also says that if I don't like conflict, killing and wars, then I should reduce my own addiction to conflict and negativity. I should find a practice that decreases the fear and defensiveness that cause me to react to anger with more anger, to negativity with more negativity. If I want a world without wars, then I shouldn't add more negativity to the world!

> In our society, this kind of straightforwardness is thought to be idealistic, impractical, and out of reach. But my own experience says that this isn't so. My own experience says that it is possible to reduce my fossil fuel use, and that it is possible to come out of conflict and negativity. What's more, the personal rewards for doing both of these things are tremendous. You can't send negativity into the world unless you suffer; conflict and negativity are manifestations of suffering. **A practice that reduces my own addiction to conflict and negativity is a practice that reduces my own suffering**. It can't be otherwise.

> In my experience, living without fossil fuels also increases my happiness. It leads to a life with less stress and distraction and more health, satisfaction, gratitude and connection.

In Peter Kalmus, I also find powerful suggestions for the eventual redefinition of the word "hope." Clearly, in his world, hope occurs in action. It grows as we engage all of our faculties to address the sobering realities of a predicament-laden world. It comes from the remarkable flexibility of Kalmus and his family as they adapt their lifestyle to be far less fixated on consumption and far more focused on connection with life.

As has been mentioned before, all of these wonderful practices for right-living are taken on not to somehow "Save the World!"… they are done in the spirit of living in a way that best honors the web of life itself.

One more visit into the world of Carolyn Baker deeply confirms this orientation. In her book, *Dark Gold: The Human Shadow and the Global Crisis,* Baker goes right to the heart of how we might live fully, with eyes and hearts wide open, even in the face of our daunting predicaments:

> We alter our perception that saving the planet depends on us, or that anything we do or do not do will manifest the "death row miracle" so hoped for by the condemned inmate. We consume less, not because it will lower greenhouse gases, but because we need less and it feels better to live more simply and perhaps express more generosity to others who have less. We seek avenues for sharing our love, and we allow our hearts to be broken open with compassion. Kindness, not entitlement, becomes our most cherished preoccupation.
>
> We savor every occurrence of beauty and blessing in our lives, and we seek to create beauty in every circumstance. We treat other species with exquisite mercy and make their extinction as gentle as possible. Gratitude, not acquisition, becomes the motivating force of our lives. Moreover, we immerse ourselves in these practices, even as we witness the withering and perhaps irreversible departure of ecosystems. We allow beauty and sorrow to intercept in the flaming crucible of our hearts. We do all of this, not because our actions will somehow reverse abrupt, catastrophic climate change, but because doing so transports us to the core of our humanity and allows us to revel in the love and beauty of other beings.

Meanwhile, we allow ourselves to consciously grieve every personal and planetary loss of which we are aware because grief surgically opens our hearts and radically connects us with the Earth community, and with all living beings, including ourselves.

I have been looking long and hard for solid tutoring, coaching, training about how to create your own support group within the context of the End of Business as Usual. Ironically there is not much out there. What is out there is based firmly in our old, business-as-usual model of group dynamics and motivations for founding and maintaining a support group structure.

There is nothing wrong with this. I am mentioning it because it seems to me that each practice and each tool or reference or resource we point to here in The Impossible Conversation, better have some depth and breadth to it, enough to accommodate the transforming purpose, mission, growth and evolution we are talking about as aspiring "bridge builders."

Outside of a few, well established personal growth programs like the one I mentioned before, for men, the Mankind Project and its New Warrior Training Adventure or a number of women's programs including, Woman Within-there aren't many programs out there that offer solid skill building in creating safe circles for support and community to grow and thrive. One of the founders of the Mankind Project, Bill Kauth, is offering a workshop designed to empower folks to build local small support groups, or tribes. Information can be found on their site, timefortribe.com.

I do have a soft spot in my heart for the work of Parker Palmer and his cadre of facilitators. On his website you will find many workshops and learning tools for people interested in heartful human community.

None of the programs I've just mentioned address the "elephant in the room" of Anthropogenic Climate Disruption or the associated systems collapses we have detailed here.

As I've mentioned before, my partners in this alliance, Living Resilience, and I are committed to bringing world-class tools to the courageous among us who are willing to take on the tough work of reconnecting: with deeper self, with others and with Earth. The important distinction here is that we couch our work in what I've been calling, the Sober Data. It is our view that any attempt to grow, heal, evolve, thrive or even muster resilience in the face of our global predicaments – without acknowledging and naming those predicaments – is a thinly veiled attempt to sustain the business as usual paradigm. Those attempts, by definition, will primarily offer some solace to people who are still firmly and exclusively planted in the business-as-usual world.

Having lived for years in very successful co-housing and group living arrangements, I have to say that Kalmus gives us as powerful and well-articulated guide for purpose-driven group life as I have ever seen.

There is no time like the present to find your people. These predicament-laden times call for each of us to find our own support team or tribe. In a culture that enshrines the image of the rugged individualist as the icon of success, most of us need all the help we can get in forming any kind of support team.

In our society filled with "rugged individualists" it could be said that building support groups, community or tribe is one of our weakest suits. Where do we even start to have the conversation with others? What do we talk about? How do we share what is important to each of us? How do we create a circle that is safe and supportive for people who may not always agree with one another?

*   *   *

By far the greatest vehicles I have found for finding other, kindred spirits with whom you can generate supportive community are: conversations and shared meals. We have already talked about the essential nature of reaching out to share about our personal concerns about our world. These conversations can happen almost anywhere, but are not very well served in noisy, public spaces.

Pot lucks are dinners in which a number of folks get together to share a meal. Each person brings a dish to share. Of course, sharing a meal doesn't have to be pot luck nor does it have to involve a full meal. The purpose of this shared meal time is to gather in a quiet location and invite a lightly facilitated sharing from all of the attendees. The focus for each session could be a different aspect of the concerns of your community, your family, your region etc.

If you are wondering where a person begins to facilitate this kind of sharing, you are welcome to start with any of the prompting questions we have used in this book for self assessment and self exploration. Additionally a reminder that Joanna Macy's and Molly Young Brown's, *Coming Back to Life*, is a book chock full of easy and evocative exercises that would quickly get the conversation moving in any fledgling support group. Now you could add Peter Kalmus', *Being the Change* to the list of strong source documents for building a support group or tribe or community.

Why I'm going to such lengths here is to summarize my concerns about the stamina and eventual effectiveness of Americans' efforts to protest and resist? Now, as never before, it is of essential importance for people to talk with one another. If we are serious about turning any portion of this daunting reality around, we must find a way to reach out and connect with others. We must somehow find the courage to engage in civil dialogue. We must find a way to actually connect, in a sincere way, with people who are different from us.

There is no way we will ever match the money or media monopoly or military might of those in power. There is, however, one power that promises to overwhelm even the greatest piles of wealth, the most seamless propaganda and the most deadly military. It is the power that I've been pointing to every time I've mentioned reconnecting with our deeper selves, with other people and with Earth.

This immense power is the one that Joanna Macy meant when she spoke of expanding our compassion and our experience of being one with the web of life. This, of course, is the Joy that Carolyn Baker and Andrew Harvey spoke of in *Return to Joy*. This is the Grace that I have been blessed to experience more times than I can count.

This is the power of people who are intentionally breaking their hearts open together—to release the immense power of our love of life itself. There is no greater power. Ironically, we have crafted a business-as-usual lifestyle that teaches us to fear that power and to avoid any action that might crack open our armored hearts.

*   *   *

Self Assessment:

How active are you in speaking with other people in your own family, community, workplace, about topics of great concern for you?

Have you articulated your highest priority concerns about the world around you to the people you love?

Are there certain people around whom you intentionally remain silent or change the subject to something lighter or less triggering?

Do you have a circle of people with whom it is safe to open your heart?

How skilled are you at creating and maintaining a safe and clear environment for an "Impossible Conversation?"

Are you aware of your own stress behaviors? …the stress behaviors of others in your family, group, workplace, neighborhood?

Are you skilled at transforming a group of stressed-out people into an aligned support group focused on encouraging resilience and reconnection?

*　　*　　*

Another great contributor to the redefinition of the word, hope, is a self described: activist for the soul, cultural revolutionary, status-quo crusher, unapologetic vegan, voracious truth seeker, ironman triathlon finisher and passionate lover of life—Deb Ozarko—represents a gradually growing group of people from around the world who have created their own powerful path to the same destination described here in *The Impossible Conversation* and beyond.

As you will see if you visit Deb's website, she is passionately alive in the midst of her clear understanding and resonating energetic awareness of the Sober Data. Deb is clear that the old, business-as-usual definition of hope has no value or meaning in these times. I love her current definition of hope—"activated presence." Even with full awareness of the imminent collapse of human and Earth systems and the eventuality of mass extinction, Deb embodies the passion, grace and joy that we touched on earlier. This is the passion, grace and joy available when we turn our intent toward full reconnection with the miraculous web of life in which we live.

In her term, "activated presence," we are invited to focus on a key component shared by all of our exemplars. In the override mode of business-as-usual, we are compelled to intensify and accelerate our activities in order to "succeed" by attaining more money, status or accomplishment. All of this is done with the background intention to override or deny any sort of signal, impress, intuition or direct perception that our actions may be off track, damaging or ill suited to the truth of the moment.

With Deb's shift to full Presence—with its shift to a primary focus on our reconnection with deeper self, others and Earth— our attention and engagement with the world is directed by a more life-aware way of being and perceiving.

I'm also enchanted by Deb's inclusion of her own mission statement. While she may not include exactly the same elements that I described in the last chapter, there is no shortage of passionate aliveness in Deb's statement:

> My mission is to inspire a movement of cultural revolutionaries who celebrate their birthright: simplicity, passion, kindness, creativity, authentic expression, and a purpose-driven life outside of the stifling confines of today's dysfunctional, distracted … and let's face it, insane cultural mindset. By shifting the paradigm from head to heart we can live a more passionate, compassionate, loving, and interconnected world that excludes no living being.
>
> In the end, all you really need to know is that I give a damn:
>
> About life.
>
> About love.
>
> About me.
>
> About you.
>
> … oh ya, and I really love to dance.

Deb recently discontinued hosting her *Unplug* podcast. For the past few years, Deb has used her podcast as an expression of her mission in life. In her online blog writings, you will discover a treasure trove of wisdom and the sharing of her direct connection to what I like to call "the truth of the moment." For a person who has fully shed the trappings and painful limitations of the business-as-usual paradigm, a rich world of beauty and grace is available to fill their senses and their heart. Deb Ozarko has abundant access to the truth of the moment in her world.

> We are living on a planet being rendered uninhabitable by our own species. There is no stopping the accelerating death spiral we are now on. To believe otherwise is delusional. No longer do I

subdue my deeper inner knowing. I speak my truth—even when it is hard to bear. Things may still look relatively "normal," but as the old adage goes, "never judge a book by its cover."

The other day I walked our old dog, Zoey along the trails of a local provincial park. Our walks are slower to accommodate her aging body. We walked along the shores of a salmon-spawning creek that led to the ocean. Under natural circumstances, the creek would be teeming with salmon by now. Under natural circumstances, the ocean would be bubbling with jumping salmon. Under natural circumstances, there would be bears, eagles, seals and otters.

On that day I saw nothing (and still nothing since). Not a single sign of life. Not one salmon. Not one seal. Not one otter. Not one bear. Not one eagle. A few seagulls and ducks, but even their numbers were smaller than usual. It's surreal and eerie.

The ocean is dying and my premonitions are playing out with dizzying speed. I've been internally guided to leave the ocean and move to the mountains. I no longer question my inner guidance. We are voluntary climate migrants. We leave the coast mid October. The sad reality is that I wouldn't consider leaving if my premonitions, my intuition, my body, and what I perceive with my own senses, was not so damned clear. It's heartbreaking. Sometimes I *think* I should stay to bear witness, but my body screams at me to move on. The body never lies.

Deb ends one of her essays with an admonition about this bold, extraordinary path of reconnecting with our deeper self and with the web of life:

The warrior's path is a lonely one. It's one of uncertainty, change, discomfort, fierce love, ruthless compassion, activated presence, truth, transformation, courage and trust. It is not for the faint of heart, but it's so worth it.

In summary, Ozarko and Kalmus have created their own unique expressions of what they love about life. They both, along with the other exemplars in this book, have found a way to disengage from the despair that is built-in to those who grip tightly to the business-as-usual paradigm. They all have found their own way of staying informed, re-creating their sense of purpose and meaning in life, and keeping their hearts broken open to stay in direct contact with core joy and grace, in the face of predicaments far greater than any humanity has seen before.

This is the invitation that awaits each of us who is courageous enough to reconnect with life.

*   *   *

The last element of Sober Data I will introduce is as important as any we have spoken about in prior chapters. This element is another metric with which we can assess the sustainability of our human operating system on Earth.

The remarkable cultural, political and environmental events of the past two years have created a sense of urgency and mandate to include a number of elements that I never imagined would be a part of this book and Informed Inquiry.

This is why you have heard so much about the interweaving of Earth systems with human systems in these pages. This is why we spent time with the powerful writings of Pope Frances and Naomi Klein. The remarkable chain of events that started so long ago but exploded into public view with the election of Donald Trump, has forced us all to grapple with our collective Shadow.

Suddenly, the people Naomi Oreskes describes as the *Merchants of Doubt*, have jumped from their influential positions on the fringes of our corporations, government and media, to the center of political, financial and cultural power in the US.

If my inclusion of the words, "contempt" and "violence," five years ago would have felt contrived and tin-foil-hat conspiratorial, today they start to make sense as we see an administration dismantling the minimal protections and regulations put in place by past administrations. We can easily see and feel the contempt for social and environmental justice as pillars of our remarkable country's legacy are torn apart. Those with power and money stage themselves and their ilk to rake in ever more wealth as half the US working population struggles to get by on fifteen dollars an hour or less, without benefits.

In any case, it is no random coincidence that the "hockey stick" shaped graphs showing non-linear acceleration of the many metrics of Abrupt Climate Change Sober Data— and species extinction numbers and degradation of habitat— all match the graphs that track this last piece of *The Impossible Conversation*. This final offering of Sober Data is the tracking of our global economic model.

So, if we put a graph showing the global output of CO_2 since 1990 next to a graph of the amount of global debt being produced in that same period, you get a direct correlation. You get a side-by-side rise in both metrics. Both graphs could be said to be equally disturbing. Both graphs show a non-linear or exponential progression. Both graphs show our human operating system in what is called, "over shoot." Our free-lunch dumping of CO_2 is clearly at a scale that is far beyond Earth's ability to process in a normal way. Similarly, the exponential growth of global debt creation is far beyond the capacity for a healthy global economy to process or repay.

This whole notion of exponential growth is the piece of this Impossible Conversation that can silence a room of climate scientists or economists. In either field this notion of troubling metrics, growing in an exponential or non-linear fashion, is jaw dropping and, frankly, terrifying.

In our Conversation here we have obviously focused on what we are calling Sober Data that includes climate and temperature metrics, sea level rise, extreme weather events, species extinction and habitat and diversity loss. Whether we are talking about the speed of temperature rise or the demise of global fisheries, exponential acceleration is not good news.

Similarly, the measures of economic activity (exponential growth), particularly false signs of growth propped up by the creation of money and debt out of thin air, have their own brand of terror for those brave enough to look behind our global economics curtain.

Both of these vital measures have been fitting into the now familiar hockey-stick-shaped graph that describes exponential growth and acceleration.

A short while ago, I described how to avoid one of the biggest pitfalls in speaking with climate deniers or "luke warmers." My suggestion was to not mention CO_2 at all. Instead invite your denier conversation mate into a mutual sharing of what you each love in life and what values and concerns you both have about those subjects or any other. You may feel inclined to offer them some of the Sober Data from chapter three from *The Impossible Conversation.*

This is a very simplistic version of the recommendations made by numerous neuroscientists as they coach us on how to connect with people who are different from us. In the case of articulating your personal species extinction or habitat loss concerns there also appear to be fewer of those pesky pitfalls that have been rehearsed and polished by every "cap and trade hating denier" out there.

No taxes or big government oversight—just a world without fisheries by 2040, without coral reefs by 2050, and without major land based wildlife by 2100.

For a much fuller and more vivid layout of our fatally flawed, denial-based, global economic system, I again recommend viewing Chris Martenson's *Crash Course* on his website, *Peak Prosperity*. Martenson's *Crash Course* is a quick and easy way for folks to get on the same page with some very understandable descriptions of how and why we are in the predicament we are in. Early on in their course, you will be shown a visually potent example of exponential growth. This piece alone will provide your pot-luck guests with plenty of fodder for vulnerable sharing of heartfelt concerns.

Why this inclusion of the exponential expansion of the economic predicament? Precisely because it too is a predicament. And, precisely because the same icons of wealth and power that are now controlling the dismantling of global environmental stewardship are the ones who have set up the entirely self-serving economic system that also teeters on the brink of utter collapse.

Perhaps you balked at my suggestion of hosting pot-luck dinners at your place to expand your circle of support and allies— with the suggested topic being something to do with this stuff we are calling, the Sober Data of Abrupt Climate Change or species extinction or global habitat destruction. If that is the case, you may want to start out with a topic that is a bit closer to home and closer to our daily concerns, like "What shape is the world economy in?" and, "How can I prepare myself and my loved ones to survive and possibly even thrive in the face of imminent economic predicaments?"

> Ours is not the task of fixing the entire world all at once, but of stretching out to mend the part of the world that is within our reach. Any small, calm thing that one soul can do to help another soul, to assist some portion of this poor suffering world, will help immensely. It is not given to us to know which acts or by whom, will cause the critical mass to tip toward an enduring good.
>
> *Clarissa Pinkola Estes*

*　　*　　*

As you will recall in earlier chapters, I suggested a couple of sources for the current use of neuroscience to explain how we have become the people we have become. Particularly, I recommended, *Don't Even Think About It*, from George Marshall. Based on the notion that we generate our defining stories and our relationships with other people in that mysterious black-box called our brain, these neuroscience researchers are searching for clues to make sense of our crazy world. And, yes, I think George Marshall does a fine job of relaying the most current iteration of neuroscience in our daily lives, particularly relating to our challenges of speaking with others who do not believe as we do.

I still don't have much of a resonance of the whole topic because, as I mentioned before, I don't see any neuroscience model that accounts for the field of propaganda, public relations or mass communications strategy. I just find it difficult to go into great detail about imagined thought strings and neural pathways when we aren't including a multi billion dollar propaganda machine that has been hard at work for years, successfully influencing the public perception of the health, facts and science on planet Earth.

A few pages earlier you might recall me laying out the history of that propaganda, public relations, sales behemoth that has become the water we swim in or the central defining story of humanity to date.

I am pleased to say that I have discovered a world-class media analyst who has looked at many of the same issues that we have covered here, and come to some similar conclusions. It may be of some relief to you, the reader, to hear that the perspective of this analyst tends to be a bit less conspiracy-tinged than my own.

In her recently released book, *The Trouble With Reality: A Rumination on Moral Panic in our Time,* Brooke Gladstone has offered us a clear and potent interpretation of and context for, our current chaotic and fractured political and cultural world. Gladstone, a long-standing host of public radio's *On The Media* program, brings her usual incisive yet well considered analysis to the questions: "How did we get to this bizarre point where facts have almost nothing to do with how we interact with each other and how we put together this human operating system?" and, "What part has our media: our news, opinion and even entertainment media contributed to our chaotic and polarized world?"

If it is not clear by now, let me say that this topic of influencing public opinion and perception is as important a subject of Sober Data as any we have covered here in *The Impossible Conversation*. Brooke Gladstone offers us a number of striking examples of current affairs that are examples of tried and true propaganda tools being used in the now turbo-charged global media environment.

Gladstone also gathers expert analysis from decades ago and distant, similar political circumstances, to help us understand some of the historical context for our current situation.

I am not asserting here that Brooke Gladstone subscribes to the *Impossible Conversation* notion of Sober Data or the accelerated timelines projected by Abrupt Climate Change advocates. What Gladstone does so well in her short book, *The Trouble With Reality*, is map out how truth and facts and integrity have become irrelevant to modern day living.

She asserts that our current leaders are quite adept at "blatantly using lies to assert power over truth itself." She goes on to quote one of the world's foremost experts on totalitarianism, Hannah Arendt, as Arendt describes part of the dynamic that occurs which allows a totalitarian government to take hold:

> ". . . A lying government has constantly to rewrite its own history. On the receiving end you get not only one lie— a lie which you could go on for the rest of your days— but you get a great number of lies, depending on how the political wind blows. "And a people that no longer can believe anything cannot make up its mind. It is deprived not only of its capacity to act but also of its capacity to think and to judge. And with such a people, you can then do what you please."

This is, for me, the heart of *The Impossible Conversation*. We are a people that has become desperately disconnected: from our own deeper, wiser selves, from Earth our home and Mother, and from each other.

We have created a way of communicating, governing and relating that is steeped in separation, judgment, contempt and ignorance, backed by threatened violence. And, within that atmosphere of contempt we show no signs of regret or irony as we sneer at facts, science or authentic connection and relationship as we busily fill up our experience with the distractions of the day and bark out epithets at those "others" who are obviously, not like us, and "to blame for our troubles."

While I am no fan of President Trump, it is not actually his daily episodes of lunacy that concern me when I speak of having concerns about the stamina of any resistance or protest movement. My concerns live behind the scenes that are now filling our media screens with utterly insane talk of Russian and American spying, horrendously obvious conflicts of interest and corruption in the Executive Branch and in the Cabinet. My real concerns are about the cynical political agendas and motivations that are being carried out in back rooms while all of the daily Trump train wreck action is crunching and writhing on our media screens of choice.

In the early chapters of this book we explored the Sober Data estimates and projections regarding global temperature rise, sea-level rise, species extinction, habitat destruction, economic systems collapse and much more. I've shared with you the evidence I've uncovered that convinces me that our corporate and governmental leaders are fully aware of the reality of Abrupt Climate Change and all of its associated collapse of systems.

I'm concerned that in the very few months of the Trump administration (and the entirely Republican government that accompanies it) we have already seen the demise of the very few structures in government and in society, that had any chance of changing our business-as-usual trajectory from its obviously gloomy, near future, chaos, to a more wholesome way of operating and being on Earth.

Here, in the pages of *The Impossible Conversation*, I've tried to share with you the simplest, most potent context and practices I can find to address the collapse of our daunting, business-as-usual paradigm. I know of no more powerful actions to take in the face of our global predicaments than to commit ourselves to reconnect with the essential sources of meaning in the human experience, and to take on a rigorous personal reinvention of purpose and mission.

I know of no more important information in our information-saturated world than the Sober Data that will keep each of us connected with the world around us and keep us fully able to discern the truth in any given moment or situation, so that we can continue to reclaim some authentic agency in life. For to forfeit our discernment about integrity, science, truth and facts, is to forfeit our ability to stand for anything of real value in life.

To turn this tide around, this tide of nearly universal disempowerment and polarization, we have the biggest challenge of all ahead of us. This ultimate challenge will be for each of us to instigate our own version of The Impossible Conversation, hundreds or even thousands of times over.

While we may well take on sincere practices that reconnect us with our own inner, vital sensitivities and we might just dive into practices that reunite us with the miraculous web of life that is our home, Earth... the greatest challenge in any of these domains of reconnection, is clearly our reconnection with other people.

This realm of creating robust, trusting, creative relatedness between human beings looks to be the most vexing aspect of the reconnection suggested here in *The Impossible Conversation*. In fact we have come full circle to my original insight and shock in the original presentation of Abrupt Climate Change data a few years ago.

It was obvious then and it is obvious now that we all are mixed bags of core reactions and motivations when it comes to grappling with our global predicaments. From our most loving, generous, heartfelt motivations, sincerely desiring for ourselves, our children and all beings to live gorgeous lives on this miraculous planet… to our most cynical, willfully ignorant and privileged, Shadow motivations… we are all imbued with an extraordinary blend of reactions, values and presence.

*   *   *

What will be the qualities of our individual and collective presence that we will choose to bring forth as we turn to face the self-created predicaments on our horizon?

Will we choose to lessen our impact on our fellow Earth inhabitants – those inhabitants that are going extinct at a rate of 150 to 200 species per day?

Will we muster the immense courage and fortitude that it will take to slow down or even stop our destructive, business-as-usual ways on this planet? If not, will we find a way to fully face the consequences of our collective action? Will we find a way to fully connect with the web of life, even as we wreak havoc within it?

Will we take on the challenge of reconnecting with our primary sources of meaning in the human experience?

Will we endeavor to build out our weak suits and reduce the size of our immense, Shadow-filled blind spots?

Will we commit ourselves to volitionally cracking open our own hearts in the name of letting loose the vital life energy, the core joy, the grace we so desperately need to face our shared predicaments?

Will we develop the profound inner tool kit that includes mastery of creating safe circles for ourselves, our loved ones, our communities? Will people experience more aliveness and resilience in the presence we generate as we step forward into a predicament-laden future?

This does appear to me to be the calling of our times. Not a panicking, terrified nation of isolated individuals, trembling in their insulated enclaves – but powerful, courageous, "bridge builders" valiantly offering their open hearts and reclaimed empowerment, to their loved ones and co Earthlings, to bring forth love and grace and resilience, in the face of our many problems, challenges and predicaments.

*   *   *

As we come to a close in this *Impossible Conversation*, please know that you are deeply appreciated for your courage and your perseverance. Those of us in this alliance, which we are calling, Living Resilience, know full well how challenging it is to be living on the leading edge of a global transformation. (www.LivingResilience.Earth and www.ImpossibleConversation.net)

We know from experience how challenging it is to generate not one purpose statement to motivate our actions in life, but three. We know what it is like to keep being, "that guy," as we share our predicament concerns and visions of possible futures with others. We know the grief and pain that can come from piercing through the collective denial and bargaining, to see and feel the damage being done to our shared biosphere and our long-honored human cultural legacy. And, all of this in the name of our unbridled profit motive.

We also know that there is a deep and nourishing wellspring of core joy and grace to be found when we crack through the layers of insulation and awkward silence that so often surrounds our hearts. When we commit to setting aside our twisted mastery of overriding life's subtler signals, and reconnect with our loves in life, we invite a return to our innate belonging with the web of life.

We call this The Impossible Conversation because we appear to be immersed in a confluence of predicaments and fatal human flaws that promise no easy solutions. In fact the predicaments, by their nature, offer no solutions at all. But, as you have seen in the descriptions of the exemplars here, this is no place to retreat into a paralyzed heap in the corner. We in this Living Resilience alliance are choosing to respond to the calling of our times by breaking our hearts open together and reconnecting with the infinite source of life energy that awaits each of us.

This is, by every measure, the end of our business-as-usual paradigm. It is the end of the many defining stories humans have carried for generations. Particularly, it is the end of any story that promises each progressive generation being more well-off than their parents.

This is a time of great mystery and uncertainty. This is uncomfortable news for a global culture that demands certainty.

What will actually happen with each type of Sober Data and projections we have detailed here? None of us knows that either. What we do know is that these predicaments and challenges we all face, stand as the ultimate motivators for each of us to actually "*BE* the changes we wish to see in this world."

If you have concluded as I have—that large-scale breakdowns in all manner of Sober Data will occur long before 2100 (that, in fact, they are starting now)—then perhaps you will join me and the other members of our informal alliance in commencing the expansion of our core capacities and inner tool kits to encourage that enhanced state of *BEING* that our lives and Earth are calling for. Perhaps you will bring forth Deb Ozarko's version of hope, activated presence.

This is a time like no other in the history of humanity. The consequences of our collective actions and our predicaments stand looking just over our shoulders, always in the background. What will be the choices we make regarding our participation in our daily lives, in our families, in our communities?

*   *   *

Wild Geese

You do not have to be good.
You do not have to walk on your knees
for a hundred miles through the desert, repenting.
You only have to let the soft animal of your body
love what it loves.
Tell me about despair, yours, and I will tell you mine.
Meanwhile the world goes on.
Meanwhile the sun and the clear pebbles of the rain
are moving across the landscapes,
over the prairies and the deep trees,
the mountains and the rivers.
Meanwhile the wild geese, high in the clean blue air,
are heading home again.
Whoever you are, no matter how lonely,
the world offers itself to your imagination,
calls to you like the wild geese, harsh and exciting –
over and over announcing your place
in the family of things."

Mary Oliver

Chapter 11 Chapter References and Resources

"The biggest gift you can give is to be absolutely present, and when you're worrying about whether you're hopeful or hopeless or pessimistic or optimistic, who cares? The main thing is that you're showing up, that you're here and that you're finding ever more capacity to love this world because it will not be healed without that. That was what is going to unleash our intelligence and our ingenuity and our solidarity for the healing of our world."

Joanna Macy

"I for one believe that if you give people a thorough understanding of what confronts them and the basic causes that produce it, they'll create their own program, and when the people create a program, you get action."

Malcolm X

References: Chapter 1.

Special Additional Reference Video: If you are pressed for time and want more detail and context about Abrupt Climate Change, Positive Feedback Loops and even a very well executed connecting of the dots to our need for a new global economic model then watch this one video:

Arctic Methane Emergency: Methane Release by the Gigaton. YouTube. Stuart Scott, United Planet Faith & Science Initiative. Paul Beckwith. Professor of Geography, University of Ottowa.

https://www.youtube.com/watch?v=FPdc75epOEw

*　　*　　*

(1) Guy McPherson: http://guymcpherson.com
McPherson's ever growing essay detailing the current state of more than 50 Positive
Feedback Loops or Self Reinforcing Feedback Loops.
http://guymcpherson.com/2014/01/climate-change-summary-and-update/

(1a) Guy McPherson. *Presentation in Wellington NZ 2016.*
This more recent McPherson presentation adds extra emphasis on the Sam Carana
projection of 4°C to 10°C by 2026.
https://www.youtube.com/watch?v=t0yd1avJrV8&t=30s

(100) *Bill Nye's Global Meltdown, National Geographic Explorer (TV),*
Aired November 1, 2015.
Bill Nye, Arnold Schwarzenegger, Guy McPherson. Arnold plays therapist to Bill
Nye's character, grieving over our global crisis regarding climate change. This is a
remarkable, breakthrough show that is the first of its kind to combine frank talk
about climate change impacts to come and how grief is a natural and appropriate
part of the human experience of those human caused impacts.
https://www.youtube.com/watch?v=ra1M7XyyIDA

(2) Paul Beckwith, M.Sc., B.Eng. http://paulbeckwith.net
Adjunct Professor of Climatology, University of Ottawa, Ontario; Ph.D. candidate
in Abrupt Climate Change.

(3) Sam Carana. *Arctic News.*
http://arctic-news.blogspot.com/p/posts.html

(3a) *February Temperature.* Particularly powerful article highlighted in Chapter 1,
Arctic News. Sunday, March 13, 2016.
http://arctic-news.blogspot.com/2016/03/february-temperature.html

Infographic and referenced article detail showing projected range of global average
on-land temperature rise. By 2016, temperature rise of between 3.9°C and 10.4°C.
(See Guy McPherson YT Video from Wellington NZ for detailed description)

A Global Temperature Rise of More Than Ten Degrees Celsius by 2026? Arctic News Blog. Sam Carana. July 15, 2016. All of the graphs, data and projections from February article with more detail and context.
http://arctic-news.blogspot.com/2016/07/a-global-temperature-rise-of-more-than-ten-degrees-celsius-by-2026.html

(4) David Wasdell: (included in greater detail in chapter 3), Director, Apollo-Gaia Project. Accredited reviewer for the IPCC's 2007 Fourth Assessment Report. Lead on Feedback Dynamics in Coupled Complex Global Systems for the European Commission's Global System Dynamics and Policy (GSDP) network.
http://www.apollo-gaia.org

A good place to start to understand his point of view:
Basis for a Carbon Budget?: A Critical Evaluation of the "Summary for Policymakers" of the IPCC AR5 WG1 (the Scientific Basis). This paper can also be viewed in video/webinar form on the Apollo-Gaia website. Extensive critique of IPCC metrics used to calculate the proposed 2C "Budget" of CO_2 emissions at the center of COP21 and all current climate mitigation negotiations.
http://www.apollo-gaia.org/AR5SPM.html

(5) James Hansen, *YouTube.* Climate Change: James Hansen at Sydney Ideas Conference. 2010. This is a solid example of Hansen's primer on climate change and his heartful activism.
https://www.youtube.com/watch?v=ntOgBMgENTU&t=1707s

(5a) James Hansen: Additional book *Storms of My Grandchildren: The Truth About the Coming Climate Catastrophe,* and, *Our Last Chance to Save Humanity.*

Censoring Science: Dr. James Hansen and the Truth of Global Warming
Mark Bowen.

(5c) James Hansen: *TED Talk.*
https://www.ted.com/talks/james_hansen_why_i_must_speak_out_about_climate_change?language=en

(5d) A sample interview with Hansen, on the Public Radio program, *Living on Earth* is instructive. I invite you to savor Hansen's manner of speaking. It is clear, and he pulls no punches. This is impressive given the intense pressure from corporate and governmental interests to distort or suppress research findings and vilify scientists who speak truth to power.

(5e) *The world's most famous climate scientist just outlined an alarming scenario for our planet's future,* The Washington Post. Chris Mooney, July 20, 2015 http://tinyurl.com/okce9tl Article detailing recent findings from James Hansen and his research team regarding the nonlinear acceleration of Arctic and Antarctic ice and climate change projections.

(5f) *Almost Out of Time:* Interview with James Hansen, Living on Earth. Radio Podcast, November 27, 2015.
http://loe.org/shows/segments.html?programID=15-P13-00048&segmentID=1

(6) Michael Mann. *The Madhouse Effect,* Michael Mann and Tom Toles. *The Hockey Stick and the Climate Wars,* Michael Mann. *Dire Predictions,* Michael Mann.

(7) Kevin Anderson. http://kevinanderson.info
Anderson is the Deputy Director of the Tyndall Centre for Climate Change Research. Interview on Radio *EcoShock,* December 2, 2015. Soundcloud.
http://tinyurl.com/glnv9cl

(7a) Kevin Anderson. (5) Interview on Radio EcoShock, December 2, 2015. Soundcloud.
http://tinyurl.com/glnv9cl

(7b) *The Ostrich or the Phoenix?* Kevin Anderson, *YouTube* video. *Earth 101 Lecture.* Reykjavik, Iceland.
https://www.youtube.com/watch?v=mBtehlDpLlU&feature=youtu.be

In this one extraordinary video lecture, Professor Anderson delivers a full-force assessment of the state of the world in terms of climate change. This is Anderson at his most brazen in his assertion that we have missed twenty-five years of opportunities to mitigate our climate damage. I would call this the one video to watch if you must limit yourself to one. It is at once deeply informative, sobering and real. This is what a scientist sounds like when he is a trained communicator, fully able to speak truth to power and committed to speaking essential truths to concerned human beings. Bravo!

(8) Professor Peter Wadhams, Professor of Ocean Physics. Head of the Polar Ocean Physics Group at the University of Cambridge. Professor Wadhams is mentioned in Guy McPherson's Wellington NZ video above and more pointedly he has suggested to McPherson and others that many of the Positive Feedback Loops

mentioned in Carana's analysis should be multiplicative rather than additive. In other words, climate impacts may be worse still if some of the PFLs should be multiplied together rather than added together. *Ice Free Arctic?* Peter Wadhams Interview with Thom Hartmann. June 2016.
https://youtu.be/m8V9WWCAC1M

A Farewell to Ice: A Report From the Arctic. Peter Wadhams' most recent book.

(9) Dr Natalia Shakhova, Lead Scientist at the International Arctic Research Centre (IARC) Actively conducting research on the East Siberian Arctic Shelf.

(9a) Dr Shakhova *YouTube* interview:
https://www.youtube.com/watch?v=PVi1lotRLRU

Dr. Shakhova expresses great concern that the massive stores of methane in Arctic tundra and methane hydrates in the Arctic Sea shelves could be released far faster than IPCC projections state. Arctic methane has not been included in IPCC reports or assessments to date yet the Arctic is warming at a far faster rate than any other region on Earth. Dr. Shakhova's in-depth study of and concern about Arctic methane release can also be tracked in Guy McPherson's ever growing website Summary essay. Dr. Shakhova also speaks frankly about the intense pressure to suppress or change her findings—pressure exerted by corporate and government representatives who, according to Shakhova, know nothing about the science of what is occurring in the Arctic.

*   *   *

Climate change may be escalating so fast it could be "game over," scientists warn. *UK Independent.* Ian Johnston. November 2016
http://www.independent.co.uk/news/science/climate-change-game-over-global-warming-climate-sensitivity-seven-degrees-a7407881.html

Journal: Science Advances. Study detailed in *Independent* article above. Friedrich, Timmermann et al. November 2016.
http://advances.sciencemag.org/content/2/11/e1501923

New research suggests the Earth's climate could be more sensitive to greenhouse gases than thought, raising the specter of an "apocalyptic side of bad" temperature rise of more than 7°C within a lifetime. Actual projected range: 4.78 to 7.36.

This study focuses on evidence that Earth's sensitivity to greenhouse gases may be more extreme than originally estimated.

*   *   *

Earth Warming to Climate Tipping Point, Warns Study,
BBC News. Mark Kinver. November 30, 2016.
http://www.bbc.com/news/science-environment-38146248

Extraordinary validation of a few important Positive Feedback Loops and Tipping Points mentioned in the works of the Level 2 advocates, e.g. Guy McPherson, et al. mentioned in chapter 1.

How Soil Carbon Loss Could Accelerate Global Warming, YouTube video. NIOO KNAW. Thomas Crowther. Netherlands Institute of Ecology. Yale University. https://youtu.be/IrKOpPJIbXA

This is a video for the lay audience, describing the geochemical processes detailed in the BBC article above.

Potential Carbon Emissions Dominated by Carbon Dioxide From Thawed Permafrost Soils, Nature Climate Change. Study- the subject of the BBC article above. http://www.nature.com/nclimate/journal/v6/n10/full/nclimate3054.html

Additional validation of the potential release of CO_2 and Methane in permafrost and Arctic environments. They project that an increase of $1°C$ (1.8F) will release an additional 55 billion tons of carbon into the atmosphere by 2050. This could trigger a "positive feedback" and push the planet's climate system past the point of no return.

They warned that as the world warmed, organisms living in the planet's soils would become more active, resulting in more carbon being released into the atmosphere, exacerbating warming. "There have been concerns about this positive feedback for a long, long time," said lead author Thomas Crowther, who conducted the research while based at Yale University, US, but now at the Netherlands Institute of Ecology.

"For the past two or three decades there have been literally thousands of studies trying to address this topic and trying to identify whether there are going to be increases or decreases in carbon uptake of the soil in relation to warming or increases in carbon loss," says Crowther.

He told BBC News: "We are the first study to take a global perspective and then map the variability and we able to say that in these areas there are going to be huge losses and in these areas there are going to be some gains. Using this approach, we can get a robust idea of the whole picture. We show that, actually, the losses are going to be really considerable."

Using data stretching over twenty years from forty-nine sites across the globe, the team observed that global carbon stocks would fall by up to fifty-five petagrams (55 billion tons) under a business-as-usual scenario, which is roughly equivalent to adding the emissions from a nation the size of the US.

Fifty-five trillion kg of soil carbon will be released by 2050 in a business as usual scenario. This will be a 17% increase in carbon emissions from already existing sources of human caused emissions.

*   *   *

Resources, Chapter Two.

Additional Book Recommendation:

"*The Madhouse Effect: How Climate Change Denial Is Threatening Our Planet, Destroying Our Politics and Driving Us Crazy,*" Michael Mann and Tom Toles. 2016

(1) *Turn Down the Heat: Why a 4C Warmer World Must be Avoided,* World Bank. November 2012.
http://tinyurl.com/nkdgp8s

Video: *Turn Down the Heat: Why a 4C Warmer World Must Be Avoided,* Erick Fernandez, World Bank. 2016. Updated presentation.
https://www.youtube.com/watch?v=zCpQJf4LgEk

(1a) *Steven Chu Shares Some Sobering Climate Change Math,* Commonwealth Club. YouTube video. December 28, 2016.
https://www.youtube.com/watch?v=zDXFixLrmic&feature=youtu.be

(2) *Global Warming: Four degree rise will end vegetation "carbon sink,"* Science Daily. University of Cambridge. December 2013.
http://www.sciencedaily.com/releases/2013/12/131216154851.htm

(2a) *Climate Change; Prepare for global temperature rise of 4°C, warns top scientist, The Guardian.* Aug 6, 2015. James Randerson.
http://www.theguardian.com/environment/2008/aug/06/climatechange.scienceofclimatechange

(2b) *Climate change catastrophe by degrees, The Guardian.* Mark Lynas. August 2008.
http://www.theguardian.com/commentisfree/2008/aug/07/carbonemissions.climatechange

(2c) *Six Degrees: Our Future on a Hotter Planet,* Mark Lynas.

*　　*　　*

References: Chapter 3.

Additional Video Content:

Climate Change: Time is Running Out. Professor Andrew T. Guzman.
YouTube clip. February 25, 2013.
Exceptional, strong layout of the interconnectedness of Earth systems. In this case the direct correlation between Climate Change impacts and the devastation of the glacier-fed water systems that the majority of humans on the planet rely on. This is also a no-holds-barred layout of how human, economic, social, political and cultural systems are intricately interwoven with the Earth systems and climate disruption.

Notice that Guzman projects ten to twenty feet of sea level rise. This was his projection in 2013. We can see that James Hansen and his research team validate those projections now, in 2016.

*(1) Overheate*d. Andrew T. Guzman. 2013.
UC Berkeley Professor, Guzman gives a remarkable level of detail about the impacts of a world at 2°C above pre-industrial temperatures. As we have seen, 2°C is a very conservative range for our now-certain projected global impacts.

(2a) The Sixth Extinction: An Unnatural History.
Elizabeth Kolbert
Half of the species of plants and animals currently in existence will die out by 2050.

(3) "Earth has lost half of its wildlife in the past 40 years"
The Guardian, Damian Carrington. September 12, 2014
Scientists at World Wildlife Fund and Zoological Society of London.
http://tinyurl.com/p3asese

(3a) "Marine Population Halved Since 1970"
Report BBC News
http://www.bbc.com/news/science-environment-34265672

(3b) "Salt-Water Fish Extinction Seen by 2048" CBS News / AP.
http://www.cbsnews.com/news/salt-water-fish-extinction-seen-by-2048/?mc_cid=a94ec71b58&mc_eid=eb2b343649

(3d) "Alarming New Coral Bleaching Event Has Begun at the Great Barrier Reef,"
Truthout. Dahr Jamail. February 22, 2017.
http://www.truth-out.org/news/item/39569-alarming-new-coral-bleaching-event-
has-begun-at-the-great-barrier-reef

(3e) "Rapid emergence of climate change in environmental drivers of marine
ecosystems."
Nature Communications. March 7, 2017.
http://www.nature.com/articles/ncomms14682

(4) "Sixth mass extinction is here: Humanity's existence threatened,"
Science Daily. Rob Jordan. June 19, 2015
http://www.sciencedaily.com/releases/2015/06/150619152142.htm

(4a) Gerardo Ceballos, Paul R. Ehrlich, Anthony D. Barnosky, Andrés García,
Robert M. Pringle and Todd M. Palmer. Accelerated modern human–induced
species losses: Entering the sixth mass extinction. Science Advances, 2015 DOI:
10.1126/sciadv.1400253

(5)"150-200 Species Extinct Each Day."
Protect nature for world economic security, warns UN biodiversity chief.
http://www.theguardian.com/environment/2010/aug/16/nature-economic-security
The Guardian, John Vidal, Environment Editor. August 16, 2010.
UN Secretary General of the UN Convention on Biological Diversity, Ahmed
Djoghlaf relays findings of the UN Environment Programme.

The Earth is in the midst of a mass extinction of life. Scientists estimate that 150-
200 species of plant, insect, bird and mammal become extinct every 24 hours. This
is nearly 1,000 times the "natural" or "background" rate and, say many biologists, is
greater than anything the world has experienced since the vanishing of the
dinosaurs nearly 65m years ago.

(5a) "Phytoplankton Population Drops 40 Percent Since 1950."
Scientific American, Lauren Morello and ClimateWire, July 29, 2010
http://tinyurl.com/mxazlh2

(5b) "22 Million Trees Killed by Bark Beetle; California Declares Emergency."
Woodworking Network, Michaelle Bradford, November 2, 2015
http://tinyurl.com/p7fa3r2

(5c) "Living Planet2016."

World Wildlife Fund. Zoological Society of London. Biannual Report.

(6) "Current Updates and Disturbing Trends,"Dahr Jamail Sixth Great Mass Extinction Event Begins; 2015 on Pace to Become Hottest Year on Record. *Truthout*. June 29, 2015.
http://tinyurl.com/npn8wyh

(7) *The World is Blue.* Documentary about Oceanographer, Sylvia Earle. Mission Blue. Activist organization committed to protecting Earth's oceans.
http://mission-blue.org

(8) "Study: Man-made heat put in oceans has doubled since 1997,"Seth Borenstein. AP. *Seattle Times*
http://www.seattletimes.com/nation-world/nation-politics/study-man-made-heat-put-in-oceans-has-doubled-since-1997-2/

*   *   *

References: Chapter Four.

*** Additional Recommended Video Content…

The Ostrich or the Phoenix: Dissonance or creativity in a changing climate. Earth 101. Professor Kevin Anderson, Professor of Energy and Climate Change, University of Manchester, Deputy Director of the Tyndall Centre. UK. https://www.youtube.com/watch?v=mBtehlDpLlU

Professor Anderson speaks in no uncertain terms about the consequences of our continuing a businessas-usual lifestyle. If you only have time for one video about the Sober Data. Watch this one.

*   *   *

(1) "Carbon Budget is only half as big as thought," *Climate News Network.*Tim Radford. February 2016. http://climatenewsnetwork.net/17592-2/

(1a) "America Now Has 27.2 Gigawatts of Solar Energy: What Does That Mean?" *Inside Climate News.* David J. Unger. May 25, 2016. http://tinyurl.com/gufpp7d

(1b) "Pledges Made at Paris Climate Talks Will Not Contain Global Warming.: *Truthdig. Climate News Network.* Tim Radford. July 2, 2016. http://www.truthdig.com/report/item/pledges_made_at_the_paris_climate_talks_will_not_contain_20160702

(2) *Open Letter.* Academics from around the globe asking world leaders to do what is necessary to prevent catastrophic climate change.

http://globalclimatechangeweek.com/open-letter/

(3) ClimateActionTracker.org

http://climateactiontracker.org

The *Climate Action Tracker* is an independent science-based assessment, which tracks the emission commitments and actions of countries.

(4) :Exxon: The Road Not Taken."

Inside Climate News. September 2015.

Exposé of Exxon's promotion and funding of disinformation regarding human-caused climate change damage— after years of funding world-class research that fully confirmed that damage.
http://insideclimatenews.org/content/Exxon-The-Road-Not-Taken

(4a) "Exxon's Oil Industry Peers Knew About Climate Dangers in the 70s Too,"
Inside Climate News. Neela Banerjee. December 22, 2015
Of course it wasn't just Exxon.

(4b) "CO²'s Role in Global Warming Has Been on the Oil Industry's Radar Since the 1960s,"
Inside Climate News. Neela Banerjee et al. April 13, 2016.
http://tinyurl.com/zf97qnr

(5) "Oil majors' climate plan gets hostile reception."
Climate Home. Ed King. April 2016.
http://www.climatechangenews.com/2016/11/04/oil-majors-climate-plan-gets-hostile-reception/

(6) "Exxon CEO: World needs oil of five Saudi Arabias by 2040,"
Climate Home. Ed King. October 2016.
http://www.climatechangenews.com/2016/10/19/exxon-ceo-world-needs-oil-of-five-saudi-arabias-by-2040/

(6a) "Exxon Mobil boss warns against tougher climate regulations,"
Climate Home. Ed King. July 2015.
http://www.climatechangenews.com/2015/10/07/exxon-boss-warns-against-tougher-climate-regulations/

(6b) "Exxon's Oil Industry Peers Knew About Climate Dangers in the 70s Too,"
Inside Climate News. Neela Banerjee. December 22, 2015
Of course it wasn't just Exxon.

(6c) "CO2's Role in Global Warming Has Been on the Oil Industry's Radar Since the 1960s,"
Inside Climate News. Neela Banerjee et al. April 13, 2016.
http://tinyurl.com/zf97qnr

(7) "Reagan, Bush 41 memos reveal sharp contrast with today's GOP on climate and the environment,"
Washington Post. Joby Warrick. December 3, 2015.
Detailed article describes fully articulated climate change concerns, possible policy strategies and includes copies of numerous, declassified, executive level memoranda.
http://tinyurl.com/jpmvw4x

"GLOBAL CLIMATE CHANGE," *Current Situation and Trends.* If climate change within the range of current predictions (1.5 to 4.5 degrees Centigrade by the middle of next century) actually occurs, the consequences for every nation and every aspect of human activity will be profound."

(Excerpt from USG declassified documents included in *Washington Post* article referenced here.) US State Department memo to the Secretary of State under George H.W. Bush, James Baker.

Pg. 5 of 9. Memorandum, February 27, 1989.

Silence of the Labs. Canada and suppression of science. YT.
https://www.youtube.com/watch?v=Ms45N_mc50Y

*   *   *

Chapter 5. The Shadows are Busy.

Extra Recommended Media Content:

Abrupt Climate Change Brief Overview Video and Article:
Earth's Relentless Warming Just Hit a Terrible New Threshold.
Bloomberg. Tom Randall. May 18, 2016.
Ironic that this very business-as-usual publication puts out a very informative overview of Sober Data, suggesting that continuing with business as usual could result in 8°C or more global temperature rise by 2100. Sound familiar?
http://tinyurl.com/hn477xp

The Origins of Totalitarianism.
Hannah Arendt. 1973.

This seminal book is required reading for anyone who intends to do anything other than blindly accept the current state of US and global politics and control. This is a long, hard read, but well worth the effort.

References: Chapter 5.

(1) Edward Bernays. Wikipedia December 2016.)

(2) Lee Camp, *Advertising is an Asshole,* (begins at: 14'15")

excerpt from YouTube video, *Culture in Decline,*episode 3. Peter Joseph.
https://www.youtube.com/watch?v=hqy3atoAB0c&list=PLP-
Mo2sArLBHnlakAi2sgVEBwwxXsAFpX&index=3
Astounding social commentary from one of America's great comedians.

(3) *Peak Prosperity.* Educational website re personal and global finance.

The Crash Course: a free offering on this site that intends to articulate some of the many ways that our current economic system is unhealthy and predicted to collapse.
Chris Martenson, one of Peak Prosperity's creators, also hosts a podcast.

(4) Why are so many Americans skeptical about climate change?
The Washington Post. Joby Warrick. November 2015.
https://www.washingtonpost.com/news/energy-

environment/wp/2015/11/23/why-are-so-many-americans-skeptical-about-climate-change-a-study-offers-a-surprising-answer/?utm_term=.0df503dd1bbc

(5) Museum.tv, website for history and analysis of TV programming. History of the Fairness Doctrine is available here.
http://www.museum.tv/eotv/eotv.htm

(6) *Climactic Change.* Robert Brulle et al. February 2017. Article Link:
http://link.springer.com/article/10.1007/s10584-013-1018-7
Details of the billion dollar industry that climate denial has become.

(6a) Video report re this article: YouTube.
Why They Deny Climate Change. TYT.
https://www.youtube.com/watch?v=1kLIAVV8g34&t=6s
Sources and amounts of money supporting climate denial.

(6c) Infographic showing six corporations control 90% of the media in America.

http://www.businessinsider.com/these-6-corporations-control-90-of-the-media-in-america-2012-6

(7) *Exxon: The Road Not Taken.*

Inside Climate News. 2015, 2016. Neela Banerjee, Lisa Song et al.
https://insideclimatenews.org/content/Exxon-The-Road-Not-Taken

The most extraordinary investigative journalism to date about our human misadventures regarding the decimation of our global habitat and cynically-hiding corporate research that could have motivated mitigation decades earlier, while funding climate denial campaigns.

(8) **What Exxon Knew About the Earth's Melting Arctic.**
The Los Angeles Times. Sara Jerving, Katie Jennings et al.
October 9, 2015.
http://graphics.latimes.com/exxon-arctic/

(9) **The Data That Turned the World Upside Down**
Vice: Motherboard column.
https://motherboard.vice.com/en_us/article/how-our-likes-helped-trump-win
Using Big Data to craft precisely the candidate that Americans will vote for.

(10) **Gaslighting: Know It and Identify It to Protect Yourself.**

Psychology Today. Stephanie Sarkis Ph.D.
https://www.psychologytoday.com/blog/here-there-and-everywhere/201701/gaslighting-know-it-and-identify-it-protect-yourself

\

*   *   *

Chapter 6. Resources and References.

(A) Deb Ozarko. Website, Podcast, Essays/Blog.
http://www.debozarko.com
Deb is a self-proclaimed "activist for the soul, status quo crusher, passionate lover of life."

I heartily recommend reading Deb's blog posts from 2016. You will find great passion, clarity and inspiration there.

(1) *Don't Even Think About It: Why our brains are wired to ignore climate change,* George Marshall.

(1a) *What We Think About When We Try Not to Think About Global Warming,* Per Espen Stoknes.

(1b) *"Can Geoengineering Save the Planet?"*
Ken Caldeira
Carnegie Institute for Science / Department of Global Ecology - Stanford University
Interview on Inquiring Minds Podcast #79 – 2014
https://soundcloud.com/inquiringminds
Caldeira is at the top of this field and freely suggests that if we use geoengineering to try to fix Climate Change problems – we will likely encounter large scale negative repercussions that may further aggravate our deteriorating climactic conditions.

(2) *Peak Prosperity Podcast.* Chis Martenson and Gail Tverberg. October 2016.
https://www.peakprosperity.com/podcast/102796/gail-tverberg-why-theres-no-economically-sustainable-price-oil-anymore

(3) *This Changes Everything: Capitalism vs the Climate,* Naomi Klein.
No other book has so clearly connected our environmental world with our human systems world. Anyone serious about teaching their children to live in our world that is dramatically changing, indeed, in every way, should read this book.

Statements from Religious Leaders:

(4) Catholic: Pope Francis, Encyclical, 2015
Laudato Si-On Care for Our Common Home
http://tinyurl.com/o6sowft

Comprehensive list of Climate Change Statements From World Religions
http://fore.yale.edu/climate-change/statements-from-world-religions/
Provided by The Forum on Religion and Ecology at Yale.
United Planet Faith & Science Initiative
http://www.upfsi.org

This organization provides an interface between religious leaders and eminent scientists in hopes of bringing these two influential forces together to mobilize action for ecological sustainability. Small sample of founding members: Evangelical climate scientist, Katharine Hayhoe, Michael Mann, James Hansen, Desmond Tutu, Dr Peter Wadhams, Dr Lise Van Susteren.

Islamic Declaration on Global Climate Change
http://islamicclimatedeclaration.org/islamic-declaration-on-global-climate-change/

Restoring Creation for Ecology and Justice
Presbyterian Church (USA 1990)
http://www.webofcreation.org/ncc/statements/pcusa.html

Faith-Based Statement on Climate Change.
Citizens Climate Lobby.
http://citizensclimatelobby.org/files/images/Faith%20Based%20Statements%20PD
F%20for%20printing.pdf

Reality's Rules: Ten Commandments to Avoid Extinction
Michael Dowd. Connie Barlow.
https://youtu.be/IC2bbpnlREg
Dowd suggests a new 10 Commandments – based in a deep love and stewardship of Earth and our relationship to life on Earth.

The Great Story
Website of Michael Dowd and Connie Barlow. Offering alternative offerings to people of faith, based on the assertion that reverence for Earth and our stewardship is actually a powerful expression of a love of God and our interrelatedness with this

biosphere.

http://www.thegreatstory.org/home.html

Katharine Hayhoe offers an introduction to her new web series regarding climate change and faith communities. One of the world's great climate communicators from an evangelical Christian.

https://youtu.be/W53uRqITk2I

*   *   *

Additional article about our Administration's lies, and America's apparent lack of care about those lies.

Why Nobody Cares the President is Lying.
Charles J. Sykes.
The New York Times Sunday Review. February 4, 2017.
https://www.nytimes.com/2017/02/04/opinion/sunday/why-nobody-cares-the-president-is-lying.html?_r=2&mc_cid=3cb33462c7&mc_eid=eb2b343649

*   *   *

Chapter 7. References and Resources:

(1) *The Psychological Effects of Global Warming on the United States: And Why the U.S. Mental Health Care System Is Not Adequately Prepared.*

2012. The National Wildlife Federation. Kevin J. Coyle, JD and Lise Van Susteren, MD.
http://www.nwf.org/pdf/Reports/Psych_Effects_Climate_Change_Full_3_23.pdf

This report estimates that as many as '200 million Americans will be exposed to serious psychological distress from climate-related events and incidents."

Chapter 8: Reconnection With Earth. References and Resources.

(1) *Navy Allowed to Kill or Injure Nearly 12 Million Whales, Dolphins, Other Marine Mammals in Pacific.*
Truthout. Dahr Jamail. May 2016.
Extraordinary piece of journalism from one of the best environmental journalists alive today.

Additional Video/Media Content Recommendation:

The Years of Living Dangerously. Season Two.
National Geographic Documentary series about climate change.

http://yearsoflivingdangerously.com

This second season is beautifully produced just like the first, but it goes quite a bit further toward The Impossible Conversation-level of abrupt climate change projections and rage-inducing efforts by corporations and governments around the world, to slow or stop any measures to mitigate our damage to our habitat.

Man vs. Earth. Prince Ea. YouTube video.
https://www.youtube.com/watch?v=VrzbRZn5Ed4

Yet another brilliant video from Prince Ea. Inspiring and motivating for those who sincerely wish to reconnect with our original Mother—Earth.

Interview With Nafeez Ahmed.
Chris Martenson's Peak Prosperity Podcast. February 19, 2017.
https://www.youtube.com/watch?v=r3T9bXYmhRg&list=PL4A2E33FCBAEF1E5B

Two of today's strongest reporters speak regarding all things environmental, political and economic. In about 55 minutes the listener will have a vivid picture of our global human and environmental systems. This is a fantastic starting point for someone wanting real information, Sober Data and solid analysis.

References: Chapter 9. Reconnecting With Deeper Self.

(1) *Coming Back to Life.*
Joanna Macy and Molly Young Brown.

(2) *Active Hope: How to Face the Mess We're in Without Going Crazy.*
Joanna Macy and Chris Stone.

(3) *New Self, New World: Recovering Our Senses in the 21st Century.*
Philip Shepherd.
https://philipshepherd.com
Essay: The Embodiment Manifesto, available on this website.

(4) *Cowspiracy.* The movie.
http://www.cowspiracy.com
Our daily choices make a huge difference.
Remarkable documentary that includes breathtaking statistics about the impacts of global animal agriculture on our health, climate change and social justice issues.

(5) *Return to Joy.*
Carolyn Baker and Andrew Harvey.

(6) *The Hope: a Guide to Sacred Activism.*
Andrew Harvey.

*　　*　　*

References: Chapter 10. Reconnecting With Others.

(1) In this YouTube video Michael Mann joins his coauthor, cartoonist Tom Toles and a renowned journalist and psychologist, to talk about our world that includes climate and science denial.
https://www.youtube.com/watch?v=nKN7wB-uMNY&t=832s

(2) , *Being the Change*: *How to live well and spark a climate revolution*.
Peter Kalmus.
http://becycling.life

(3) *Coming Back to Life*.
Joanna Macy and Molly Young Brown.

(4) *The Crash Course*, Chris Martenson
https://www.peakprosperity.com

Recommended journalists and journalism sites:

Inside Climate News.

The Guardian.

The Washington Post. Chris Mooney.

George Monbiot.

Nafeez Ahmed.

Daily News Digest, Carolyn Baker

Chris Hedges. Truthdig.

Dahr Jamail. Truthout.

Derrick Jensen Resistance Radio w/Dahr Jamail – February 19, 2017. https://www.youtube.com/watch?v=A3Qargg1XS8&t=544s

An extraordinarily useful interview by author and activist, Derrick Jensen, with the remarkable Truthout.org journalist, Dahr Jamail. Jamail offers one of his in-depth updates regarding the current state of affairs of our shared global habitat. He also shares a bit from his upcoming book, *The End of Ice.*

Both Jensen and Jamail (Truthout) are on my short list of sources for both inspiration and sober updates regarding climate change and collapse of human and Earth systems.

Climate Change Denial:

Understanding Climate Change Denial / edX
University of Queensland
Web based course. MOOC.
This is a great course! A must see for anyone who plans on talking with someone who doesn't believe in science.

Climate Crocks (website) http://climatecrocks.com
Frequent updates re climate change science.
Numerous video clips that humanize climate scientists:
Climate Change Elevator Pitch/video series

Merchants of Doubt: How a Handful of Scientists Obscured the Truth on Issues from Tobacco Smoke to Global Warming. (book and documentary)
Naomi Oreskes and Erik Conway. 2010, Bloomsbury Press.
Supporting organization/website: www.takepart.com

The Hockey Stick and the Climate Wars: Dispatches from the Front Lines.
Michael E. Mann. 2012. Columbia University Press

A highly regarded overview of climate science as it pertains to climate change research. Professor Mann also details some of the cynical attacks on scientists that have become all too common in this polarized world.

How Statistics Are Twisted to Obscure Public Understanding.
Aeon Online. Pam Weintraub. July 11, 2016.
http://tinyurl.com/jkzeupl

Cynical Government/Corporate Policy re IPCC Manipulation:

IPCC reports 'diluted' under political pressure to protect fossil fuel interests.
The Guardian Nafeez Ahmed. May, 2014.
http://www.theguardian.com/environment/earth-insight/2014/may/15/ipcc-un-climatereports-diluted-protect-fossil-fuel-interests

Additional article on corporate pressures and influence on IPCC proceedings, reports and Calculations.

The Lie We Live   YouTube video
Powerful overview of our global situation.
Spencer Cathcart, January 27, 2015
https://www.youtube.com/watch?v=ipe6CMvW0Dg

PR/Advertising/Contrived Need
The Century of the Self. (CBC documentary)
https://youtu.be/eJ3RzGoQC4s

The Corporation (documentary)
 Recently updated, profound detailing of the structure, ideology and methodologies that make up what we call a corporation.
https://www.youtube.com/watch?v=Z4ou9rOssPg

Dark Money: *The Hidden History of the Billionaires Behind the Rise of the Radical Right.*
Jane Mayer. 2016. Random House.

The Dark Side: *The Inside Story of How the War on Terror Turned Into a War on American Ideals.*
Jane Mayer.

The New Confessions of an Economic Hitman.
John Perkins.

An extraordinary expose of the dark, cynical forces at work behind the scenes on a global scale. From foreign policy to trade agreements between nations and corporations Perkins shows us the shadowy world of his former trade, the economic hitman. Essential reading for all of us who still maintain that world governments and corporations are in any way looking out for the interests of the common people.

Astounding first-hand stories of just how powerful American corporate and government influence can be as it muscles its way into resource-rich countries around the world. Even more daunting is the implicit threat of stunning violent force that will be used against any person or country that does not get with our program. Perkins includes a long list of suggestions for "What can I do?" He is also a board member with the Pachamama Alliance, a powerful place to start if you are looking to find kindred spirits around the world and effective ways to get into informed action together.

This Changes Everything: *Capitalism vs the Climate*
Naomi Klein

No other book has so clearly connected our environmental world with our human systems world. Anyone serious about teaching their children to live in our world that is dramatically changing, indeed, in every way, should read this book.

Shock Doctrine, *The Rise of Disaster Capitalism.*
Naomi Klein.
This book preceded *This Changes Everything* and details the cynical motivations and structures within our society that leverage large scale profiteering and power mongering that is occurring in the wake of every major disaster event in the US and in the world at large.

The Shock Doctrine, video.
Naomi Klein. YouTube video re: Global Neoliberalism. Markets.
The Big Think. Video series of Klein's observations and philosophy.
https://www.youtube.com/watch?v=bcQJIQmasdo

Days of Destruction, Days of Revolt.
Chris Hedges and Joe Sacco.
A deeply moving book full of clear and stark examples of the kind of government and corporate campaigns to dominate and profit from the lower classes in the US.

A very strong complement to Naomi Klein's, **Shock Doctrine**.

DEAN SPILLANE WALKER

Dean started his life-long love affair with Earth by hiking in the mountains of California and Baja California and surfing and diving on the Southern California coast. Dean's decades-long career in transformation-based, experiential training started with: Werner Erhard and Associates, The Breakthrough Foundation, On The Edge Productions, SportsMind, PSI, LifeSpring, SuperCamps, Youth at Risk, YES!, and many more.

With later work in his own training groups: InSpirit, Presence and now, Living Resilience, Dean is committed to bringing his whole heart and love of life to facing humanity's greatest predicaments.

Made in the USA
San Bernardino, CA
16 June 2017